1980

SURRENDER IN PANAMA

SURRENDER IN PANAMA:

The Case Against the Treaty

Hon. Philip M. Crane

Introduction by
Ronald Reagan

CAROLINE HOUSE BOOKS / Green Hill Publishers, Inc.
Ottawa, Illinois

To my eight children: Catherine Anne, Susanna Marie, Jennifer Elizabeth, Rebekah Caroline, George Washington V, Rachel Ellen, Sarah Emma, and Carrie Esther—my faith in the future. May they, and unborn generations, be ever vigilant to the need to keep our nation strong, just, compassionate, free, and a beacon of hope to those who live in the perpetual night of tyranny throughout the world.

PREVIOUS WORKS
by Congressman Philip M. Crane
The Democrats Dilemma (1964)
The Sum of Good Government (1976)

CONTENTS

Acknowledgements

My very special thanks go to the thousands of dedicated American patriots who are working so hard to preserve our title to the Panama Canal. Their help and encouragement to me has been enormous.

I particularly wish to thank those friends whose aid and advice contributed greatly to this manuscript: Richard S. Williamson, Aram Bakshian, Jr., Edward J. Milne, Jr., Richard Viguerie, Bill Rhatican, Morton Blackwell, and Jeff Gaynor.

Finally, I must acknowledge my debt and gratitude to an outstanding American for whom I have held the greatest esteem and respect for many years: Ronald Reagan. Governor Reagan raised the issues of American sovereignty over the canal with force and eloquence at a time when a surrender was thought improbable. The present crisis would not be upon us had we heeded his wisdom.

P.M.C.

Introduction
by Ronald Reagan

Ever since he staged a media extravaganza in Washington, D. C., to mark the signing of the new Panama Canal treaties, President Carter has been saying that once the American people know "all the facts" about the treaties they will support them and want them ratified.

The American people already knew some important basic facts about the Panama Canal and the Canal Zone before the new treaties were signed. Now, once they know "all the facts" about the treaties and the circumstances leading to their signing, I think they will do just the reverse of what Mr. Carter expects: they will oppose ratification in even larger numbers than they do now.

Congressman Phil Crane has put between these two covers all the facts anyone needs to make a reasoned decision about the Panama Canal treaties now before the Congress.

He traces the history of the canal, the role of the Frenchman Phillipe Bunau-Varilla (if it hadn't been for him, the canal might have been built in Nicaragua); how Panama was born (if it hadn't been for the United States, Panama would probably still be a province of Colombia); and why the charge of "colonialism" is an empty one.

The author examines the question of sovereignty; the United States acquired the right to act in the Canal Zone as if sovereign, to the exclusion of the exercise of those rights by the Republic of Panama. Treaty advocates nearly always omit that latter condition of the existing treaty when arguing for a new one. The fact is that only one nation—the United States—can exercise sovereignty in the Canal Zone unless that right is given away, as the new treaties would do. But it is that right which is the bedrock foundation for American ability to operate and defend the canal. If we give it away, our presence in the area is then only at the sufferance of the Panamanian government. It could nationalize the canal on a moment's notice and order us out, *with the full backing of provisions of the United Nations charter*. We would be powerless to do anything about it—except fight, and it is hard to believe that any American wants a confrontation under such circumstances. By keeping the rights of sovereignty in the Canal Zone, we cannot be summarily kicked out at the whim of a Panamanian regime. Considering the volatile nature of Panamanian politics over the years, the fact of the present military dictatorship which squelches human rights, and the evidence that Fidel Castro (and, behind him, the USSR) covets much greater influence over Panama, it is clear that the new basic treaty's provision relinquishing the rights of sovereignty represents a fatal flaw.

This book raises important questions about the defense role the canal plays in hemispheric security; about its commercial value to ourselves and our neighbors. It answers many of them, but leaves others—nagging ones—for the treaties' proponents to answer. . . if they can.

It looks at key elements in the development of these treaties, such as the Tack-Kissinger Memorandum of 1974, in which the then–secretary of state seemed to be agreeing, in advance, that the Panamanians could have what they wanted. The effect of Special Ambassador Sol Linowitz's six-month appointment on the speed of treaty negotiations is studied. The announcement of the new treaties was made just hours before his appointment expired; to have it renewed, Mr. Carter would have had to submit it to the Senate for ratification. This would have meant public hearings and a close examination of Mr. Linowitz's business relationships—relationships the author tells you about.

You will learn from these pages who is anxious to have the treaties ratified and why. You will learn why legal experts say that the House of Representatives must play a role in the congressional approval process (it involves a basic Constitutional principle).

In recent months there have been persistent efforts to rewrite the history of the Panama Canal. Some have been made out of ignorance or incomplete research; others have no doubt been willful. *Surrender in Panama* strips away whatever confusion has been built up as a result of this. It is thorough; it is methodical. It is also highly quotable.

Though the American people may not have had *all* the facts

about the canal till now, most have known some vital basic ones for a long time. In early 1976, as I began my campaign for the presidential nomination, I was surprised to find that, in state after state, the issue would come up in town hall–type meetings. The people knew that our nation had built the canal; had helped Panama achieve independence and to reach one of the highest per capita income levels in Latin America; had maintained the canal and operated it fairly for more than sixty years; and had helped guarantee the security of the hemisphere by defending it. What they couldn't understand was why we are negotiating its giveaway under threat of blackmail by a military dictator and under a drumbeat of international propaganda by the far left designed to make us feel guilty and to retreat still further from a role of international leadership.

"Why?" was the question the people kept asking me. I was not the person to answer that question, of course, for I did not support the giving away of the canal then and I do not support it now. It is for President Carter and the supporters of his new treaties to answer that question.

Once he does and "all the facts" are known and Congress takes the logical steps of turning down these treaties, what then? I believe it is important that we find workable alternatives which will protect our security and that of the hemisphere and will also recognize the aspirations of the Panamanian people.

One alternative ready to be put into action is the Terminal Lake-Third Lock plan, which would modernize and increase the capacity of the canal. It would take a decade to complete and would cost between $1 and $2 billion. Panamanian contractors and workers could be used extensively in the project to insure that a great deal of the benefit of the expenditure would go directly to the people of Panama and not to the ruling clique which stifles human rights. Once completed, the project would make it possible for all but a few of the world's very largest ships to transit the canal.

In recent months, scholars, legal experts, engineers, and foreign affairs specialists have brought forward other alternatives. Some may not survive close scrutiny, but certainly all are worth laying on the negotiating table for discussion. Among them are:

—International participation on the canal governing board. In addition to the group of permanent U.S. seats, some Panamanian seats might be added, as well as some term seats to be rotated among canal-user nations.

—Turning over Panamanians who violate laws in the Canal Zone to Panamanian courts.

—Adjusting the boundaries of the Canal Zone to turn over to Panama any land not needed for operations or watershed protection.

—Building one or more new vehicle bridges across the canal to improve access by Panamanians to either side.

No doubt, in renegotiations other alternatives will be discussed. We should approach all of them with an open mind, but we should also make it clear—as past negotiators apparently did not—that the United States must retain practical control over the canal for the security of the entire hemisphere.

Chapter 1:
Why Is Panama an Issue?

From the very beginning, Panama has been a source of confusion and controversy. When Christopher Columbus sighted the Isthmus of Panama during his fourth voyage of discovery, he was convinced that he had reached India, and spent several weeks prowling along the coast, looking for the mouth of the Ganges River. Naturally he didn't find it, and left disappointed. As Samuel Eliot Morison so humorously put it in *The Oxford History of the American People*, "America was discovered accidentally by a great seaman who was looking for something else; then discovered it was not wanted; and most of the exploration for the next fifty years was done in the hope of getting through or around it." Getting "through or around" Panama—a dense, disease-ridden tropical forest—and digging the monumental canal that would link the Atlantic and Pacific oceans took not fifty, but four hundred years. And getting through or around the current issue of Panama is almost as difficult today.

Today, 475 years after Columbus first set eyes on the narrow strip of jungle waste that connects North and South America, Panama is less understood than ever. The rights and wrongs of the United States' role in helping to establish an independent Panamanian republic and constructing and running an American canal in the first place; the economic, military, political, and psychological importance of the canal today; the practical and moral force of the arguments on both sides of the issue—all these crucial considerations seem to have been lost in a sea of half-baked emotionalism and oversimplification every bit as turbulent and confusing as the unknown waters Columbus navigated in his unsuccessful search for the riches of the East Indies.

Sad to say, some of the worst offenders in distorting or obscuring the real issues about Panama and the canal have been those with the highest responsibility to deal candidly with the American

1

people: the White House and the State Department. Along with much of the print and electronic media, the Carter administration has painted America as the villain in Panama. The story of the canal, we are told, is a legacy of national shame; our presence in the Canal Zone was secured through an immoral use of force and is the last vestige of hated colonialism in Latin America. Besides, we are told, if we don't haul down the flag and leave quietly now, we face the haunting prospect of fighting an endless and costly guerrilla war against Panamanian "freedom-fighters" and saboteurs who could cripple the canal overnight.

A politically naive Joint Chiefs of Staff has been trotted out to assure the Congress that the new treaties—which would surrender the Panama Canal to a country currently ruled by a corrupt, pro-Castro dictator and reward him with millions of dollars for the privilege of so doing—are in our best national interests. And as if that were not enough, we are also told that the canal is obsolete anyway, so why all the fuss?

Now the fact is that all of these arguments are not only misleading but demonstrably false. Yet they have been swallowed whole by many distinguished politicians and journalists, by three presidential administrations (Nixon, Ford, and Carter), and may—if enough voters do not get the truth in time—lead to a dangerous and disgraceful American surrender in Panama. To their credit, the American people have instinctively rebelled against the idea of giving away, under blackmail, a vital waterway that was paid for with American money and built and run by American expertise under sovereignty signed over to America by legally binding treaties. To put it bluntly, millions of average citizens have smelled a rat, and every sampling of public opinion taken on the subject shows the American people strongly opposed to giving away the canal.

However, as a great newspaperman, Arthur Hays Sulzberger, once remarked, "a man's judgment cannot be bettter than the information on which he has based it," and too much of the information on Panama conveyed by television, press, and government has been shallow. Jimmy Carter says that when the public has the facts, it will support the giveaway. The purpose of this book is to meet that challenge by bringing the evidence—the facts about Panama and the canal—directly to a concerned public. It is a long story and occasionally a complicated one. But taking it issue by issue, fact by fact, the reader can judge for himself whether President Carter is right or whether the case against surrendering the canal and zone by ratifying the new treaties is not overwhelming on political, military, economic, constitutional, and moral grounds.

Why is Panama such an important issue? In order to answer this question, we have to ask several other questions:

—How did the American involvement in the canal come about?

—What did the government of Panama agree to in the first place?

—What is the importance of the canal today? Is it vital or obsolete?

—Who really speaks for the Panamanian people in a country governed by a military dictator who overthrew a freely elected government?

—What do the new Panama treaties actually do? What do they surrender in terms of American rights and interests?

—What will they cost us economically?

—What will they cost us strategically?

—How much, if any, truth is there to the "red herring" issues raised by proponents of the treaties: the threats of sabotage, terroism, guerrilla war, and enraged Latin American opinion that will inevitably result unless we surrender the canal?

—Whose canal is it, and how can it best continue to serve as an efficient, fairly run waterway serving not only the American and Panamanian people, but all peaceful maritime traffic?

In the following seven chapters, I attempt to answer each of these nine key questions in detail, with further documentation in the appendexes which follow. The purpose of this opening, overview chapter is to state the overall case in summary: the basic case against surrender which the balance of this book will flush out with fuller facts, figures, and expert testimony. To begin, how did the United States first get involved in Panama?

Origins of American Involvement

The vision of an Atlantic-to-Pacific canal is an old one, but nature and disease made it an impossible dream until the beginning of the twentieth century. In Spanish colonial days, and in the opening years of Latin American independence, the theory of a transoceanic canal had often been discussed, but no practical measures were taken to construct one. America's first diplomatic step towards the canal concept was actually a negative one—the 1850 Clayton-Bulwer Treaty between the United States and Great Britian, which agreed that neither power would obtain or maintain exclusive control over any future Atlantic-Pacific canal, while both powers guaranteed its neutrality. Despite this limiting agreement, American interest in a canal remained lively, and in January 1875, a U.S. Navy expedition under Commander E. R. Lull steamed out of Norfolk, Virginia, in search of a suitable route for a possible canal through the Isthmus of Panama.

Three years later, the government of Colombia (Panama was then only a geographical expression, a poverty-stricken, pestilential province of Colombia racked by chronic internal disorder) granted a French company headed by Ferdinand de Lesseps, the creator of the Suez Canal, a 99-year concession to build a sea-level waterway across Panama. Natural obstacles, yellow fever, and corrupt financial practices led to scandals and the company's bankruptcy in 1891. By 1902, remnants of the failed venture were up for sale.

Meanwhile, in November 1901, Britain and America signed the Hay-Pauncefote Treaty, which granted the United States exclusive rights to construct, *maintain* and *control* a canal through the Isthmus of Panama. The way was now cleared for positive American action, and serious negotiations began between the American and Colombian governments. The result was the Hay-Herrán Treaty (January 22, 1903), which provided for American acquisition of a canal zone across the isthmus. However, the treaty ran into stiff opposition in the Colombian Senate, which delayed ratification. Meanwhile, matters were coming to a boil in Colombian Panama.

Like most Latin American countries of the period, Colombia was riven with dissent and political instability. Coups and countercoups were common; there had been more than forty changes of government since independence from Spain in 1810. Civil war, sometimes hot, sometimes cold, prevailed. Against this backdrop of unrest, the long-simmering local resentment of Panamanians against the central Colombian government burst into open rebellion in November 1903. It was a typically farcical revolution, one of many in the history of Latin America, but this time the results were to

4

prove of great historical importance. Spurred by fear that the United States would choose an alternative canal route in Nicaragua because of Colombian obstructionism, the Panamanians proclaimed themselves an independent republic on November 3. The United States recognized Panama three days later and signed the canal treaty twelve days after that. Thus the Republic of Panama and the American Zone (and ultimately the canal) were virtually Siamese twins. Neither would have arrived without the other.

Much ink and even more hot air has been expended on the rights and wrongs of the revolution in Panama. A blatant case of Yankee imperialism and American interventionism, say the critics—including, ironically, many outspoken Panamanian nationalists. The irony lies in the fact that in denouncing America's early recognition and support of Panama's independence, Panamanian critics are, in effect, questioning the legitimate origins of their own country as a sovereign state. Either the United States recognized a government with a just claim to existence (and thus with legitimate authority to negotiate the subsequent acreement on the canal) or the government of Colombia was the injured party, and Panama is an outlaw state from birth, unentitled to any legal consideration at all.

The unvarnished truth is that Panamanian independence was the work of a small group of wealthy, influential Panamanians and foreign commercial interests, not of the United States government. The bloodless coup owed its success to a handful of local conspirators who, working with officials of the Panama Railway Company, managed to talk the two officers commanding Colombia's ragtag, 500-man security force into a train ride to the other side of the isthmus, where they were briefly jailed and subsequently paid off to salve their wounded pride. While an off-shore American naval presence lent credibility to U.S. support of Panamanian independence, the only official American "intervention" consisted of a landing party of forty-two marines; far from facing a hostile reception from the natives, the marines went through their brief paces without firing a shot in anger. The United States had, moreover, a perfect legal right to land troops in Colombia to protect the rights of transit across the existing railroad—a right granted by Article 35 of the Bidlack Treaty of 1846. The whole coup had been carried out by a group smaller than a professional football team, and without a drop of blood spilled.

5

The main reason the Panamanians had staged the coup in the first place was to secure—not to prevent—an American canal on the isthmus. So it comes as no surprise that one of the first orders of business that the provisional government of the new-born republic set for itself was negotiating and ratifying a treaty with the United States ensuring America's role in bringing a canal to Panama, a canal that would turn an impoverished tropical backwater into a thriving commercial center and one of the healthiest and wealthiest countries in Latin America.

What the 1903 Treaty Said

The result was the Hay–Bunau-Varilla Treaty (November 18, 1903), agreed to by the United States and the provisional government of Panama. It granted the United States "in perpetuity" the ownership of a zone five miles wide on each side of the projected canal. The United States stood guarantor of the canal's neutrality in return for the right to fortify, defend and govern it, and paid Panama $10 million for rights to the terrority along with an annual subsidy of $250,000 as a compensation for the loss of the annual franchise payment to the Panamanian railroad, which had previously been paid to Colombia. The amount of the annual subsidy has increased over the years to the present figure of $2.3 million. On February 13, 1904, a Panamanian constitution was adopted, creating a president and a unicameral legislature. On February 26 the treaty was ratified, and on April 23, the United States purchased the property of the bankrupt French Canal Company for $40 million. Subsequent negotiations and treaties compensated Colombia for the loss of Panama and secured Colombian recognition of Panama's independence and American rights to the Canal Zone.

Inevitably, the precise meaning of the Hay–Bunau-Varilla Treaty has been the subject of heated debate among Latin American nationalists, revisionist historians, and others who would like to see America surrender all claim to the Panama Canal. But the words of the treaty itself are clear and to the point. The crux of the matter—the question of whom the Canal Zone belongs to in terms of legal authority and physical possession—is spelled out in Articles 2 and 3 of the treaty.

Under Article 2, the Republic of Panama "grants to the United

States in perpetuity the use, occupation and control of a zone of land and land under water for the construction, maintenance, operation, sanitation and protection of said Canal . . . ." As to the actual exercise of sovereignty, the treaty is equally explicit and comprehensive. Under Article 3, Panama grants the United States "all rights, power and authority within the zone mentioned . . . which the United States would possess and exercise if it were the sovereign of the territory . . . to the entire exclusion of the exercise by the Republic of Panama of any sovereign rights, power or authority."

In other words, in clear and incontrovertible language, Panama recognized the United States' exclusive, sovereign rights over the Canal Zone from the outset. Those rights have been upheld, in fact and in law, ever since, as the more detailed discussion of the treaty and subsequent court rulings, interpretations, and· diplomatic agreements show (see Chapter 3). This, in summary, is the ironclad legal basis for current and perpetual American possession of the canal. In deciding whether to surrender this possession by a new treaty, we must also consider the practical importance of the canal today and in the years ahead.

Do We Still Need the Canal?

The epic achievment of Colonel William C. Gorgas, who eliminated malaria and yellow fever from the Canal Zone, and the magnificent accomplishment of the Army Engineers under Colonel George W. Goethals, who constructed the elaborate system of dams and locks that still stands as a monument to American skill and endurance, is a story most Americans know from their school days. When the first ocean steamer passed through the canal on August 3, 1914, a new chapter had begun in the history of navigation and commerce, and a new symbol of American prestige had arisen.

That is all fine and good, say those who advocate surrender of the canal, but the importance of the canal is a thing of the past. Today it is an increasingly costly anachronism, a diplomatic embarrassment, and a militarily indefensible white elephant. In the age of the supertanker and the aircraft carrier, the Panama Canal is too small and too expensive. The number of American ships using it is dwindling, and its days as a major factor in global strategy and

7

commerce are numbered. We stand to gain much more in Latin American good will and gratitude by surrendering the canal, they say, than we will lose in military and economic clout, or global prestige.

As rhetoric, these arguments sound plausible; but the facts tell a different story. To begin with, supertankers and aircraft carriers, while indeed too bulky to use the canal, are not the wave of the future. The current trend in both military and commercial ship design is toward smaller, more specialized vessels that take advantage of modern container-technology and weapons systems. The result is that while the number of ships passing through the canal has remained fairly constant in recent years (following the major increases in the 1950s and early 1960s), the actual *tonnage* has continued to rise. More cargo is being carried through the canal today in fewer and more specialized ships, thanks to modern technology and design. By 1980 tonnage passing through the canal will reach a projected record of 160.3 million tons; by 1985, 184.9 million. Seventy percent of all the ships transiting the Panama Canal are heading to or from American ports, and 17 percent of all U.S. seaborne commerce passes through the canal. And with the growing importance of North Slope Alaskan oil for our fuel-hungry East Coast, the Panama Canal could become even more important to America's economic survial in the years ahead. Estimates are that 500,000 barrels of North Slope oil per day will be transported through the canal. Forty-five percent of all Alaskan oil will come through the canal by 1980.

According to recent reports, the major North Slope oil producers are already planning to route fleets of medium-sized tankers through the Panama Canal. Until such time as new West Coast refineries are constructed or older facilities are converted to process Alaska crude—or until a new pipeline system can be built to channel the crude overland to the Midwest and New England—the canal will be a crucial energy artery and, as such, should remain in American hands, under complete American control. Even the briefest stoppage—whether caused by inefficient operation or deliberate political action—could deliver a body blow to the American economy. Surrendering the canal would leave our prosperity hostage to the whims of a small, unstable Latin American dictatorship. Actual closure of the canal aside, manipulation of canal fares, which have been kept at bargain levels through efficient American management, could drive up the cost of shipment drastically enough to create serious problems not only for us but for a number of our Latin American and Pacific neighbors, many of whom are even more dependent on the smooth, economical functioning of the canal than we are. Colombia, Ecuador, Peru, and Nicaragua all depend on the canal for carriage of from one-third to three-fourths of all their trade; 42 percent of the canal's westbound tonnage goes to Japan, with 23 percent of its eastbound tonnage originating there. Other important friendly Pacific trading nations, like Australia and New Zealand, also depend on the canal to carry on trade with key East Coast American and European markets. Total ocean-going transits in fiscal year 1977 is estimated at 12,200 (34 daily). By the year 2000, this is expected to increase to 17,000 vessels (47 daily).* Changes in how the canal is run could have a profound effect, then, on world commerce, especially on countries whose economies are closely tied to the cost of raw materials.

In its efforts to sell the public on the new treaties, the administration and its spokesmen at the Pentagon have also tried to downplay the strategic importance of the canal today. Much has been made of the fact that, in its current state, the canal cannot accommodate vessels more than 950 feet in length, 40 feet in draft, and 106 feet in beam, which is considerably smaller than some of our carriers and warships. Despite President Carter's repeated assurances that he intends to cut back the military budget, we are also told that current American naval strategy is based on a two-ocean navy, thereby reducing the canal's importance.

While it is true that America's thirteen aircraft carriers are too large to pass through the canal, this argument overlooks the fact that the remaining 470 U.S. combat vessels, including nuclear submarines, all are capable of using the canal. And the figures prove that they *use* that capability. Between 1972 and 1975, for example, there were approximately 750 U.S. naval transits through the canal. History shows that the canal and control of it is even more important in wartime than in peace. Between 1965 and 1970, the peak years of direct American involvement in the Vietnam

*H. R. Parfitt, Canal Zone Government and President of Panama Canal Co., Report to Panama Canal Subcommittee of House Committee on Merchant Marine and Fisheries, July 25, 1977.

War, 95 percent of all American military cargo was carried by ship, and as much as 70 percent of annual cargo destined for Vietnam during the war moved through the canal.

With the trend in military design away from massive carriers and battleships and toward nuclear submarines, cruisers, and frigates, the canal becomes more rather than less relevant to American strategic security. In an age when small, swift military "police actions" have at least temporarily replaced the likelihood of all-out conventional wars, speed of response and quick logistical support of our farflung, overextended navy are of the essence. Contingency plans in the event of a NATO crisis, for example, call for the movement of sixty ships from the Pacific fleet to the Atlantic. Hanson Baldwin cites the movement of marines from the West Coast through the canal in 1962 as the basis of Khrushchev's willingness to negotiate quickly for fear of a U.S. invasion of Cuba. Closure of the canal, even for a few days, could cripple our ability to make a limited miliary response in an emergency. To give two graphic examples of the time and distance savings involved, a voyage from Norfolk, Virginia, to Yokohama via the canal is 5,666 miles shorter than the route around Cape Horn, and a voyage from San Francisco to New York via the canal is 8,000 miles and up to thirty days shorter than the cape route. In a national emergency, this could mean precious time and countless lives saved. At all times it represents a substantial financial saving in an era of skyrocketing fuel costs. The next obvious question, then, is whether the treaties now under debate could potentially endanger control, access, and efficient running of the canal, and what rights and advantages they would force us to surrender.

What Do the New Treaties Surrender?

The basic form of the present treaties took shape four years ago. The treaties now before the Senate are the result of four years of negotiation by an American team headed by Ambassador Ellsworth Bunker, begun under President Nixon and concluded under President Carter, who is now pushing for their ratification.

Key provisions of the new treaties would:

—Immediately end American sovereignty in the Canal Zone—the Panamanian flag goes up and the American goes

10

down at once;

—Phase in Panamanian participation in the running of the canal between now and the year 2000;

—Increase substantially Panama's "take" of canal earnings immediately upon ratification of the treaties;

—Yield title to over half the territory of the zone during the transition period, at the end of which all title and control of the Canal Zone will be surrendered to Panama.

A separate and all too vaguely worded agreement purports to provide for joint American-Panamanian defense of the canal. Far more explicit is the commitment to an immediate large increase in canal tolls to provide the Panamanian government with annual revenues of over $60 million, as compared to the present subsidy of $2.3 million a year. Key provisions intended to guarantee America's right to intervene to protect the canal, ensure preferential passage for U.S. warships in time of major conflict or war, preserve the neutrality of the canal, and keep it open under all circumstances (barring natural disasters) are couched in such vague terms, and have already been interpreted so differently by American and Panamanian spokesmen (and sometimes even by the same spokesmen before different audiences) as to raise grave misgivings even among those who might support in principle the idea of a new, more liberal agreement.

For example, despite the ostentatious friendship at the signing ceremonies for the treaty at the Pan American Union in Washington, D.C., and despite repeated assurances from White House, State Department, and Pentagon sources that all is well, Panama's chief treaty negotiator, Dr. Romulo Escobar Bethancourt, in an address to the Panamanian National Assembly, virtually declared the security provisions of the agreement worthless. Dr. Escobar's speech is more fully analyzed in Chapter 6 and is reprinted in full in Appendix 3; these crucial points stand out: (1) he denied that the Neutrality Treaty and its protocol granted the United States any defense rights after the year 2000, and stated that America will not be the guarantor of the canal's neutrality; (2) he denied that U.S. warships would be given preferential passage, even in time of war, after the year 2000; (3) he expressed the Panamanian view that it would not be necessary for his country to abide by the Neutrality Treaty in cases of foreign attack or "internal disorder";

11

(4) he denied that Panama was bound by treaty to keep the canal open if it was not "making money" or in the event of "internal disorder."

Given this interpretation of the treaties by the head of the Panamanian negotiating team, ratification can mean only one of two alternatives, both of them unacceptable. Either the United States accepts a limited and shrinking role in running the canal between now and 2000 and a virtually nonexistent one afterwards, thus surrendering total control to a tiny dictatorship, or it faces the prospect of having to intervene in force somewhere down the road, risking a global crisis and perhaps even war in order to regain the basic rights currently guaranteed under the terms of the Hay–Bunau-Varilla Treaty. Clearly, the cost of the new treaties is unacceptably high economically, and in terms of providing our enemies with a sublime opportunity to accuse the U.S. of restoration of gunboat diplomacy.

Economic Benefits to Panama

Under the current arrangement, the Panama Canal Company has a proven record of efficient, equitable, inexpensive operation. The Panama Canal toll structure is geared to recovering costs and maintenance. As such, its rates are comparatively low (about half those of the Suez Canal). The Canal Zone budget today stands at $260 million, of which $2.3 million goes to the government of Panama in annual subsidy. Under the new treaty, the current advantageous toll rates would be forced up in order to pay the Panamanian government a bounty of 30¢ for each ton of shipping weight that passes through the canal. This additional charge will cost the Canal Company an estimated $48 million a year in new fees to the Panamanian government by 1980. In addition, the new agreement proposes a fixed annuity to Panama of $10 million, plus another $10 million if canal revenues permit, plus service charges. These payments, which will total at least $60 million a year by 1980, will have to come from toll revenues; this in turn will mean higher tolls, higher shipping costs, and, ultimately, higher costs to the consumer on a wide range of goods and services. In 1976, the governor of the Canal Zone testified that tolls, currently about $1.50 per ton, could not increase by more than 30 percent without making use of the canal prohibitive to many commercial shippers; yet the Canal Company will not be able to meet yearly payments to Panama under the new treaties without quickly breaking the 30 percent limit—and with no end in sight for further increases. Even Ambassador Sol Linowitz, senior American negotiator of the agreement, has acknowledged that tolls will increase by from 25 to 30 percent upon ratification. At that rate, bankruptcy and closure of the canal could be a distinct possibility once Panama obtains full control.

With 70 percent of the 12,000 ships annually passing through the canal either leaving or calling at American ports, closure would paralyze 17 percent of all U.S. export and import shipping tonnage; alternate land or sea routes would saddle American companies with an estimated 33 percent in new shipping costs, and this, of course, would feed the inflationary cycle at the consumer level, further driving up the cost of living for the average American. The effect on the price of major raw materials and fuels, and the damage it could inflict on resource-poor industrial economies like Japan, could be even more devastating. And even the drastic alternative of building a new sea-level canal elsewhere in Central America is no longer open to us if the new agreement is ratified, for under its terms we surrender not only our right to the old canal, but also our right to build a new one without Panama's consent.

The Strategic Cost of Surrender

The Carter administration's self-imposed strait jacket on military spending leaves little flexibility once existing military expenses and research and development costs are met. Yet the insecurity of the new canal once American sovereignty has been surrendered would require extensive new naval expenditures merely to maintain our current level of preparedness and ability to respond, given the higher fuel costs, reduced mobility, and need for more naval craft to perform the same services that a smaller number of vessels would be able to do as long as American control of the canal was complete and American access unquestioned. Then there is the matter of land forces. We currently have 9,300 U.S. combat and support personnel stationed in the Canal Zone; at one point during World War II, U.S. forces in the zone totaled 67,000. Once these

American troops are phased out, the only thing standing between chaos and disruption in Panama and the Canal Zone will be the politicized Panamanian National Guard and police, smaller in number than our current garrison with three-fourths of their number lacking even basic infantry training. This pathetic rabble would be incapable of guarding and defending the Canal Zone from attack or sabotage even if it wanted to, and there is every reason to believe that, in a crisis, their loyalties would lie not with any abstract treaty commitments, but with whatever dictator or faction happened to be dispensing Panamanian salaries and graft at the moment.

Quite aside from the security which the current American military presence in the zone provides for the canal, yielding it would also mean the loss of a vital American presence in the Caribbean, an area already menanced by Cuba's Castro, a Marxist government in Guyana, and the recent rise to power of a pro-Marxist regime in Jamaica. The American military presence in Panama has long acted as a check to potential communist aggression in Central America and the Caribbean, and its withdrawal would mark the end of Panama as an ideal site for the jungle training of U.S. troops and those of friendly Latin America neighbors who also face the threat of potential communist infiltration. This too would be part of the strategic cost of surrender in Panama.

But above all, loss of American control of the canal would further aggravate the great American naval dilemma of our time, aptly described by former *New York Times* military analyst Hanson Baldwin as "the same strategic bind" the U.S. Navy was in prior to World War II: that "it is a one-ocean navy [in size and power] with two-ocean responsibilities." Without unquestioned command of the canal, the beleaguered navy's job would be so sorely taxed as to put in question its ability to meet its national security responsibilities. Chapters 4 and 7 will examine this and other military problems in detail, and include the opinions of some of our country's most respected military authorities on the Panama issue.

Finally, there is another potential military price of surrender, the possible need to intervene in the Canal Zone with massive force if a crisis arose at some date after the American pull-out—an eventuality that uninterrupted American control and a steadily maintained American military presence would preclude. Although advocates of the new treaties set up the specter of a "native uprising" of en-

14

raged Panamanian students and nationalists as one of the reasons for an American retreat, it is precisely an American withdrawal, and the power vacuum it would leave in its wake, that is most likely to encourage internal disorder in Panama and terrorist or sabotage activities within the Canal Zone. Yet this bogus issue of sabotage and guerrilla warfare is one of the main red herrings dangled before the Senate by President Carter and his spokesmen. Incredibly, on at least one occasion, Panamanian dictator Torrijos actually threatened to lead the charge against the canal personally if the U.S. Senate refused to ratify the new treaties. This myth of the "Panamanian Putsch" and massive sabotage (which even the highly organized World War I German intelligence service, not to mention Hitler's crack espionage corps and their Japanese confreres, failed to pull off during two world wars) will be discussed further in Chapter 7.

The Moral and Constitutional Case Against Surrender

Even if the new Panama Canal treaties were intrinsically sound —and I believe that the evidence and analysis in this book will prove that they are not—there is at least one major constitutional argument against simple Senate ratification as the sole means for their approval. There are sound constitutional grounds, including precedents and the opinions of some of our country's leading scholars (see Appendix 2), for maintaining that the House of Representatives should also have a share in deciding the fate of the canal. Bear in mind that besides paying $10 million to Panama for sovereignty in the Canal Zone and $40 million to the French Panama Canal Company for its rights, we also paid almost $90 million to more than 3,000 individual landowners for their property rights and, a few years later, $25 million to Colombia to compensate that nation for its loss. In return, Colombia recognized Panamanian independence and our clear title to the canal and the zone.

Now, inasmuch as the Hay–Bunau-Varilla Treaty and these other instances of compensation for property and claims all establish the zone as U.S. territory, the House of Representatives, as well as the Senate, should be involved in the final decision over the appropriations of this agreement. The constitutional intent is clear: Article

IV, Section 3, Clause 2 of the Constitution states that the Congress—not just the Senate—shall have power to ". . . dispose of and make all needful rules and regulations respecting the territory or other property belonging to the United States." Both past practice and various Supreme Court decisions indicate that this is an exclusive, rather than concurrent, grant of power; in fact, there have been several past cases when small alterations in the Canal Zone territory have taken place. In each instance, the House has passed implementing legislation. If the House is entitled to a voice in the disposal of small segments of the Canal Zone, as legislative precedent indicates, it is certainly entitled to a voice in disposing of the entire zone, locks, stock, and barrel. Hence, simple ratification of the agreement by the Senate, without implementing legislation from the House, will not meet the explicit requirements of the Constitution. In other words, without the approval of the House, neither the Senate nor the administration has the right to give away the canal—and there is every reason to believe that, given the say it deserves in this matter, the House of Representatives will oppose surrender in Panama.

Constitutionality aside, there is a deep moral issue at stake in Panama. In the past decade, the United States went through something very close to a collective national breakdown. Assassinations, rioting, war, campus violence, Watergate, and the tragic, humiliating collapse of Indochina have all contributed to a global climate in which most of the world—but especially those nations and those ideologies who wish us ill—are watching the United States through wolfish eyes, searching for any trace of irresolution or weakness of purpose. In Korea, in Taiwan, throughout Africa, Asia, Europe, the Middle East, and Latin America, wherever freedom is on the line and men must choose, America's image, strong or weak, will help to determine their fate. And the weaker our image becomes, the greater the danger of miscalculation, of adversaries pushing us too far in the belief that we will take any amount of pressure and abuse without standing up for what is right.

No one put it better than Teddy Roosevelt, the man whose driving vision made the Panama Canal a showcase of American vitality and know-how, and whose leadership, more than anyone's, first won the United States a respected place as a major power.

T. R. was a man of letters as well as action. In one of his

books, *The Strenuous Life,* he warned of the dangers of apathy and retreat, of passive surrender in the fact of challenge:

> If we seek merely swollen, slothful ease and ignoble peace, if we shrink from the hard contests . . . then bolder and stronger peoples will pass us by, and will win for themselves the domination of the world.

In Eastern Europe, in China, in Cuba, in Angola, and in Indochina, we have seen all too well what can happen when boldness and strength are on the side of evil. This is no time for America to abandon a just claim to a symbol of our national resolve and a vital safeguard of economic and military security for the entire free world.

There must be no surrender in Panama.

Chapter 2:
How We Got There

Historical Perspective on Panama,
the Canal, and the United States' Involvement

The first explorer to recognize, at least partially, the importance of the Isthmus of Panama was a dashing Spanish adventurer by the name of Vasco Nunez de Balboa. His career as a discoverer began quite by accident. After a brief and unsuccessful career as a planter in Santo Domingo, young Balboa went bankrupt. To elude his angry creditors he hid in a barrel which was subsequently rolled on board one of several Spanish ships about to embark for parts unknown. Discovered, the stowaway offered his services as a common sailer. The commander of the expedition accepted his offer, little suspecting that the ambitious Balboa had grander ambitions than serving as a lowly tar, and would soon replace him.

Gold and tales of gold—native legends of an Eldorado on the western side of the isthmus, situated in a mysterious southern sea—were the lure that drew Balboa and his newly established command to Panama. It was a motley force, consisting of a single ship, nine dugout canoes, two hundred Spaniards, a handful of Indian porters, and, for some unknown reason, a pack of hounds. Quite by chance, in September 1513, Balboa landed near Acla, where the isthmus is narrowest. Leaving behind a guard party on the coast to protect his ship, Balboa and the rest of his men plunged into the Panamanian jungle, slashing their way westward in search of the unknown sea and, they hoped, the land of gold. Historian Jean Descola has left a vivid word picture of their march to discovery:

> Imagine these men from Castile and Estremadura, helmeted and armored as on a Spanish battlefield, fraying a passage with sabre-blows through the dense Panamanian forest! For the first time men were forcing a way through this jungle of trees so

densely packed and lianas so tangled that it was like a fortress that had to be demolished wall by wall. It was dark there even at full moon . . . . To cover a hundred miles took this heroic band twenty days. Insect bites—there were spiders as large as tortoises, and serpents which were indistinguishable from the roots—Indian ambushes, and the polluted waters of the swamps accounted for half the expedition. . . . On the morning of the twentieth day the detachment reached the foot of a hill. A keen breath suddenly succeeded to the suffocating smell of the jungle. Balboa inhaled deeply at this breath of seaweed and salt. He seized his sword and, slowly and alone, climbed the slope of the hill. At the foot of the further slope, something immensely blue mirrored the blaze of the tropic sun: it was the sea.

Balboa had discovered the Pacific Ocean and thereby established the potential geographical importance of Panama. Three days later, the *Adelantado* (governor) of the Southern Sea became the first white man to come into physical contact with the unknown ocean:

At low tide, he strode forward towards the sea. His armor, his helmet and his naked sword flashed in the sunlight. He held aloft the banner of Castile and Aragon. He entered the sea until it was half-way up his body and took possession, in the name of Ferdinand and Isabella, sovereigns of Castile, of León and Aragon, of this southern ocean with all its ports, islands and coasts. And he took care to specify possession "royal, corporeal, present and eternal."

While Spanish possession of Panama was not eternal. it did endure for three centuries. On a subsequent expedition, Balboa even foreshadowed the idea of a canal by dismantling four ships, carting them by native bearer to the western side of the isthmus and reassembling them to sail in Pacific waters. However, Balboa never did discover the land of gold which he sought, for the excellent reason that it didn't exist, and even his triumph as a discoverer was short lived. On his return to Acla he was arrested by jealous Spanish rivals, put in irons and tried for treason. Later the same day, the discoverer of the Pacific was ignominiously beheaded in the dusty town square. Balboa was dead, but his vision of the isthmus as the link between the Atlantic and the Pacific only slept.

Panama under the Spanish

During the early years of Spanish rule, Central America was treated as the poor cousin of the richer Spanish conquests to the north in Mexico and to the south in Peru. Earthquakes, the almost inpenetrable jungle, and disease all mitigated against extensive permanent settlement on a large scale, and Panama and the rest of Central America were viewed mainly as a narrow corridor, hazardous but necessary, through which caravans of mules and Indian bearers hauled some of the gold and silver that, carried back to Spain in the galleons of the royal treasure fleet, supported Hispanic might in Italy and the Netherlands.

Gradually, however, a chain of towns and fortified posts were established across the isthmus, beginning with the port city of Panama on the Pacific coast and ending with the port of Nombre de Dios on the Atlantic coast. Just as tales of Indian gold had drawn the *conquistadores* to the New World, the rich yield of the Spanish mines now attracted marauding English swashbucklers. In 1572, Nombre de Dios was sacked by the most celebrated of the Elizabethan seadogs, Sir Francis Drake; a century later, the last of the great buccaneers, Sir Henry Morgan, seized and laid waste to Panama itself, carrying off treasures of gold and silver bullion so immense that it required 175 mules and bullocks to carry it. Because much of it was lost or buried along the march, Morgan's Treasure found its way into folklore, to be unsuccessfully sought by treasure hunters to this day.

Despite these occasional treasure raids and Indian and slave uprisings, Spanish authority in Central America went largely unchallenged for three centuries. It is from this period—the early 1500s to the early 1800s—that modern Panama can trace most of its cultural roots. The sparse original Indian population was soon overrun by large numbers of Spaniards and imported African slaves. Intermarriage was common, and most modern Panamanians are of mixed Spanish, Negro, and Indian descent, sharing the language (Spanish) and religion (Catholicism) introduced, often at swordpoint, by the *conquistadores*. Many of the wealthy families who make up today's small Panamanian oligarchy can trace their ancestry back to the early years of the Spanish rule.

From time to time during the years of Spanish rule, the idea of an isthmian canal was put forward, but the lethargic Spanish government made no decision to build one until 1814, more than 300 years after Balboa first crossed the isthmus. By 1814, however, Spain's imperial power in Central America was on the brink of collapse, a casualty of the Napoleonic Wars in Europe and the rise of nationalism thoroughout Latin America. Native leaders like Bolivar, San Martin, and O'Higgins, inspired by the example of the United Stetes, had launched their struggle for independence. In the revolutions which followed, Spain had no time or resources to spare for construction of a canal; indeed, the next champion of the canal concept would be the father of Latin American independence himself, Simon Bolivar. In 1822, Bolivar, full of high hopes, called for a Pan-American congress. His goal was a league of independent Latin American states, each internally sovereign but all united against foreign foes and dedicated to forwarding hemispheric cooperation and political and economic development. The result was the Congress of Panama; as Bolivar's scholarly biographer, Dr. Gerhard Masur, wrote, "Bolivar had long ago chosen Panama as the haven for the American federation. While he was still trying to lay its foundations, he also prepared for the building of the Panama Canal."

Once again in the tangled history of Panama, however, the dreamer proved unable to realize his dream. Lofty visions of a progressive, unified Latin America crumbled in the midst of squalid rivalry, greed, and grasping personal ambition. The occasional pattern of Latin American political excess and instability had begun, and Bolivar would soon express his disgust at the emerging trends toward violence, chaos, and tyranny:

> We have tried all system, and nothing has proved effective. Mexico has fallen; Guatemala is destroyed; there are new revolutions in Chile. In Buenos Aires they have killed the President. Bolivia has had three presidents in two days, and two of them have been murdered.

All of which is still a partially accurate description of the political climate in Latin America 150 years after Bolivar wrote it. For those concerned with the reliability of any new canal treaty agreed to by the military dictatorship in present-day Panama, another line of Bolivar's carries an even more disturbing timeliness. In Latin

21

America, he wrote, *"Treaties are mere scraps of paper,* constitutions are books, elections are battles, freedom is anarchy, and life is a torture."

Thus the likelihood of a Panama Canal being built for and by Latin Americans died a-borning, along with the notion of a peaceful, stable Latin American federation. Bolivar himself barely outlived the failure of his life's work. Only 47, but a broken, bitter man, he died in exile on December 17, 1830. A month before his death he wrote the bottom line to his disillusionment with Latin American independence. Latin America, he said, "is ungovernable. Those who serve the revolution plough the sea. The only thing to do. . . is to emigrate."

Beginnings of U.S. Interest in a Canal

Simon Bolivar was not the only man interested in building an interoceanic canal through Central America in the 1820s. In 1826 United States Secretary of State Henry Clay proposed to the assembled Latin American nations at the Congress of Panama that a joint U.S.–Latin American effort be made to build a canal.

> What is to redound to the advantage of all America should be effected by common means and united exertions, and should not be left to the separate and unassisted efforts of any one power. . . . The benefits ought not to be exclusively appropriated to any one nation. . . .

In 1835 the Senate passed a resolution urging President Andrew Jackson to enter into negotiations with other nations with a view to building a canal and securing free and equal navigation rights to all nations. The House of Representatives passed a similar resolution in 1839, urging the same course on Jackson's successor to the presidency, Martin Van Buren. By the middle of the nineteenth century, the opening of the American West and the discovery of gold in California created further interest in a canal; in 1846, the United States signed a treaty with Colombia (then called New Granada) which guaranteed the United States "the right of way or transit across the Isthmus of Panama upon any modes of communication that now exist or may be hereafter constructed." In exchange, the United States guaranteed the neutrality of the isthmus and Colombia's sovereignty and title to the territory. But political developments elsewhere in Central America soon distracted the United States and delayed practical implementation of the treaty.

As the United States grew from an economically and militarily insignificant coastal enclave into a transcontinental power with burgeoning industry and trade, Great Britain, the greatest maritime trading power of the time, began to take a renewed interest in American affairs in general, and the possibility of a Central American canal in particular. While America had its hands full fighting the Mexican War, the British exerted their influence to gain control of an alternative canal route through Nicaragua. The result was a stalemate formalized by the Clayton-Bulwer Treaty of 1850. Under the terms of the agreement, Britain and the United States both pledged never to obtain or maintain exclusive control over a ship canal, or to fortify it, or to assume or exercise dominion over any Central American territory through which such a canal might be built.

It was a stand-off; America had pledged itself not to obtain exclusive control of a canal in return for Britain's relinquishing its de facto control over the possible Nicaraguan route. As long as the Clayton-Bulwer Treaty remained in force, official, direct United States control of a canal project was out of the question; once again, American interest in the canal idea waned. The only direct U.S. concern with the isthmus now revolved around the transisthmian railway, which private American developers completed in 1855. In the following years, when the political situation in Colombian Panama broke out into open disorder, American troops were landed, at the express request of the Colombian government, to prevent disruption of rail traffic; that was as far as U.S. involvement went. The existence of the transisthmian railroad, plus the completion in 1869 of the transcontinental railway in the United States, made Panama a nonissue as long as no third power attempted to gain influence in the area and build a canal. Such interference was not long in coming.

It took the form of a colorful French diplomat, engineer, and entrepeneur, Vicomte Ferdinand Marie de Lesseps, the man who in 1854 had gained the concession to build a canal through the Isthmus of Suez in Egypt. The Suez Canal had been completed, under Lesseps's direction, in 1869. Many of the crowned heads of Europe

23

were present for the gala opening, here described by a wide-eyed reporter for *The Illustrated London News*:

> On November 17, a procession of some fifty vessels, including the steam-yachts of the Empress of the French, the Emperor of Austria, and the Viceroy, with a Prussian frigate, a Russian vessel of war, various steam-boats, pleasure-yachts, and merchant ships, went through the northern half of the Canal, from Port Said to Ismalia. . . . It is impossible not to contemplate this magnificant achievement without emotion. . . .

It was the proudest moment in Lesseps's long and checkered career. Hailed by the press as "one of those great men of practical invention and administrative execution," he was showered with honors, including France's highest, the Grand Cross of the Legion of Honor. Elation turned to bitterness in 1875, however; following the collapse of France's Second Empire and taking advantage of a bankrupt Egyptian government's desperate need for ready cash, Prime Minister Benjamin Disraeli secured controlling interest in the Suez Canal for Great Britain. With control of the Suez Canal in British hands, an embittered Lesseps set off in search of a new challenge. He found it in Panama.

In 1878 a French company organized by Lesseps obtained a concession from Colombia to build a sea-level waterway across the isthmus. Suddenly, Panama was back in the headlines. The United States government began to take renewed interest. Unsatisfied with Lesseps's assurances that this canal would "always be kept free from political influence," Secretary of State William Maxwell Evarts issued a strong protest:

> Our Pacific coast is so situated that, with our railroad connections, time [in case of war] would always be allowed to prepare for its defense. But with a canal through the isthmus the same advantage would be given to a hostile fleet which would be given to friendly commerce; its line of operations and the time in which warlike demonstration could be made, would be enormously shortened.

In a line that is particularly timely today, Secretary Evarts stressed an overwhelming argument for American control of the canal that still applies: "*All the treaties of neutrality in the world might fail to be a safeguard in a time of great conflict.*"

Undeterred, the French company continued to sell stock and, in 1881, actual work on the canal began. In the same year, President Chester A. Arthur attempted to modify the Clayton-Bulwer Treaty with Great Britain to give America a freer hand in dealing with the canal question, but Britain refused to revise the treaty.

Nevertheless, in 1887, while French work on the isthmian canal continued, a syndicate of American private investors began a rival project in Nicaragua; in 1889 Congress gave is sanction by incorporating the enterprise as the Maritime Canal Company of Nicaragua. Meanwhile, in Colombian Panama, a mixture of corruption and disease succeeded where American influence had failed. In February 1889, Lesseps's Compagnie du Canal Interocéanique collapsed, triggering a major financial and political scandal and an attempted cover-up on the part of the deeply implicated French government.

Thousands of individual Frenchmen, from financiers to peasants, had invested 1.5 billion francs in the bankrupted company. Now it was all lost, and it would take four years of litigation and investigation to clear up the mess, during the course of which it was discovered that Lesseps and his associates had spent thousands of francs to buy the support of the Parisian press and members of France's Senate and Chamber of Deputies. Appearances were not improved when one of the company's kingpins, Baron Jacques Reinach, was found dead the day after he was summoned for trial. Lesseps and his associates were ultimately tried, found guilty and disgraced, and work on the canal ground to a stop.

The failed French attempt to build a Panama Canal had been immensely costly in lives and treasure. Of a labor force that averaged 10,000 men a year, 20,000 had perished of malaria, yellow fever and other tropical diseases; as for the degree of corruption involved, while $260 million had been disbursed by the company, on close scrutiny it was discovered that only $40 million of this amount had actually been spent for legitimate concessions and work on the canal. The remaining $220 million had gone into graft. All that remained of Lesseps's grand vision was a useless stretch of ditch and the silent wreckage of rusting machinery. Another brief, static interlude descended on the sleepy Isthmus of Panama.

Three years after the failure of the French company, and in the absence of the threat of new foreign competition, the American-owned Maritime Canal Company of Nicaragua followed Lesseps's firm into bankruptcy. Its capital had never amounted to more than $6 million, and this had quickly been swallowed up by the cost of laying the beginnings of a railroad and starting excavations on the proposed canal. It is an ironic historical footnote that, except for the fact that the company happened to run out of money during the financial panic of 1893, it might easily have raised enough fresh capital to complete a Nicaraguan canal, in which case Panama would probably have remained a stagnant provincial backwater of Colombia, the isthmian canal would probably never have been dug, and General Omar Torrijos would probably be earning a meager living instead of trying to shake down the American people for millions of dollars.

The Turning Point in American Involvement

The turn of the century also marked the turning point in America's involvement in the isthmus, and our emergence as a global power. On February 15, 1898, the U.S.S. *Maine* was blown up in Havana harbor. While the true cause of the explosion is still debated by historians, the practical result of the sinking of the *Maine* was a cresting wave of war fever, stirred up in part by yellow press lords like William Randolph Hearst. To the rallying cry of "Remember the *Maine*!," the United States declared war on Spain on April 21, 1898. A string of American naval and military victories ended with the complete humiliation of Spain, including the loss of Cuba, the last Spanish colonial foothold in the Western Hemisphere, and a heightened American profile in the Caribbean and extensive American involvement in the Pacific, including occupation of the Philippines. The United States was now a major naval power with strategic interests in both the Atlantic and the Pacific, and the ninety-day rush of the U.S. cruiser *Oregon* around Cape Horn during the war had brought home the advantage of a Central American interoceanic canal to millions of average Americans who followed the war in the sensationalized pages of the mass-circulation dailies.

In his 1898 message to the Congress, President William McKinley articulated the growing public interest in, and the increasing practical need for, a canal:

That the construction of such a maritime highway is now more
than ever indispensable to that intimate and ready intercommuni-
cation between our eastern and western seaboards demanded by
the annexation of the Hawaiian Islands and the propective expansion of our influence and commerce in the Pacific, and that our
national policy now more imperatively than ever calls for its
control by this Government, are propositions which I doubt not
the Congress will duly appreciate and wisely act upon.

Already in 1896, Secretary of State Richard Olney had made
overtures to the British foreign office with an aim to modify or
abrogate the Clayton-Bulwer Treaty. At first the British rebuffed
the American approach but, when Britain became entangled in the
costly and upopular Boer War (October 12, 1899–May 31, 1902)
and ran into increasingly hostile reactions from other major European powers, the importance of winning American good will sof-
tened the British stance on the canal.

The result was the Hay-Pauncefote Treaty of 1901 (for a full text
of the treaty, see Appendix 1). Thanks to the skilled diplomacy of
American Secretary of State John Hay, and the newfound British
respect for American importance in global affairs, the way was finally cleared for direct United States control of a canal across Central America. Hay-Pauncefote abrogated the restrictions of the
Clayton-Bulwer Treaty and provided that a canal could "be constructed under the auspices of the Government of the United States,
directly or indirectly." America would "have and enjoy all the
rights incident to such construction, as well as the exclusive right
of providing for the regulation and managment of the canal."

The creation of an American-controlled canal was now a virtual
certainty, but the question of where it would be built remained
open. The sentimental favorite with American public opinion was
still the Nicaraguan site, Panama being associated in the public
mind with the abortive French attempt led by Lesseps. In 1894, the
remnants of the French company had been dusted off and reor-
ganized as the New Panama Canal Company. Lacking the resources
to resume work on the canal itself, the company's sole hope lay in
finding an affluent buyer; a high-powered and none-too-scrupulous
lobbying campaign was launched in Washington to sell Congress
on the Panama route.

In 1897, the Walker Commission was appointed to consider the
canal question and, although many of its technical findings sup-

ported the isthmian over the Nicaraguan route, in 1899 it recommended Nicaragua. Once again, the matter might have been permanently settled and the Panamanian issue laid to rest forever; but the "Panama lobby" rallied enough congressional support to pass an 1899 law directing the president to name a commission with a mandate to consider all possible canal routes. Once again, Panama was back in the running. In the meantime, to increase American leverage and keep as many options open as possible, the State Department in 1900 signed protocols with the Costa Rican and Nicaraguan governments under which both countries agreed to negotiate canal treaties with the United States at such times as the president was authorized by Congress to acquire a route through their territories.

This new development sufficiently worried the Colombian government; to avoid being left out in the cold, it sent a minister to the United States to negotiate a canal treaty. In 1901, the Walker Commission issued its final report, still in favor of the Nicaraguan route. This was all that was needed to stop the New Panama Canal Company from holding out for a higher bid. In January 1902, it telegraphed Washington a concrete offer to sell its rights and property in Panama for $40 million, a figure which the Walker Commission had ruled acceptable. Within two weeks, the commission issued a "Supplementary Report" recommending the Panama route "due to changed circumstances."

After some heavy horsetrading between congressional partisans of both sites, the Spooner Act was passed on June 2, 1902, authorizing President Theodore Roosevelt to acquire the assets of the New Panama Canal Company for the offered price of $40 million, and to obtain a strip of Colombian territory not less than six miles wide in which to construct and operate a canal, along with any additional territory and rights the president deemed necessary to the project. However, if these terms could not be met "within a reasonable time" the president was then directed to resume negotiations for a Nicaraguan canal.

The Hay-Herrán Treaty

These events occured at an unfortunate time in Colombia's volatile history. Beset by civil war, administrative collapse, and near bankruptcy, and with the country in a state of siege, Colombia was being governed by executive decree. The Colombian government was torn between its desire to be the site of the canal and its fear that a hastily negotiated treaty, ratified by decree in the absence of the Colombian Congress, would offend national pride and trigger further civil unrest.

The desperate need for cash, the long-term economic benefits which a canal would inevitably bring, and the very real possibility that the province of Panama—which had rebelled several times in the past—would break away and deal directly with the United States outweighed other considerations. In a letter to acting head of state José Manuel Marroquín, Colombia's representative in Washington, Carlos Martinéz Silva, spelled out the danger of Panamanian secession:

> . . . the Panamanians of position and financial resources will never willingly submit to the opening of the canal in any other place than at the isthmus. They understand very well that the adoption of the Nicaragua route will be the moral and material ruin of Panama; and this sacrifice, which will have no compensations, may very well prove superior to the concept of platonic patriotism.

With the home government's hands full dealing with civil war, Colombia's negotiators in Washington had to act on their own initiative in a highly charged atmosphere. Marroquín and his regime were in an unenviable position, as he himself pointed out in a letter written in July 1902:

> Concerning the canal question, I find myself in a horrible perplexity; in order that the North Americans may complete the work by virtue of a convention with the Government of Colombia, it is necessary to make concessions of territory, of sovereignty, and of jurisdiction, which the executive power has not the power of yielding. . . .
> History will say of me that I ruined the isthmus and all Colombia, by not permitting the opening of the Panama Canal, or that I permitted it to be done, scandalously injuring the rights of my country.

As a sap to the national pride—and perhaps to salvage his personal and political standing in the event of a nationalist backlash—Marroquín instructed his negotiators to proceed, but repeatedly stressed that any agreement reached would have to be ratified by the Colombian Congress. The final draft of the treaty was primarily the work of Secretary of State John Hay and Colombia's chief negotiator in Washington, Tomás Herrán, and is known to history as the Hay-Herrán Treaty (a full text of the Hay-Herrán Treaty appears in Appendix 1). In its overall terms, it closely resembles the subsequent treaty under which the United States and the newly independent Panamanian nation agreed to construct the canal. Its principal provisions:

—Granted the United States a 100-year lease, renewable at the sole option of the United States, on a zone of land ten kilometers wide across the Isthmus of Panama in return for a payment of $10 million and an annual subsidy of $250,000;

—Granted the United States exclusive right to construct, maintain, operate, and protect the canal;

—Authorized the new Panama Canal Company to sell its rights and properties to the United States;

—Recognized Colombia's nominal sovereignty over the Canal Zone;

—Established three types of judicial tribunals (Joint, Colombian, and United States) to handle future legal disputes;

—Gave Colombia responsibility for defending the canal and the railway except "under exceptional circumstances."

The "exceptional circumstances" gave the United States broad powers to ":'act in the interest of their protection, without the necessity of obtaining consent beforehand of the Government of Colombia." If this proviso seems hard on the Colombians, it is only fair to point out that the Colombian government, at that very moment in the midst of a civil war, had amply proven its inability to maintain order unassisted—a situation every bit as true of the corrupt military dictatorship in Panama today as it was of Colombia at the turn of the century.

When the civil war in Colombia simmered down and an uneasy truce achieved in November 1902, President Roosevelt decided that the time had come for decisive action. Never one to mince words, T.R. instructed Secretary of State Hay (who once described himself as merely "a fine figurehead" when serving under the dynamic Roosevelt) to issue a stiffly worded warning to Herrán on January 21, 1903:

> I am commanded by the President to inform you that the reasonable time provided in the statute for the conclusion of the negotiations with Colombia for the excavation of an isthmian canal has expired, and he has authorized me to sign the treaty. . . . I am not authorized to consider or discuss any other change.

Herrán was trapped between a rock and a hard place. If anyone was going to throw a wrench into the negotiations now, he seems to have concluded, it would have to be the Colombian Congress, not him. The day after he received the Hay ultimatum, Tomás Herrán signed the treaty. Predictably, swift ratification by the U.S. Senate followed on March 17, 1903. Now all that stood between the theory and the reality of the canal was the Colombian Congress.

It wasn't much, but it was enough to upset the apple cart. Congressional elections were held in Colombia in March 1903, and President Marroquín set June 20 as the date for a special session to consider the treaty. The nationalist backlash which Silva, Herrán, and Marroquín had feared and predicted was not long in coming. Five months elapsed between the signing of the treaty and the special session, and the air was filled with charges of "sell-out" and "imperialism." The five major popular objections to the treaty were:

1. The loss of Colombian territory involved;
2. The loss of sovereignty and national face;
3. Questionable constitutionality of granting control of Colombian territory, in perpetuity, to a foreign power;
4. Greed, in the form of demands for a higher price; if rape was inevitable, Colombians might not enjoy it, but they certainly intended to charge as much as possible for it;
5. A vague but general fear and resentment of the specter of "American imperialism."

Proponents of the treaty, led by the Colombian foreign minister, warned that the United States was the only country or organization willing and able to take on the herculean task of building and running the canal. Saying no to the U.S. meant saying no to an isthmian canal forever, they argued; the American government flatly stated that unless it was granted clear control over the zone, it wanted no part of it. There simply was no room left for compromise.

31

As is so often the case in Latin American politics, emotionalism carried the day; on August 12, 1903, the Colombian Senate, in a unanimous vote, rejected the Hay-Herrán Treaty and the legislature adjourned without taking any further action.

Revolution in Panama, 1903

To borrow a phrase from the late Everett Dirksen, the fat was now in the fire. If public opinion in the Colombian capital was strongly against the treaty, the emotional, economic, and regional sentiments of the province of Panama were even more violently in support of it. Neglected by the central government, ignored by the rest of the country, and now seemingly deprived forever of the one means of vitalizing a stagnant local economy, the Panamanians took unilateral and revolutionary action, as Silva had predicted they might, and as their delegates to the special session had warned they would if Colombia rejected the treaty.

In seventy-five years of independence from Spain, the Panamanians had made numerous bids to break away from Colombia. All had been crushed, but now the Panamanians had a powerful friend in the form of the United States. During the course of the Colombian Senate debate, as it became clear that the treaty would be rejected, a small group of prominent Panamanians—investors hoping to realize a handsome profit by selling the New Panama Canal Company to the United States—met secretly to plot for independence. When revolution broke out, there was no local opposition; control of the railway, hastily granted American recognition, a landing party of forty-two U.S. Marines in dress whites, and an off-shore U.S. naval presence preempted Colombian suppression of Panamanian independence. It was a bloodless coup with the sole exception of one unfortunate casualty, neither American, Colombian, nor Panamanian; but an unfortunate Chinese who managed to walk into a token artillery barrage—one small bang in a massive chorus of Colombian whimpers.

Years later, President Roosevelt, who was not in the habit of hiding his light under a bushel, would boast: "I took the Isthmus, started the Canal, and then left Congress—not to debate the Canal, but to debate me. . . . But while the debate goes on the Canal does too." This bit of Rooseveltian swagger has probably done a great deal of damage to America's image in Latin America and certainly must have stoked the fires of Panamanian resentment. Yet the true story behind Panamanian independence, as this account makes clear, is one in which the United States played a secondary role at best.

The fact that some Panamanians actively organized and fought for independence—bloodlessly as it turned out, but with the threat of being tried and executed for treason if they failed—and the equally obvious fact that the vast majority of their countrymen either gave them passive support or remained neutral, show that there was, if not an overwhelming enthusiasm for independence, little Panamanian support for the central Colombian government. Those expecting a stronger outpouring of public enthusiasm should bear in mind the experience of the American Revolution. Historians estimate that American sentiment during the Revolution was almost equally divided: approximately one-third actively supporting independence, about another third remaining loyal to the British Crown, and a slightly larger group straddling the fence, waiting to see which side would come out on top.

In Panama, as in the United States, the forces of independence prevailed. The American colonies won with the help of vast subsidies from France, two French expeditionary forces, and the French navy; Panama with forty-two U.S. Marines who didn't even get their uniforms dirty, and a few U.S. naval craft, most of which never even touched shore.

What really matters is that once Panama became an independent state overwhelmingly in favor of reaching a canal agreement with the United States, the last obstacle to a treaty had been removed. Panama won its independence; the United States was now about to win its canal. The die was cast.

Chapter 3:
What Panama Agreed To

The Basis for American Rights to the Canal

There is an old saying that there are two species of creatures who seem to be coming when they are going, and going when they are coming: crabs and diplomats. All too often in the annals of diplomacy, "clever" negotiators of the Kissinger variety deliberately obfuscate in the hope that if a treaty or agreement is made sufficiently vague, both parties can honor it without much inconvenience. This kind of warped thinking is amply illustrated in the new Panamanian treaties, and reflects the elitist view which George Bernard Shaw once described as the "axiom of diplomacy that the people must not be told the truth. . . . In the end, lying becomes a reflex action with diplomatists."

Fortunately for the United States, Henry Kissinger did not negotiate the Hay–Bunau-Varilla Treaty of 1903. It defines American rights to the canal in plain, straightforward language, which is probably one reason it has lasted for seventy-five years while such devious, Kissingeresque agreements as the Vietnam settlement of 1973 have collapsed in a matter of months, often leaving American credibility and prestige in tatters.

Philippe Bunau-Varilla was the former chief engineer of the French Canal Company. He played an instrumental part in winning American support for Panamanian independence and, in return for his help, the leaders of the Panamanian independence movement agreed to make him their chief negotiator for a canal treaty with the United States. Meeting in Washington with Secretary of State Hay, Bunau-Varilla worked out the formula which remains in force today and provides the sound legal basis for America's rights to the canal.

On November 18, 1903, Bunau-Varilla and Secretary Hay signed the convention for the American building of a canal to connect the

Atlantic and Pacific oceans. Revisionist historians and advocates of American surrender in Panama have since made much of the fact that two further negotiators appointed by the Panamanian provisional government. Ministers Boyd and Amador, arrived in Washington too late to participate in the discussion and signing of the treaty. Such historians point to the letter of instructions from the Panamanian government which Boyd and Amador carried with them, addressed to Bunau-Varilla. The letter empowered Bunau-Varilla "to adjust a treaty for the canal construction by the United States," but added that:

> . . . all clauses of this treaty will be discussed previously with the delegates of the junta [provisional government]. M. Amador and Boyd. And you will proceed in everything strictly in accord with them.

However, any objections which the Panamanian government may have had to Bunau-Varilla's unilateral action, and any question as to his authority to sign the agreement on behalf of Panama, were settled once and forever when, on December 2, 1903, the provisional government itself ratified the treaty.

In general, the treaty was modeled on the previous Hay-Herrán agreement, although the area of the proposed zone was increased; the United States was empowered to construct a canal through a territory ten, rather than six, miles wide. Panama granted the United States the right, at all times, to use American armed forces to defend the canal. From the moment of ratification, America became the de facto and de jure master of the Canal Zone, explicitly granted full sovereign powers within its boundaries, as Article III of Hay–Bunau-Varilla makes clear (for the full text of this treaty, see Appendix 1):

> The Republic of Panama grants to the United States *all the rights, power, and authority within the zone* mentioned and described in Article II of this agreement and within the limits of all auxiliary lands and waters mentioned and described in said Article II *which the United States would possess and exercise if it were the sovereign* of the territory within which such lands and waters are located *to the entire exclusion of the exercise by the Republic of Panama of any such sovereign rights, power, or authority*. [Emphasis added.]

Seldom in the often-muddled history of diplomacy has an agreement been more clear and specific in saying exactly what it meant. As Bunau-Varilla pointed out in his book, *Panama Canal,* published ten years later, "to cut short any possible debate, I decided to grant a concession of sovereignty *en bloc.*" The Panamanian secretary of government, Tomás Arias, recognized this cession of sovereign powers in a diplomatic note to the United States government dated May 25, 1904:

> The government of the Republic of Panama considers that upon the exchange of ratification, on February 26, 1904, of the Treaty for opening the inter-ocean Canal across the Isthmus of Panama, *its jurisdiction ceased over the Zone.* [Emphasis added.]

Jurisdiction, says Merriam-Webster's *New Collegiate Dictionary,* is "the authority of a sovereign power to govern or legislate," and even Henry Kissinger has recognized the legal basis for America's sovereign powers in the Canal Zone. In advocating the new treaties with Panama, he has stated that they will "restore" Panamanian sovereignty over the zone, thus conceding that, in 1903, effective sovereignty passed to the United States, where it still resides until such time as the U.S. choose to restore it to Panama.

In the Winter 1977 issue of *Orbis,* veteran American diplomat and international law authority Charles Maechling, Jr., flatly refutes the claim of Ambassador Ellsworth Bunker and other advocates of the new treaties that "under the law we do not have sovereignty in Panama." While the Bunker statement echoes other attacks on America's right to the canal, Mr. Maechling writes,

> . . . it does not fit the traditional definition of sovereignty under international law. Brierly and Brownlie, the two leading authorities on public international law, agree that sovereignty (a) is territorial in scope and (b) consists in essense of a bundle of jurisdictional rights, of which the primary one, in Brownlie's words, is "jurisdiction, *prima facie* exclusive, over a territory and the permanent population living there." If one applies this test to the Canal Zone. . . the attributes of sovereignty exercised by the United States are self-evident. . . .

Mr. Maechling groups the evidence of American sovereignty into three general categories: government, laws and courts:

Government: The United States is the exclusive governing authority in the Canal Zone. The zone government is by law an agency of the federal government whose chief executive officer, the governor, is appointed by the President of the United States.

Laws: The United States Congress is the exclusive legislative body of the Canal Zone, and in this capacity it has enacted a civil code and a variety of supplemental statutes. By specific inclusion, Congress makes various provisons of U.S. law applicable to the zone.

Courts: A system of United States courts, consisting of magistrates' courts of limited jurisdiction and a U.S. district court for the Canal Zone, administers justice in the zone. U.S. courts have consistently refused to recognize the jurisdiction of Panamanian courts within the Zone, ruling that this would constitute the "exercise of a sovereign right in the Canal Zone which is prohibited by the treaty."

Mr. Maechling concludes that the United States' legal claim to sovereign power in the Canal Zone

easily fits every definition of sovereignty under international law. . . each inclusion or exclusion of the zone from the application of U.S. law, and each narrowly limited cession of jurisdiction, is itself *the product of U.S. congressional legislation or executive order. Each limited transfer of jurisdiction has been an assertion of U.S. sovereignty, not a denial of it.* [Emphasis added.]

In other words, the very yielding to Panama of certain small pieces of control proves that the United States has full control—de facto sovereignty—in the first place. This view has consistently been borne out in court. In 1907, in the case of *Wilson v. Shaw,* the Supreme Court ruled that the canal is American territory and stated that:

It is hypercritical to contend that the title of the United States to the Canal Zone is imperfect and that the territory described does not belong to this nation because of the omission of some of the technical terms used in ordinary conveyances of real estates.

Nor are more recent judicial affirmations of America's sovereign powers in the Canal Zone wanting. In 1972, in the case of *The United States v. Husband,* the Supreme Court upheld a lower court decision that the Canal Zone is "unincorporated territory of the

United States'' over which the Congress has ''complete and plenary authority.'' These rulings, and the learned opinions of some of America's foremost legal thinkers (see Appendix 2), not only establish American power of sovereignty over the Canal Zone, they also prove that modification of the status of the zone, as contemplated in the proposed new treaties, requires the concurrence of *both* houses of Congress, not just Senate ratification.

Reaffirmation of American Powers of Sovereignty

In urging rapid Senate approval of the Hay–Bunau-Varilla treaty without any amendments, Secretary of State Hay wrote to Senator Spooner on January 20, 1904, that:

> As it stands now as soon as the Senate votes we shall have a treaty in the main very satisfactory, vastly advantageous to the United States. . . not so advantageous to Panama. If we amend the treaty and send it back there [to Panama] some time next month, the period of enthusiastic unanimity, which . . . comes only once in the life of a revolution, will have passed away, and they will have entered on the new fields of politics and dispute. . . . If it is again submitted to their consideration they will attempt to amend it in many places, no man can say with what result. . . .

By quickly ratifying the treaty without amendments, the Senate avoided this problem and both nations officially approved the treaty exactly as it had been agreed to by Hay and Bunau-Varilla. However, Hay was right; the ''period of enthusiastic unanimity'' was indeed short-lived. Once Panamanian independence was secure and the American commitment to build and operate the canal was firm, some Panamanians began to reinterpret the treaty they had ratified. No matter how much they changed their interpretations, however, there was one part of the treaty that no Panamanian government has ever disputed: they have all pocketed the American subsidies and other benefits granted under the terms of Hay–Bunau-Varilla. Wanting to have one's cake and eat it too has long been a characteristic of Panamanian diplomacy.

When, later in 1904, Panama questioned the degree of American control granted under the treaty, Secretary Hay issued a comprehensive reply to the Panamanian minister's note:

If it could or should be admitted that the titular sovereign of the Canal Zone is the Republic of Panama, such sovereign is mediatized [i.e., converted] by its own act, solemnly declared and publicly proclaimed by treaty stipulations, induced by a desire to make possible the completion of a great work which will confer inestimable benefit upon the people of the isthmus and the nations of the world. . . . Under the stipulations of Article III, if sovereign powers are to be exercised in and over the Canal Zone, they must be exercised by the United States. Such exercises of power must be, therefore, in accordance with the judgment and discretion of the constituted authorities of the United States, the governmental entity charged with responsibility for such exercise, and not in accordance with the judgment and discretion of a governmental entity [the Republic of Panama] that is not charged with such responsibility and by treaty stipulations acquiesces in "the entire exclusion of the exercise by it of any sovereign rights, power, or authority" in and over the territory involved.

Article II provided that "the Republic of Panama grants to the United States in perpetuity the use, occupation, and control of a zone of land and land under water for the construction, maintenance, operation, sanitation, and protection of said canal."

The Panamanian authorities now contend that the words "for the construction, maintenance, operation, sanitation, and protection of said canal" constitute a limitation on the grant; that is, that the grant is confined to the purposes so stated. The position of the United States is that the words were not intended as a limitation on the grant but as a declaration, and are appropriate words of conveyance.

As has been shown, this interpretation, upheld by the United States Supreme Court, is the legal basis for the present American position in Panama. As the powers of sovereignty were granted by Panama to the United States "in perpetuity" they are ours as long as we choose to keep them. While the United States has allowed Panama a powerless but face-saving claim to "titular sovereignty" over the territory of the zone, this in no way affects the sovereign *powers*—the actual control and possession of the zone by the United States. As William Howard Taft, then secretary of war, reported to the Senate Committee on Interoceanic Canals after a November 1904 visit with Panamanian President Manuel Amador:

[Article III] is peculiar in not conferring sovereignty directly

39

upon the United States, but in giving to the United States the powers which it would have if it were sovereign. This gives rise to the obvious implication that a mere titular sovereignty is reserved in the Panamanian government. Now, I agree that to the Anglo-Saxon mind a titular sovereignty is like what Governor Allen of Ohio once characterized as a "barren ideality," but to the Spanish or Latin mind, poetic and sentimental, enjoying the intellectual refinements, and dwelling much on names and forms, it is by no means unimportant.

So Panaa was welcome to claim an empty "titular sovereignty," one which had no actual force, in law or in reality, and in no way limited the total control of the canal granted by treaty to the United States. In 1924, Secretary of State Charles Evans Hughes repeated this American stance in a convention with Panamanian Minister Alfaro. He summarized his statement in a memorandum:

> This government would never recede from the position it had taken in the note of Secretary Hay in 1904. This government could not and would not enter into any discussion affecting its full right to deal with the Canal Zone and to the exclusion of any sovereign rights or authority on the part of Panama. . . . This must be regarded as ending the discussion of that matter.

While the 1903 treaty had undergone two major revisions—the General Treaty of Friendship and Cooperation of 1936 and the Treaty of Mutual Understandings and Cooperation of 1955 (see Appendix 1), neither in any way amended or modified Articles II and III of the original agreement, the crucial passages conferring power of sovereignty on the United States in perpetuity. This fact was brought home during the hearings the Senate Foreign Relations Committee held on the Treaty of Mutual Understandings and Cooperation of 1955, as illustrated by the following exchange between Senator Alexander Wiley and Assistant Secretary of State for Inter-American Affairs Henry Holland:

> *Senator Wiley:* As I understood from you, Secretary Holland, there is nothing in this present treaty that would in the slightest degree depreciate all the attributes of sovereignty that we possess.
> *Mr. Holland:* That is true; and so true is it, that in the course of the negotiations the Panamanians advanced several small requests, which one by one, had considerable appeal, but all of

which we refused because we did not want to leave one grain of evidence that could a hundred years hence be interpreted as implying any admission by the United States that we possess and exercise anything less than 100 percent of the rights of sovereignty in this area.

Was the Treaty Unfair?

When any nation goes to the bargaining table it does so with the determination to act in its own best interests and to derive as many benefits as possible from the ensuing negotiations. Our 1903 agreement with Panama was no exception. There is no doubt about it: the Hay–Bunau-Varilla Treaty was very favorable to the United States, a shrewd bargain. But there was absolutely nothing illegal or unethical about it, and the benefits that the Republic of Panama has derived from it over the years are impressive. The United States did for Panama what the Spanish, Simon Bolivar, the French company, and the Colombians had all failed to do: built and operated a magnificent interoceanic canal that pumped commercial vitality and opportunity into the stagnant economic bloodstream of Panama. We also rid the country of the scourges of malaria and yellow fever, brought good jobs and opportunity to thousands of needy Panamanians, and promptly paid increasingly large subsidies to the Panamanian government—all after helping Panama to win independence in the first place. To the extent that Panama exists and is a viable state today, it is because a strong America, which could have taken what it wanted without giving anything in return, has been a generous friend of Panama from the moment of ratification of the 1903 treaty.

But, as Aristotle observed three centuries before the birth of Christ, gratitude soon grows old. All of us have known at least a few testy and resentful characters who find it harder to forgive a favor than an injustice. Thanks to the constant prodding of political demagogues—and the certainty that the United States will react with fairness, compassion, and restraint, even when provoked—many Panamanians have whipped themselves into an unthinking frenzy of jingoism and anti-Americanism. Their specialty, as ably demonstrated by that past master of political contortionism, Panamanian dictator Omar Torrijos, is to bite America's hand while

41

simultaneously demanding bigger and bigger American handouts.

Ironically, if anyone has a right to feel bilked, it is the Colombians, not the Panamanians. After all, they were the big losers in 1903. But under the terms of the Thompson-Urrutia convention, signed in April 1914, Colombia agreed to recognize Panamanian independence in return for a $25 million indemnity from the United States. The agreement ran into opposition in the United States Senate but, in 1921, it was ratified in amended form and accepted the following year by Colombia. This treaty further emphasized the strength of American rights by asserting that title to the Panama Canal and railroad "now vests entirely and absolutely in the United States without any encumbrances or indemnity whatever." Thus, with the recognition of the status quo in Panama and the Canal Zone by the nation which had previously held sovereign power over both, America's legal claim to the waterway was rendered watertight. Having established this clear-cut standing in law, we must now determine how important the Panama Canal is to the United States today. Given our proven right to sovereign powers in the Canal Zone, is it in our best interests to retain those powers or to surrender them?

Chapter 4:
The Importance of the Canal Today

The importance of the Panama Canal was recognized almost immediately around the world. Macmillan's *International Geography*, published in London in 1911, proclaimed that previously insignificant Panama had become "the most important republic in Central America," due to "the work being carried on in constructing the great ship-canal which is to unite the Atlantic and Pacific across the narrowest part of the isthmus joining North and South America."

> A belt of country 5 miles wide on each side of the route of the canal has been ceded to the United States, and for sanitary and quarantine purposes the towns of Panama on the Pacific and Colón on the Atlantic side are under the same administration. The two ports have been united by a railway 47 miles long since 1855. The health of the Canal belt has been improved in a remarkable degree, yellow fever and malarial fever, formerly responsible for a very high death-rate, having been practically stamped out by the destruction of the mosquitoes which carried the infection.

This victory over infection, almost as impressive as the construction of the canal itself, was the work of a great American medical officer, William Crawford Gorgas. After becoming an army surgeon in 1880, Gorgas gained fame for his work against yellow fever while serving in Havana, Cuba, where he was chief sanitary officer from 1898 to 1902. It was during this period that his colleague, Walter Reed, also serving in Cuba, discovered the link between mosquitoes and the fever. Armed with this knowledge, Gorgas was named chief sanitary officer for the Panama Canal Zone, where he served from 1904 to 1913, and it was his untiring efforts that rid the area of disease. No native Panamanian has alleviated as much suffering among his countrymen as this dedicated American army surgeon.

The actual building of the canal was the work of another brilliant American military man, Colonel George Washington Goethals of the Army Engineers. Appointed chief engineer of the Panama Canal Commission in 1907, Goethals oversaw the construction of one of the great engineering marvels of world history. There was nothing particularly novel about the excavation and dredging of the canal except the vast size of the work; but the building of great dams to form artificial lakes at different levels, and the elaborate system of massive locks, were an innovative achievement on a scale never before attempted. Each lock consisted of two parallel chambers which effected a double tracking of the channel, allowing vessels going in opposite directions to use the same flight of locks at the same time. Starting on the Atlantic side, the canal was dug at sea level to Gatun, where three sets of locks were built to raise ships 85 feet, level with man-made Gatun Lake. Crossing the lake to Gamboa, through the Gaillard or Culebra Cut, a lock was built at Pedro Miguel to lower transiting craft 31 feet to the Miraflores Lake, which led to the site where two locks were built to lower the ships 54 feet to Pacific sea level.

The work was grueling and hazardous, plagued by frequent landslides, which continued even after the canal was opened in 1914. In 1915, a massive slide in the Gaillard Cut caused the canal to be closed for seven months while the channel was dredged and widened 300 feet. In the years since, constant dredging and close observation of local weather and seismographic conditions have kept the canal open continuously. Improvements have been added, such as the massive concrete dam built in 1935 on the Chagres River to create Madden Lake, another man-made body of water that provides storage for 22 million cubic feet of water and prevents the danger of a water shortage in the canal.

Vital Statistics of the Canal Today

Although the distance from Cristóbal to Balboa, the two terminal cities of the canal route, is only 36 miles as the crow flies, the canal itself is approximately 51 miles long. Passage through it by a ship sailing from New York to San Francisco saves 7,873 miles. The canal, still operates on the basic plan developed by Goethals seventy years ago. The lock chambers are filled or emptied by letting water run downhill in one direction or the other from Gatun Lake. Since the lake is 85 feet above sea level, no pumps are needed; the water flows from one level to another through enormous tunnels, 18 feet in diameter, which are located in the walls of the locks.

The individual lock chambers are 110 feet wide, 70 feet deep, and 1,000 feet long; their minimum water depth is 40 feet. Vessels passing through the lock chambers are pulled by four to eight of the canal's 55-ton locomotives, nicknamed "mules," of which there are 57. It takes two minutes for a lock gate to open or close and eight minutes to fill or empty a lock chamber. Total transit time through the canal averages between seven and eight hours (compared to 25–30 *days* around Cape Horn). The lock chambers hold 8.8 million cubic feet of water each; 52 million gallons of water are used during the course of a single canal transit.

The Canal Zone consists of 647 square miles, 372 of which are land area, housing the men, machinery, and technology required to keep this great waterway functioning. As of 1975, population of the Canal Zone stood at 43,900, including 5,500 Panamanians. Of the 34,400 U.S. citizens in the zone, 27,500 were either uniformed or civilian employees of the armed forces; the balance were civilians and their dependents employed by the Panama Canal Company or the Canal Zone Government.

How the Zone Is Run

The Canal Zone is governed and operated by two independent United States agencies, each ultimately responsible to the Congress and the president. As organized by Congress in 1950, these two agencies are the Panama Canal Company and the Canal Zone Government.

The Company is defined as "a body corporate and an agency of the United States for the purpose of maintaining and operating the Panama Canal and conducting business enterprises incident thereto and incident to the civil government of the Canal Zone." As owner of the Company, the United States is represented by the president or his designated representative—traditionally the secretary of the army, who is also responsible for appointing the members of the Company's board of directors, which is in turn directly responsible for the management of the canal. Specific duties of the Company include the actual passage of vessels through the canal, ship repairs, management of the railroad, transport of supplies from the United States to the Canal Zone, and supplying electric power, water, communications, and living quarters for employees.

The Canal Zone Government is responsible for civil and military administration of the zone and is headed by a governor of the Canal Zone, who also serves as president of the Panama Canal Company, thus providing a personal link between the two independent but cooperating agencies. The governor is appointed by the president of the United States for a four-year term. From the beginning, this system of American control and government of the Canal Zone has been a model of efficiency, fairness, stability, and integrity. Meanwhile, in the first seventy-one years of its existence, the Republic of Panama has changed governments some sixty times, and only four of its presidents have managed to serve out their full four-year terms. General Torrijos, the present dictator of Panama, seized force at gun point and has been a consistent violator of human rights. The havoc that his corrupt, inept regime, or its successors, could wreak if America surrendered the canal is all too obvious, quite aside from possible outside interference, such as pressure from Cuba, which would be sorely tempted to fill the power vacuum once America hauled down the flag and retreated.

How economically crucial is the open and efficient running of the canal? As can be seen from Chart 1, three of our Latin American neighbors depend on the Panama Canal for transit of approximately three-quarters of all their seaborne trade. Small wonder then, that many Latin American leaders, although afraid to speak out in public for fear of being branded hemispheric "Uncle Toms," have privately expressed the hope that America will hold on to the canal and not surrender it to the caprices of a Panamanian petty tyrant. As a leading Colombian journalist told veteran American diplomat Spruille Braden, "The best thing that ever happened to Colombia was to be rid of Panama! Continued ownership and operation of the canal by the United States is imperative for our security on the west and the trade of our Pacific ports."

Chart 1

Trade Through the Panama Canal for Selected North and South American Countries
(long tons)

Country (Latest Year)	Total Seaborne Trade[1]	Trade Through the Panama Canal[2]	Percent of Seaborne Trade Through Canal
Brazil (1974)	131,465,499	1,239,300	0.9
Chile (1972)	15,099,596	4,270,885	28.3
Colombia (1974)	4,748,765	3,695,133	77.8
Costa Rica (1974)	2,867,959	694,195	24.2
Ecuador (1974)	12,850,699	9,409,305	73.2
El Salvador (1974)	1,847,343	1,395,622	75.6
Guatemala (1973)	2,190,829	706,957	32.3
Honduras (1972)	2,740,013	207,840	7.6
Mexico (1974)	21,878,866	3,381,529	15.5
Nicaragua (1972)	1,358,916	842,861	62.0
Panama (1974)	5,202,481	2,945,231	56.6
Peru (1974)	14,023,866	7,002,310	49.9
Venezuela (1973)	192,285,122	7,680,639	4.0
United States (1976)	650,700,000[3]	78,100,000	12.0

1. Source: *U.N. Statistical Yearbook, 1975*.
2. Source: Panama Canal Company.
3. Source: *Survey of Current Business*, U.S. Department of Commerce

Proponents of the new treaties have consistently tried to downplay the importance of the Panama Canal today. They are particularly fond of pointing out that the canal cannot accommodate vessels more than 950 feet long, 106 feet in beam and 40 feet in draft (the Panama maximum or ''Pan-Max'' as it is known in nautical circles), and that the number of individual Panama vessel transits has declined to a zero growth rate in recent years. However, as Charles Maechling, Jr., points out in the *Orbis* study cited in Chapter 2, the real indicator of the canal's importance is how many tons of cargo—not how many vessels—pass through it:

... world cargo *tonnage* has risen dramatically and with it ton-

47

nage transiting the canal—from 114 long tons in 1940 to over 140 million long tons in 1975, with a sharp drop to 117.4 million in 1976 after the Suez Canal reopened [an event, incidentally, which could be reversed at any moment in the volatile Middle East]. Clearly, more cargo is being carried in fewer and more specialized ships, but the notion that this trend is universal, or will continue indefinitely, is not borne out by projections. . .

The new classes of medium-size container ships, automated bulk carriers and barge-carrying LASH vessels are still comfortably within "Pan-Max". . . . As technology, rather than size, becomes the key to shipping modernization for all but bulk trades, turn-around time will become more crucial than ever.

This, in turn, will make the Panama Canal more, not less, important to global commerce. As for the United States economy, Mr. Maechling rightly points out that even a brief closure of the canal could have "catastrophic consequences on shipping costs, especially fuel."

Seventeen percent of U.S. ocean-borne commerce passes through the canal and 70 percent of all ships transiting the canal have the United States as their destination. Shipping costs of exports and imports now amount to $3 billion a year. Even if these figures were halved to reflect U.S. exports alone, the effect of a sudden rise in export costs on the U.S. trade balance [already in record bad shape according to late 1977 figures] would be drastic.

As Maechling notes, the impact would be particularly strong in crucial bulk commodities, and in the economical transport of new yields of Alaskan crude oil to energy-hungry East Coast ports:

. . . in 1975 coal and coke represented 18 percent of the tonnage: petroleum products 17 percent; grain 13 percent; and ores, 9.5 percent. Eastern coal and western oil, carried in conventional-size bulk carriers, are now the canal's most important shipments. If, as predicted, North Slope Alaskan oil creates a glut on the West Coast at the same time that fuel shortages worsen on the East Coast, the canal will play a vital equalizing role for domestic energy prices. It has recently been reported that Standard Oil of Ohio and other North Slope producers are already programming medium-sized tankers (maximum of 60,000 dead-weight tons) to use the Panama Canal, at least until West Coast refineries are converted to process the high-sulfur Alaskan crude, or until new pipelines are built to supply the Middle West and New England.

48

Charts 2 and 3, prepared from research assembled by the Legislative Reference Service of the Library of Congress, give a clear idea of the massive amounts of important commodities tonnage exported from and imported to the United States via the canal:

Chart 2

Major U.S. Exports Transiting the Panama Canal
(Fiscal Year 1977)

Commodity	Long Tons		
	Atlantic-Pacific	Pacific-Atlantic	Total
Borax	2,177	463,702	465,879
Caustic Soda	275,442		275,442
Chemicals and petrochemicals	851,215	38,984	890,199
Clay, fire, and china	288,902	8,298	297,200
Coal and coke	12,240,710	—	12,240,710
Food in refrigeration	217,875	281,263	499,138
Fertilizers, various	580,684	12,149	592,833
Grains:	20,630,823	806,850	21,437,673
Barley	134,230	451,261	585,491
Corn	10,723,089	19,125	10,742,214
Rice	148,303	252,547	400,850
Sorghum	2,509,110	—	2,509,110
Soybeans	4,325,846	449	4,326,295
Wheat	2,640,960	71,490	2,712,450
Other and unclassified	149,285	11,978	161,263
Lumber and products (excluding pulpwood)	15,382	521,670	537,052
Metal, scrap	1,242,486	276	1,242,762
Oil, vegetable	193,856	53,872	247,728
Paper and products	216,394	128,670	345,064
Petroleum and products:	469,397	1,384,402	1,853,799
Lubricating oil	234,878	4,057	238,935
Petroleum coke	136,059	1,177,030	1,313,089
Other and unclassified	98,460	203,315	301,775
Phosphate	3,624,099	7	3,624,106
Pulpwood	81,952	319,098	401,050
All other and unclassified	3,745,315	1,209,882	4,955,197
	44,676,709	5,229,123	49,905,832

Chart 3

Major U.S. Imports Transiting the Panama Canal
(Fiscal Year 1977)

Commodity	Long Tons		
	Atlantic-Pacific	Pacific-Atlantic	Total
Bananas	—	544,701	544,701
Chemicals and petrochemicals	52,698	187,877	240,575
Coffee	7,865	211,965	219,830
Fertilizers, various	135,726	27,038	162,764
Food in refrigeration	29,703	546,306	576,009
Lumber and products (excluding			
pulpwood	4,834	2,098,627	2,103,461
Machinery and equipment:	187,255	807,152	994,407
Autos trucks, and accessories	176,561	722,755	899,316
Other and unclassified	10,694	84,397	95,091
Manufactures of iron and steel	294,651	5,453,123	5,747,774
Metals, various	43,792	355,597	399,389
Molasses	—	499,762	499,762
Oil, coconut	—	243,482	243,482
Oil, vegetable	996	237,545	228,541
Ores:	451,108	3,276,584	3,727,692
Alumina/bauxite	304,622	515,817	820,439
Iron	15,787	1,854,539	1,870,326
Lead	20,587	125,073	145,660
Other and unclassified	110,112	781,155	891,267
Petroleum and products:	3,205,606	1,271,618	4,477,224
Crude oil	2,528,776	787,496	3,316,272
Gasoline	156,089	78,451	234,540
Jet fuel	373,452	—	373,452
Residual fuel oil	46,631	295,948	342,579
Other and unclassified	100,658	109,723	210,381
Salt	261,584	421,040	682,624
Sugar	—	2,263,372	2,263,372
All other and unclassified	645,801	3,341,153	3,986,954
	5,321,619	21,786,942	27,108,561

50

Strategic Security Importance of the Canal Today

Perhaps the most credible source on the strategic importance of the Panama Canal today is Admiral John S. McCain, Jr., former U.S. commander-in-chief in the Pacific. Because he is retired, Admiral McCain can speak his mind freely without fear of recrimination from the Carter administration or its minions in the Pentagon and State Department. And that is exactly what he did in a statement presented to the Senate Judiciary Committee's Subcommittee on Separation of Powers on July 29, 1977. "Throughout my active career," Admiral McCain stated, "I have been a student of sea power in the defense of the United States." Admiral McCain goes on to state that "during the war in Vietnam, the Panama Canal transited 1,505 U.S. Government vessels in Fiscal Year 1968; 1,376 in 1969; and 1,068 in 1970. These vessels were indispensible in the conduct of the war, and could not have been effectively used without the Canal." The admiral concluded his testimony by a stern warning that "Soviet Russia [is] making every effort to gain control of the Canal . . . the loss of sovereign control over the Canal Zone would result in transforming the Caribbean and the Gulf of Mexico into Red Lakes."

And Admiral McCain added a foreign policy note that seems to have escaped the White House masterminds behind the surrender of the canal:

> In Latin America, the national qualities that win respect are strength and decisiveness. It is time for our country to stop cowering, cringing and to act the part of a great and powerful nation with a positive and constructive program. We have nothing to be ashamed of.

Admiral McCain is not alone among this nation's most distinguished military men in opposing surrender in Panama. In a joint June 6, 1977 letter to President Carter, four former U.S. chiefs of Naval Operations—Admirals Robert B. Carney, Arleigh A. Burke, George Anderson, and Thomas H. Moorer—joined in unanimously warning of the folly of surrender:

> Dear Mr. President: As former chiefs of Naval Operations, fleet commanders and naval advisors to previous presidents, we believe we have an obligation to you and the nation to offer our

51

combined judgment on the strategic value of the Panama Canal to the United States. Contrary to what we read about the declining strategic and economic value of the canal, the truth is that this interoceanic waterway is as important, if not more so, to the United States than ever.

Of prime importance to all four former chiefs is the ability that total control of the canal gives the United States to transfer naval and commercial shipping from ocean to ocean in the shortest possible time—a capability "increasingly important now in view of the reduced size of the U.S. Atlantic and Pacific fleets."

Looking back on past military crises affecting the United States and forward to possible future confrontations, the chiefs stated that their experience has been:

> That as each crisis developed during our active service—World War II, Korea, Vietnam and the Cuban missile crisis—the value of the canal was forcefully emphasized by emergency transits of our naval units and massive logisitic support for our armed forces.

These distinguished naval officers properly stressed the enormous strategic value of having the jurisdiction to deny emenies the use of the waterway in wartime, a control which will disappear upon ratification. This would, in their words, "create an immediate and crucial problem and prove a serious weakness in the overall U.S. defense capability, with enormous consequences for evil."

"Enormous consequences for evil . . . serious weakness in U.S. defense"—these are the grave and considered opinions of four of the most distinguished commanders ever to wear the uniform of the United States Navy. Pivotal to their concern for the safety of the canal if American sovereignty is surrendered, is the nature of "the present Panamanian government." The next chapter will take a close look at the corrupt Panamanian dictator and his coterie of pro-Marxist advisers who stand to gain the most from an American surrender in Panama.

Chapter 5:
Who Speaks for Panama?

Two contrasting scenes often spring to mind when considering the Panama Canal debate. The first is a large, festive gathering at the palatial Pan American Union building in Washington, D. C. The date is September 7, 1977, and leaders from twenty-five American republics have gathered to witness the signing of the two new canal treaties. The blaze of the sparkling crystal chandeliers is reflected in brightly polished rows of medals; the cameras whir and click; a hush falls over the large hall.

President Jimmy Carter, the self-proclaimed crusader for human rights, signs the treaties surrendering the Panama Canal and calls them a "symbol of equality" and "mutual respect." The beneficiary of this equality and respect is a short, swarthy man with a stiffly martial bearing. General Omar Torrijos is signing the treaties on behalf of Panama where, although he is not a self-proclaimed champion of human rights, he is the self-proclaimed "Maximum Leader of the Revolution."

A broadly grinning President Carter announces that the ceremony has opened "a new chapter in our relations with all nations of this hemisphere," and then the elected leader of the United States and the military dictator of Panama embrace. On his way home to Panama, Omar Torrijos sends a message to another hemispheric leader with whom he has exchanged even more ardent bearhugs, but who was unable to attend the ceremony in Washington—Fidel Castro:

> As I fly across Cuba's skies on my return to my fatherland, I greet you with friendship, as always. It is my wish that the Cuban people, under your skillful leadership, may continue on their march toward Latin American progress. In Latin America your name is associated with feelings of dignity linked to the elimination of all remnants of shameful colonialism.

The other scene that comes to mind is far less grandiose. It, too, involves a Panamanian, but he is not a swaggering military boss, and it takes place thousands of miles away under a far northern sky. The man's name is Leopoldo Aragon. He is a respected Panamanian journalist living in exile in Sweden after suffering illegal arrest, imprisonment, and torture in Panaman at the hands of the G-2, General Torrijos's dreaded security police. A foe of oppression of all kinds, Mr. Aragon has crusaded for human rights in America and behind the Iron Curtain, as well as in his native land. He is a scholarly man and perhaps he has read the ancient Greek dramatist Aeschylus's words on freedom and the human spirit: "Death is better, a milder fate than tyranny."

At any rate, he has considered his course carefully. In a letter to his wife and daughters living in America he wrote: "I know what I have to do. . . . I feel it with all the depth of conviction that a man can have. . . . And I am going to do something that can be instinctively understood. . . ." On September 1, 1977, six days before President Carter embraced Omar Torrijos at the glittering signing ceremony in Washington, Leopoldo Aragon's last journey took him to the steps of the American embassy in Stockholm. In front of the embassy, in a brief, fiery burst, Leopoldo Aragon immolated himself. He used his last weapon—his life—to focus world attention on the dictatorial abuses of the Torrijos regime.

In a message later read over network television by commentator Jack Anderson, Mr. Aragon denounced the murder, the massive human rights violations, the drug smuggling, and the financial corruption of the Panamanian dictatorship. And he warned that the United States will regret any agreement it makes with a man like Omar Torrijos.

Portrait of a Police State

In deeply moving testimony before the International Relations Committee of the House of Representatives on October 11, 1977, Leopoldo Aragon's widow, Rose Marie Aragon, recounted not only the grim story of her husband's jailing, torture, and exile at the hands of Torrijos's security police, but 181 other cases of Panamanian violations of human rights—ranging from murder, torture, imprisonment without trial, terror bombings, and arbitrary arrests to disappearances and forced expatriations. These specific cases, Mrs.

Aragon emphasized, "are only a small part of the known violations by Torrijos in 1976." However:

> Let us look at the numbers. In one year 181 persons are known to have had their human rights violated in Panama's tiny population of 1.7 million. Translating that number . . . [to] the U.S. population is the equivalent of human rights violations of more than 21,000 citizens.
>
> Gentlemen: I think it is abundantly clear that Panama shows a consistent pattern of gross violations of internationally recognized human rights. . . .

"Let my people decide freely," was Leopoldo Aragon's dying plea. His act of sacrifice, he said, was to "call attention to the enormity of the deprivation of human rights and political freedoms under the Torrijos dictatorship."

The Aragons are far from alone in denouncing Torrijos's tyranny, although official U.S. spokesmen, in their efforts to shove through treaty ratification, have consistently ignored or minimized evidence of Torrijos's abuses. Particularly damning evidence of the nature of the Torrijos regime was given to the House International Relations Committee by Dr. Winston Robles, Director of the Panamanian Commission for Human Rights. Although Dr. Robles favors a newly negotiated canal treaty, he firmly opposes any agreement between the U.S. government and the current Torrijos regime. "The new treaty," Dr. Robles testified, "does not solve 'the causes of conflict' between the two countries. On the contrary, it adds a few new ones. . . . Among other things, it is going to condemn future generations of Panamanians to live under a dictatorship. . . ."

In his carefully prepared, detailed statement to the committee, Dr. Robles painted a grim picture of life in Panama under Torrijos:

> In 1968, through a military coup, for the first time in their history, Panamanians found themselves under the brutal rule of one of the most corrupt and arbitrary dictatorships of Latin America. . . .
>
> Following the coup, the University of Panama was closed for a year. All political parties were banned. Newspapers and radio stations were seized and all the independent media controlled. Many Panamanians were tortured, incarcerated, murdered or simply disappeared. . . .
>
> Today Panamanians live in constant fear. Telephones are

tapped, mail intercepted, houses searched in the dark of night, people arbitrarily arrested, and the population intimidated by an organization of paid informers.

Arrests are made on the grounds of "insults to the General" or "disrespect of the authorities" because of private conversations in which there was criticism of the government or its officers. . . .

The government, using every imaginable resource—intimidation, blackmail, bribery (to name a few)—maintains strict control over labor unions, professional associations, farmers organizations, and other organized groups. . . .

The government, its officers and its friends are involved in all kinds of legal and illegal businesses. The involvement of high-ranking officers in drug traffic is well known.

Before the coup, Panama maintained for many years the highest sustained rate of economic growth in Latin America and one of the highest in the world. Today, the military are the social, political and economic aristocracy of a country in bankruptcy. There was a negative 1% growth in 1976, and unemployment was the highest in the history of the country.

Dr. Robles makes grave charges, but all of them are documentable, as we shall show later in this chapter. However, in order to better understand the rise of Omar Torrijos and what it portends for Panama and the canal, we must first review a few vital facts and statistics about the country itself.

Conditions in Modern Panama

As we have seen, politically speaking Panama is an artificial modern creation, brought about because of its strategic location rather than any distinctly Panamanian culture, language, or tradition. A narrow, serpentine stretch of land, it is 180 miles long, varying in width from a minimum of 30 miles to a maximum of 120, and bisected by the ten-mile-wide Canal Zone under U.S. rule. Only a quarter of Panama's land surface is habitable, much of the craggy mountain forest being too rugged and dense for cultivation or permanent settlement on a large scale; only 16 percent of the arable land is actually under cultivation. There is some light industry but Panama is truly a "banana republic"—the yellow fruit is still the largest single national export. Out of a population of 1.7 million, it is estimated that most of the national wealth remains in the hands of forty influential families, nicknamed *los Dorados*,

56

"the golden ones." Though Torrijos has succeeded in involving numerous members of his own family and friends in the financial action, there is no evidence that the plight of the mass of peasants and urban poor has been significantly improved by the "Maximum Leader of the Revolution."

However, while by United States standards the poverty is abysmal—with an annual per capita income of $939—Panama is affluent by regional standards. It is the wealthiest country in Central America and one of the wealthiest in all Latin America. Much of this wealth is derived, directly or indirectly, from the efficient American running of the canal. At least one-third of Panama's foreign exchange is drawn from the Canal Zone. The zone is also responsible for 20 percent of Panamanian jobs, while operation of the canal contributes an estimated 14 percent to the Panamanian gross national product.

In 1974 Panamanians received $234.6 million in salaries, pensions, and payments for goods and services from the U.S. government and its agents. All of this is above and beyond the annual U.S. subsidy of $2.3 million to the Panamanian government. Between 1970 and 1975, Panama also received a total of $212.4 million in United States assistance in the form of grants and loans; A.I.D. funds for 1976 alone amounted to approximately $22.6 million. In 1973, U.S. assistance to Panama amounted to over $41 per capita for every man, woman, and child in the little country. Nevertheless, 25 percent of Panama's population still lived a grim subsistence existence as squatters six years after Omar Torrijos's rise to power. Sixty-six percent of the high (41 per thousand) annual birthrate is illegitimate. An estimated 15 percent of the population is illiterate.

Over the years, most Panamanian political leaders have been drawn from the ranks of *los Dorados*, the small, wealthy elite. Direct military intervention was rare; officers of the National Guard usually passively supported the leading candidate or maintained political neutrality in return for patronage and graft. Looking at a chart of senior government officials since Panamanian independence is more like reading a series of intertwined family trees than following the political evolution of a stable democracy. Again and again the same family names—Arosemena, Chiari, Arias, Boyd, de la Guardia and others drawn from the ranks of the *Dorados*—recur.

The pattern still held true in 1968 when, after a particularly bitter presidential election, Dr. Arnulfo Arias was elected president. It was Dr. Arias's third time around; he also served as president from 1940–1941 and again from 1949–1951. On both previous occasions, the volatile President Arias's term of office had ended prematurely as the result of coups. After only eleven days in office in 1968, history repeated itself. One of the key issues in Dr. Arias's campaign had been corruption and so, on assuming office, one of his first steps was a house cleaning of the senior ranks of the National Guard. Unfortunately for Dr. Arias, the would-be purgees were better organized than their intended purger. Before Arias could get rid of them, they got rid of Arias. For the third time in his presidential career, Arnulfo Arias was sent packing, this time as the result of a small conspiratorial ring of officers including an obscure lieutenant colonel by the name of Omar Torrijos.

Although the junta named Colonel José Pinilla provisional president on October 13, 1968, the practical power went to Torrijos, who was appointed commander of the National Guard. After making the usual empty promise that "new elections would soon be held," José Pinilla swiftly began to fade into the background; when an attempt was made to oust Torrijos from his key post in December 1969, all pretense was dropped. At the head of his guardsmen, Torrijos arrested his foes and seized the reins of power. From that moment on, Omar Torrijos has been the absolute dictator of Panama. Where did he come from? What sort of a man is he? What does he believe in? Is he an opportunist, a fanatical patriot, a Marxist, or a blend of all three? To understand his politics, it is necessary to understand the man.

The Rise of Omar Torrijos

Like so many demagogues before him, Omar Torrijos is fond of painting himself as a "man of the people." Time and again, he has claimed that he is the son of simple peasants when, in fact, his father, an emigrant from Colombia, was a middle-class intellectual, a school teacher who rose to become a provincial director of schools. Torrijos, then, was a child of the economically modest middle class intelligentsia, neither a man of the peasant masses nor a member of the inner circle of the *Dorados*. He was born on February 13, 1929, in the little town of Santiago, in the Panamanian province of Veraguas. Some of Torrijos's Panamanian critics claim that the dictator was an early and ardent Marxist. According to the September 1976 report of the Panamanian Committee for Human Rights, Torrijos was a member of the "partisan Marxist organization Young Veraguas" while attending the Normal School of the Province of Veraguas.

There is some circumstantial evidence to bear out early communist links. For example, when, in 1959, as a captain in the National Guard, Torrijos engaged in antiguerrilla activities against Marxist insurgents, he was denounced by them as a "traitor to the cause." Less conjectural is the long list of Torrijos relatives and cronies with direct communist ties, including his brother, Moises Torrijos, described by the Panamanian Committee for Human Rights as "a Marxist since his youth," and a member of the Panamanian Communist Party's Central Committee. Also cited as a member of the Central Committee is Torrijos's brother-in-law, Marcelino Jaen, who played an instrumental role in the 1968 coup and, under Torrijos, became president of the leftist-dominated National Legislative Commission.

The Torrijos family is a versatile one, however. Brother Moises, for example, has managed to spare enough time from his political activities (and his assignment under Torrijos as ambassador to Spain) to amass a large fortune and to be implicated in a drug-smuggling scandal which will be discussed later in this chapter.

Key officers of Torrijos's National Guard, especially the notorious Manuel Antonio Noriega, commander of the G-2 security police, maintain close ties with Cuba's C-2 secret police. Even the late syndicated columnist, Drew Pearson, who was anything but a redbaiter (he and Senator Joe McCarthy once engaged in an impromptu fist fight at Washington's prestigious Sulgrave Club), was concerned about Torrijos's tangled web of Marxist relationships; on November 19, 1968, Pearson, who had a wide network of official and unofficial intelligence sources in Latin America, described Torrijos as a communist.

Whether as a result of conviction or opportunism, this much is sure: the more tightly Torrijos has consolidated his grip on internal power in Panama, the more closely he has developed his ties with

the Soviet Union and Cuba; and the more his political pronounce-
ments, couched in "antiimperialist" and "revolutionary" jargon,
have begun to sound like the orthodox party line.

The growth of communist influence in Panama under Torrijos
was graphically chronicled by a leftist Argintinian journalist, Luis
Guagnini, in *Third World Magazine*, vol. 1, no. 4. Up until the
1968 coup, Guagnini reported, communist influence in Panama had
been minimal. But by September 1974, the Panamanian People's
[Communist] Party had dramatically increased its power over key
facets of Panamanian society:

> . . . from five labor unions in 1968 it now controlled thirty-
> eight. From 40 thousand high school students belonging to the
> Student Federation of Panama (FEP)—under the direction of the
> People's Party—in 1968, it now boasted 110 thousand stu-
> dents. . . .

In the spring of 1966, Comrade Castellanos of the Panamanian
People's Party had delivered a brief but significant address to the
Twenty-third Congress of the Soviet Communist Party meeting in
Moscow. A text of his speech, translated into English, was sub-
sequently published in the *Bulletin* of the World Marxist Review
Publishers, Prague. In the style of its rhetoric and the outline of its
objectives it bears an eerie resemblance to the current Torrijos line
and policies:

> . . . The people of Panama believe that the victories of the
> Soviet Union, the socialist camp, the world communist move-
> ment and the national liberation struggle, are fresh devastating
> blows to U.S. imperialism, the common enemy.
> The presence in Panama of U.S. imperialism goes against the
> interests of our people. Hence the varied and complex forms of
> struggle waged by nearly all the social sections of the country.
> Headed by the Communists, the patriotic and anti-imperialist
> forces demand:
> —an end to the U.S. monopoly on our geographic position;
> —reunification of the Canal Zone with our national territory and
> its transfer under the jurisdiction of Panama;
> —the repeal forthwith of the 1903 treaty;
> —and the subsequent nationalization of the Panama Canal.

Well might Panama's veteran communist leader, Rouben Dario
Souza, boast during a 1974 visit to Bulgaria that the Panamanian

armed forces had fallen under the influence of the "people's forces" and that the little republic was now in a transitional period making steady progress "towards revolutionary goals." As evidence of this "progress," Torrijos had banned all free political parties, jailed, harassed or exiled opposition leaders, and then allowed the previously banned communists to operate openly.

Praise from Moscow was not long in coming. In a dispatch Tass (the Soviet news agency) carried in the October 6, 1975, issue of *Pravda*, the Soviet leadership lauded Torrijos for "carrying out a program of profound social reform and genuine economic development." And *Pravda* hastened to add what was already all too obvious to experienced observers of Panamanian affairs: "Panamanian Communists were playing an active part in the revolution on the isthmus."

In a November 4, 1975, interview in the Soviet government newspaper *Izvestia*, the Panamanian dictator proclaimed: "We are conducting a struggle for national liberation." If peaceful means failed, he threatened, "we will be compelled to seek other means." After speaking glowingly of his "diplomatic relations with brotherly Cuba," Torrijos added, "New steps in this direction, including with the Soviet Union, are on the agenda. We think that the links between us will be wide and mutually profitable."

On July 19, 1977, Panama signed an economic pact with the Soviet Union and reportedly discussed construction of a new sea-level canal with Soviet financing, and the establishment of a Soviet naval base. Was Torrijos merely flirting with the Soviets to pressure the United States into new concessions, or was he a confirmed Marxist following the dictates of the party line? Either way, he was playing with fire—and the man who was giving him most of the matches was his "brotherly" friend and neighbor across the Caribbean, Fidel Castro.

Torrijos' Cuban Connection

Omar Torrijos and Fidel Castro are, at best, an odd political couple and their courtship was rather stormy. In his early days in power, Torrijos made the customary anti-Castro noises and, in turn, was denounced with characteristic understatement by Radio Havana and Castro's controlled press as "The abominable canal man, the gorilla Torrijos, who promoted himself to general and has his chest covered with embroidery and medals. . . ." In a statement submitted to the Senate Foreign Relations Committee, Dr. Herminion Portell-Vila, Director of Radio Free Americas, recounted how enmity turned to friendship between the Cuban guerilla and the Panamanian "gorilla":

> All this changed when the Panamanian leftist lawyer Romulo Escobar-Bethancourt [Torrijos's canal negotiator] . . . gained influence over Torrijos. . . . Soon the Torrijos regime helped organize excursions to Communist Cuba so that Panamanians might observe a communist dictatorship in action. . . . In 1972, Castro sent delegates, posing as students, to attend the VIII Congress of the Federation of Panamanian Students. Actually, they were specialists in propaganda, political repression and socialist "reform." That was the year in which Panama voted in favor of diplomatic relations with Communist Cuba at a meeting of the Organization of American States. But it also was the year in which the rubber-stamp National Assembly of Panama proclaimed Torrijos "The Maximum Leader of the Revolution." By mid-1974, Communist Cuba and Panama had restored diplomatic relations.

But the real turning point came in 1976, when the "gorilla" paid a personal visit to the guerilla, as Dr. Portell-Vila explains:

> On January 10, 1976, it was dictator Torrijos himself, accompanied by scores of newsmen, diplomats, policemen and military, who visited Castro. He went from Havana to Santiago de Cuba for a spectacular gathering, followed by a special tour of Cuban military installations around the U.S. naval base at Guantanamo Bay. The idea was to link the Panama Canal and Guantanamo Bay as "terra irredenta" to be rescued from the United States.

In an interview on French television on September 2, 1977, Torrijos boldly announced: "I greatly admire Fidel Castro because he changed his country's social structure despite the risk this entailed," and a few weeks later viewers of the November 1, 1977, *CBS Reports* documentary, "The Battle Over Panama," saw a film clip of the Panamanian dictator modestly declaring his own spiritual kinship to Castro with the words: "I've waited twenty-two years for a man to come to Panama . . . a man like Fidel Castro, who kicked the gringos out. Now that time has finally come."

With these moves came a heightened Cuban presence on the isthmus. Within three months of Torrijos's Cuban visit, the Cuban embassy in Panama had increased its staff to sixty, a suspiciously large number to conduct routine trade and diplomatic relations between two small countries (the staff of the American embassy in Panama, for example, only numbered forty-five). The first print of the cat's paw had been made on Panamanian territory—could the rest of the cat be far behind? The historical precedents are not encouraging from an American point of view. As Captain Paul B. Ryan points out in his outstanding Hoover Institute study, *The Panama Canal Controversy: U.S. Diplomacy and Defense Interests*:

> Since 1959 Castro had acquired ample experience in exporting military aid. Backed up by the powerful Soviet armed forces, Castro had positioned Cuban brigades, battalions, combat teams, and aid missions in Africa (Guinea-Bissau, Zaire, Zanzibar, Equatorial Guinea, Somalia, Congo-Brazzaville), the Middle East (South Yemen, Syria), and the Far East (North Vietnam, Laos). In 1976 Cuban technical and quasi-military missions were serving in Jamaica, Guyana, and Peru. Military commentator Robert D. Heinl has pointed out, "Besides serving as an increasingly professional arm of intervention for the Kremlin, Cuban forces are . . . the only military component in the hemisphere, other than the United States, capable of overseas intervention."

Since there is no way of reading Omar Rorrijos's mind, we cannot be sure of his motivation in courting Castro. As Captain Ryan explains, it could all have been a cynical political maneuver since, for the Panamanian dictator, the visit was "a godsend, serving to distract attention at home from his failures to make progress in the dormant canal treaty talks and to improve the sagging economy." If so, the price of temporary political popularity on the home front has been high. Torrijos was playing the Caribbean version of a political game that had already ruined more than one would-be national Metternich: Cuban roulette. Why was he taking the chance?

Panamanian Bankruptcy under Torrijos

A large part of the answer, political philosophies aside, is economic. Revolutions, much less a population of 1.7 million people, do not live by hot air alone. True to the mold of old-fashioned Latin America *caudillos* like Peron of Argentina and would-be Marxist messiahs like Allende of Chile, no sooner had Torrijos consolidated his grip on power than he proceeded to spend, expropriate, misappropriate and bungle his country into bankruptcy. Nationalization of many efficiently run private companies and plantations led to an erosion of business and investor confidence, and Torrijos's ineffectual attempts to buy popularity by massive "bread and circuses" government spending inflicted severe damage on the once-thriving Panamanian economy.

It can best be summed up in one simple word: debt—massive, crippling national debt. At the time of the Torrijos-backed coup in 1968, Panama's total official overseas debts stood at a manageable and, by world standards, modest $167 million. Under Torrijos, indebtedness has sky-rocketed nearly *one thousand percent* to a massive $1.5 billion. Debt-service ratio alone now consumes an estimated 39 percent of the entire Panamanian budget, as compared to only 7 percent in the United States to service our own enormous debt. The stagnation of the Panamanian economy under Torrijos's mismanagement, coupled with his heavy-handed violations of human rights, culminated in a ten-day wave of violet protest against his regime in September 1976.

"Dictator in Panama Facing Major Crisis," read the September 23 headline in *The New York Times*. The *Times* attributed the riots to public disaffection with the oppressive regime's press censorship, outlawing of political dissent, and persecution of dissidents, coupled with economic ills and a severe drought. At a time when many Panamanians were hard-pressed by rising food costs, Torrijos's decision to sell Panamanian rice to Castro's Cuba at below market price (reported in E. J. Kahn, Jr.'s "Letter from Panama" in the August 16, 1976, issue of the *New Yorker* magazine) may have been the last straw.

At any rate, a quick scenario of violence began to unfold the day after Torrijos abruptly announced increases in the domestic price of the two Panamanian staples, bread and milk, on September 9, 1976. Clashing students and protestors from the far left, far right, and moderate center were soon joined by swarms of slum dwellers. Captain Ryan describes the ensuing chaos in *The Panama Canal Controversy*:

By September 16 several thousand people were caught in the disorders. The rioters smashed windows, damaged public utilities, and created havoc in the streets. But a startling fact is that the mobs ignored the Canal Zone—firm evidence that General Torrijos' government, not the *Yanquis*, was the target. Observers recalled the storming of the U.S. embassy (with the National Guard looking on) on September 23, 1975. On that occasion some students, hurling rocks at embassy windows, had simultaneously accused General Torrijos of complicity in dealing with Washington.

But no such contradictory actions were evident in the 1976 riots. So great was the fury focused on Torrijos that the general was forced for the first time to send in the National Guard. Scores were injured as soldiers used tear gas, rubber truncheons, and anti-riot dogs on the demonstrators. Other guardsmen, armed with shotguns, fired fusillades of pellets at the crowds. Ten days later, after some 300 to 500 rioters had been arrested, order was restored.

Characteristically, Torrijos tried to blame it on his usual, all-purpose bugaboo, "Yankee imperialism." The National Guard arrested three men—one of them a U.S. Army private—and charged them with fomenting the whole thing! Throughout the turmoil, the Panamanian Communist Party had stood firmly by its patron, Torrijos; tyrants and totalitarians have a shared interest in suppressing *unplanned* uprisings. But Torrijos had other important friends in court—some of them from a most unexpected quarter.

In Bed with the Bankers

One of the most amusing—though potentially disastrous—phenomena of the twentieth century has been what I call the "Nearsighted Capitalist Syndrome"—the unseemly spectacle of industrialists and bankers underwriting the very forces which seek to destroy them in the long run. There is nothing new about the syndrome; it's been around almost as long as communism itself. Thus, only four years after the Bolshevik revolution, once Lenin and his cohorts had succeeded in demolishing the industrial and financial base of the Russian economy, the Kremlin bosses turned to gullible Western capitalists to bail them out. That Lenin should ask for help was not surprising; that he should have received it in spades *is*. Yet that is exactly what happened. No sooner had Lenin announced his alleged abandonment of "pure communism" in 1921 then a gadarene rush of Western money and technology poured into Russia to prop up the failing Soviet economy. Lenin, despite his outwardly grim visage, must have had a hidden sense of humor, since he labeled this strange bedfellow arrangement with Western financial interests "industrial cohabitation with the capitalists." Sense of humor or not, he never lost sight of his ultimate aim: "As soon as we are strong enough to overthrow capitalism," he proclaimed, "we shall immediately seize it by the throat." Which, of course, is exactly what happened.

But hope—especially the hope of a quick killing on a speculation—springs eternal in certain bankers' breasts, and there are some people who simply will not learn from experience. Thus today, on a smaller scale, "capitalist cohabitation" is propping up the corrupt, Marxist-oriented Torrijos regime despite the grim lessons of the past.

It isn't Moscow or Havana that is keeping the bankrupt Panamanian government afloat; it's the New York banking community— and the same group, eager to keep favor with General Torrijos because of the hundreds of millions of dollars in credit and investment they have sunk into his regime, is pushing hard for ratification of the new treaties, despite their obvious flaws and neglect of America's own best interests.

Perhaps the moral of this little story was best summed up the British humorist, Ben Buncombe, who quipped: "As far as the New York banking community is concerned, when it comes to interest there is no such thing as principle." Quips aside, the largest holders of Panamanian debts are American banks.

According to a memorandum submitted by the Library of Congress to the Separation of Powers Subcommittee of the United States Senate, foreign branches of U.S. banks had claims against Panama amounting to $1.886 billion as of December 1976, and domestic offices of U.S. banks had $886 million in short- and long-term claims against Panama as of March 1977. Astounding as it may seem, the Torrijos "revolution" in Panama is being underwritten by American capitalists. Thus the November 8, 1974, issue of the London-based publication *Latin America* reported that in 1973 an international consortium headed by a subsidiary of the First National Bank of New York had forked over a $115-million loan to the Torrijos government, which used it to refinance its mountainous existing foreign debts and fund popularity-buying public works projects.

The list of American industrial and financial giants with investments in Panama (totaling $1.6 billion in 1975) reads like a page from the *Wall Street Journal*: Texaco, Eastman Kodak, Esso Standard, Firestone, Goodyear, IBM, Bank of America, First National City Bank of New York, and Chase Manhattan Bank. And—wonder of wonders—where did the then former governor of Georgia, Jimmy Carter, receive his first tuition in foreign affairs? As a member of the Trilateral Commission, a group of influential scholars, politicians, and labor and business leaders founded in 1973 by none other than David Rockefeller of the Chase Manhattan Bank. The commission has proved to be quite a nursery for Carter administration foreign policy talent, especially where Panama is concerned. Since becoming president, Carter has appointed fifteen of its member to important government posts, many of them with duties that heavily involved them in the canal treaty negotiations. These include Secretary of State Cyrus Vance, National Security Council Director Zbigniew Brezinski, Deputy Secretary of State Warren Christopher, and—perhaps most significantly—treaty negotiator Sol M. Linowitz, who, besides being a member of the Trilateral Commission, has another reason for reminding us of the familiar song lyric, "It's a small world after all." In a September 1977 report to his constituents, Representative Steve Symms of Idaho raised some pertinent points about Ambassador Linowitz's suitability as a canal negotiator:

> The giveaway of the United States' canal in Panama was engineered by a negotiator who was never confirmed by the Congress and whose serious conflicts of interest should have disqualified him from the post.
>
> Negotiator Sol Linowitz was appointed for a six-month term not requiring Senate confirmation, confirmation that he probably would not have received *because of his close association with a bank that is owed large amounts of money by the debt-ridden Panamanian government*. Apparently Linowitz was appointed for a short period of time to avoid Senate confirmation hearings and he managed to reach the final giveaway agreement and sign the treaty just four hours and forty minutes before his appointment expired.
>
> Linowitz's connections with a prominent bank in Panama are

just one more indication of the way the Panama sell-out was engineered. *Linowitz has been a director and former chairman of the executive board of the Marine Midland Bank. The Panamanian government currently owes that bank at least $10 million. . . .*

And then Representative Symms gets to the heart of the matter—the potential conflict of interest that should have barred Ambassador Linowitz from negotiating the surrender of the canal:

There are strong indications that the Panamanian government is having a difficult time meeting its loan obligations and a full 40 percent of this year's national budget is earmarked for debt repayment. *One of the few ways of increasing the national income significantly was for Panama to assume control of the canal or to at least increase the income the country received from the canal. Bankers who have invested heavily in Panamanian projects stood to lose a great deal of money if a treaty agreement was not reached and an additional source of income was not tapped.* . . . I strongly object that the giveaway was engineered by a negotiator who was never approved by the Congress and who had such an obvious professional interest in securing a favorable agreement for the Panamanian government.

In my testimony before the Senate Subcommittee on Separation of Powers (September 8, 1977), I tried to sum up this problem without casting any aspersions on Ambassador Linowitz or anyone else, but still demonstrate the clear, vested interest which many large American financial pressure groups have in ratification of two treaties which are definitely not in America's best interests:

. . . what it appears we really have here is not just aid to a tinhorn dictator in the form of new subsidies and canal revenues the treaties would give to the Torrijos regime, but a bailout of a number of banks which should have known better than to invest in Panama and, in any event, should not escape responsibility for having done so. If liberals can oppose bailing out Lockheed and conservatives can oppose bailing out New York City, then there is no reason why all of us should not oppose bailing out Panama and those bankers who inadvisedly lent financial support to its dictator. Certainly, American taxpayers should not be made to bear the burden for the mistakes of others.

There are even seamier financial goings-on in Torrijos's Panama, however, and this chapter on the regime President Carter wants to yield sovereignty over the canal to—and on the man who heads it—would not be complete, without an examination of the Panama connection in the international heroin trade.

The Torrijos Heroin Connection

If there is one moral and social problem that has plagued the United States—especially our young people—in the 1960s and 1970s, it has been drug addiction. Thus it must have come as a rude shock to millions of Americans watching the CBS Morning News on October 14, 1977, when, after routinely announcing that "Panama's leader, General Omar Torrijos, will spend about an hour with President Carter today to clear up conflicting interpretations of the canal treaties," anchorperson Lesley Stahl added that, "While the White House was preparing for the visit yesterday, questions arose in the Senate over whether Torrijos's family is involved in drug trafficking. Phil Jones has a report."

And he certainly did. Along with print journalists, congressional staff investigators, and Panamanian exiles, Jones had unearthed a sordid story which adds to the long list of reasons why the United States should do nothing to prop up the politically and morally rotten regime of General Torrijos. Here is the story, as Phil Jones reported it on the CBS Morning News:

> It is known that one drug seizure in the early 1970s led back to Panama, and Moises Torrijos, the brother of Chief of State Omar Torrijos. As a result of that seizure a secret indictment was issued against Moises, who is the current Panamanian ambassador to Spain. The indictment has never been unsealed because Moises has never been found in this country.

A long, winding trail of administration evasion and sidestepping followed this shocking revelation, but a Justice Department statement finally conceded that for the past seven years, U.S. narcotics officials have been receiving allegations concerning members of the Torrijos family's playing a part in the smuggling of narcotics into the United States.

According to Jones, CBS had obtained a copy of a Drug Enforcement Agency investigation report filed in March 1975, which suggested that Omar Torrijos himself might be involved:

> The report . . . states that a Romero Rivas, a Panamanian businessman, was in partnership with General Torrijos in narcotics trafficking . . . [although] the DFA says its investigation established no business links between Rivas and Omar Torrijos.

Whether or not Torrijos was personally involved, someone in Panamanian officialdom has been facilitating the shipment of vast quantities of illegal drugs through Panama to the United States. A congressional report issued in 1973 estimated that at one point approximately 20 thousand American addicts were getting their daily fix via Panama; and in 1976 the Panama Committee on Human Rights report gave a detailed account of the cases involving Moises Torrijos.

According to the committee, Rafael Richard, Jr., a Panamanian with no diplomatic position, was mysteriously issued a diplomatic passport under orders of the Panamanian minister of foreign affairs, Juan Antonio Tack, who subsequently handled preliminary canal negotiations with Henry Kissinger. Richard entered New York in July 1971 under diplomatic immunity, carrying a suitcase which contained 70 kilos of heroin. The suitcase had been given to him by Moises Torrijos, who was then serving his brother's regime as ambassador to Argentina. Just to keep everything in the Panamanian diplomatic corps, it develops that while young Richards, then 23 years old, was not a diplomat himself, his father was Torrijos's ambassador to Nationalist China. Further details on Torrijos's Panamanian heroin connection, along with evidence of Panamanian violations of human rights and governmental corruption, will be found in Dr. Gustave Anquizola's annotated *Violation of Human Rights and Civil Liberties in Panama*, compiled for the Council for Inter American Security and reprinted in Appendix 4.

When CBS correspondent Bernard Kalb questioned General Torrijos about the drug-smuggling case involving his brother, the Panamanian dictator, instead of issuing a blunt denial, delivered an oddly rambling denunciation of "this campaign that is more a political campaign than a judicial campaign, that you would get even to the personal insult to come and tell me even that I am a thief, that it would start searching into my private life. . . ." And then the general ended grandly with his old proletarian fib: "The only thing they could say is that I am the son of two poor peasants."

It may not have occurred to anyone at the time but, in similar circumstances (and with considerable more truth) Al Capone could have said exactly the same thing.

There is much more that could be said about Omar Torrijos and the corrupt, vicious police state he has built in Panama with the help of his Marxist allies. But I believe this chapter makes it all too clear what kind of man it was that President Carter embraced at the Pan American Union on September 7, 1977, and why the Congress must reject the ill-considered treaties that would surrender the Panama Canal to Omar Torrijos and to his political heirs. In Chapter 6 we will examine exactly how, and under what terms, the surrender is spelled out in the treaties themselves.

Chapter 6:
What the Treaties Say—and What They Mean

It would be a mistake to think that the basic issue of sovereignty over the Canal Zone remained dormant between 1903 and the start of the present treaty negotiations. Almost from the beginning, there were many Panamanians who resented the cost—but not the rewards—of the bargain their government made with the United States. And, with the passage of years, opposition to what came to be known in ultranationalist circles as the "Bunau-Varilla Treason" became a standard prop in the political life of the small republic. Jingoist politicians denounced the 1903 treaty as the work of an unscrupulous foreigner and conveniently ignored the fact that, besides being ratified by the official leadership of Panama, the treaty received the concurrence of every *cabildo* (town council) in the country—the closest thing to a unanimous plebiscite possible at the time.

Regardless of this, saber-rattling—without ever drawing the saber from its rusty Panamanian scabbard—became a convenient gesture for isthmian political leaders, who found that denouncing the Yankee presence in the zone was the ideal means of distracting the mass of poor Panamanians from the sorry plight of their own country and the chronic neglect of the average Panamanians' welfare by the *Dorado* ruling class.

Summary of the 1936 Treaty

While successive American administrations held firm on the issue of sovereign power in the zone, two treaties—the General Treaty of Friendship and Cooperation (Hull-Alfaro) of 1936 and the Treaty of Mutual Understanding and Cooperation of 1955—conferred substantial new benefits on Panama and attempted, without noticeable effect, to salve Panamanian national pride. Unfortunately, neither friendship, understanding, nor cooperation seems to

72

have been strengthened in any lasting, appreciable way by these two treaties; the secondary concessions they contained only whetted the appetites of those Panamanians desiring total American surrender in Panama, and those who enjoyed extracting from the States the maximum possible amount of greenbacks.

Both treaties are printed in full in Appendix 1 and need only be summarized here. In essence, the Hull-Alfaro Treaty of 1936, while in no way yielding sovereignty in the zone, withdrew all American claims to jurisdiction in internal Panamanian affairs. We were no longer pledged to guarantee the independence of Panama; this, in fact, meant that Panama ceased to be an American protectorate. We also yielded our right to acquire land beyond the confines of the zone for the "protection of the Panama Canal"—a concession which was soon to be regretted.

The annual subsidy to Panama was increased to $430,000, and much of the tempting zone market was opened to Panamanian businessmen, a rich territory previously monopolized by American ship chandlers and commissaries. In all, fourteen concessions were granted to Panama, with the result that opposition to the treaty was strong in the U.S. Senate, so strong that it was not ratified until 1939.

The prospect of a world war, which seemed so distant to Americans in 1936, soon loomed large, and the pro-Axis antics of Panamanian President Arnulfo Arias (the same man who was driven from office by the 1968 military coup two presidential terms later) and his refusal to American requests for new defense sites, led to a steady deterioration in U.S.-Panamanian relations. It was only nine months before Pearl Harbor that Arias finally yielded to American pressure and consented to U.S. occupation of a series of defense positions outside the zone. In October 1941, Arias, who had dreamed of throwing out the Americans, was himself thrown out by the Panamanians in a quick, bloodless coup. Fleeing for his life, Arias settled in Argentina, where another would-be Latin American *Duce*, Juan Peron, provided him with a secure refuge during the war years.

Summary of the Treaty of 1955

After the war Arias returned to Panama, which had reached the end of a sustained economic boom caused largely by the massive American military presence during the war years. The withdrawal of the large wartime American garrison in Panama had been cheered by the ultranationalists, but it made a serious dent in the Panamanian economy. In 1948, Arias lost a close, bitterly contested election to Domingo Diaz, who died only one year into his term. Diaz was succeeded by his vice-president, who was rapidly turned out of office by Colonel José Remon, commander of the National Guard, who first installed Roberto Chiari as president and then, a mere four days later, deposed him.

In a stormy bit of Latin American politics, a crowd of Arias supporters then conducted their hero to the presidential palace and installed him as president for a second time. However, true to his old impulses, Arias soon tried the national patience by decreeing dictatorial powers for himself. He was voted out of power by the National Assembly. Arias tried to hold out, and only yielded when Colonel Remon's National Guardsmen actually fired on the palace.

In October 1952, Remon was inaugurated Panama's fifth president in four years; observers hoped that the period of postwar chaos had come to an end. However, on January 2, 1955, Remon was murdered by a gunman at a race track—all of which gives an idea of the atmosphere of near anarchy which has long characterized isthmian politics and could become a chronic problem if the stabilizing American presence in the zone is ever removed.

In an effort to calm matters, President Eisenhower had begun talks for a new Panama treaty in 1953. It took two years to work out the details, and the final product took another three years to win complete congressional approval in the form of Canal Zone legislation authorizing equal wage scales, retirement benefits, and equal employment opportunities for Panamanian and U.S. workers in the zone. Other key provisions of the 1955 Treaty:

—Raised the annual subsidy to Panama from $430,000 to $1.93 million;

—Gave Panama title to $25 million worth of previously American-owned property;

—Provided for completion of a $19-million bridge over the canal;

—Gave the United States the right to use its Rio Hato base for military training. The 79,000-acre area has been an important anti-guerrilla training area for U.S. and friendly Latin American troops ever since.

In summary, the Treaty of 1955 conferred a number of material benefits on Panama without making any concession of sovereign power. As such, it merely encouraged the Panamanians to make further financial demands without diminishing the resentment of the ultranationalists, who were now joined by the communists in calling for total American withdrawal.

More important than either treaty was a rhetorical concession made by the Eisenhower administration several years later. In September 1955, the government of Panama had formally requested that the Panamanian flag be flown in the Canal Zone. Students and other dissidents subsequently rioted in support of the Panamanian demand. In response, Deputy Under Secretary of State Livingston Merchant proclaimed U.S. recognition that "titular sovereignty over the Canal Zone remains in the Government of Panama." This statement, while emotionally hazing the issue of American sovereignty, did nothing to change the real situation (only abrogation of the 1903 treaty could do that) but it egged on Panamanian extremists who, four days after the Merchant statement, again rioted in force, requiring American military action to defend the zone. The flag question was ultimately settled in 1963, when it was agreed that the Panamanian flag would be flown side by side with the American flag by civilian authorities within the zone.

Beginning of Negotiations for a New Agreement

There were further riots in 1964 which cost three American and twenty-one Panamanian lives. Captain Paul B. Ryan, in *The Panama Canal Controversy*, states that:

> There is no doubt that Communists trained in rioting techniques were active in the January 1964 riots. Witnesses placed a trio of Panamanian Communist leaders at the center of the three-day action. The arsenal of fire bombs, small arms and ammunition was evidence that the leaders had made careful preparations well in advance. . . . Helping to spearhead nationalistic demonstrations were scores of Panamanians who had received training in revo-

lutionary tactics in Cuba. Undoubtedly it was this group that directed the snipers and arsonists in the affair of January 1964.*

While the riots failed to obstruct the orderly operation of the canal, they succeeded in their political objective. In December 1964, President Johnson, after consulting with former Presidents Eisenhower and Truman, committed the United States to negotiating a new treaty. Actual talks began in January 1965, leading to the joint U.S.-Panamanian announcement in June 1967 of completion of draft treaties. Neither government acted on the drafts at the time, however, and they were formally rejected by the Torrijos dictatorship in August 1970. Discussion of alternative proposals continued, and a real turning point was reached in 1973, when President Nixon appointed veteran diplomat Ellsworth Bunker to head a new American negotiating team. The basis for the present treaties was formalized on February 7, 1974, when Secretary of State Henry Kissinger and Panamanian Foreign Minister Juan Antonio Tack signed a statement of principles based on the Bunker negotiations. The so-called Kissinger-Tack agreement on principles agreed to:

—Abrogation of the Hay–Bunau-Varilla Treaty of 1903, on which American sovereign powers are based, and;

—Formulation of a new treaty restoring Panamanian sovereignty in the Canal Zone while supposedly preserving American "control" over the canal for at least twenty-five years.

The outline for America's surrender in Panama had been worked out quietly among the diplomats; it took the 1976 presidential campaign to make it a burning public issue.

Panama Hits the Headlines

Perhaps Isaac Goldberg best summed up the shady side of foreign affairs in his celebrated snippet of doggerel:

*Both Ambassador Bunker and Joseph Califano, then counsel to OAS, acknowledged communist influence in the 1964 riots. Califano stated, "We know that some of the leaders in the rioting were known and identifiable Communists."

> Diplomacy is to do and say,
> The nastiest thing in the nicest way.

Certainly, Henry Kissinger had hoped that the Panama surrender would be engineered smoothly and discreetly, behind the scenes. And so it might have been, if Gerald Ford had been unopposed in the 1976 race for the Republican presidential nomination. Instead, prodded by Ronald Reagan's charges that the Ford administration was in the process of giving away the canal, Gerald Ford declared that the United States would "never give up" control of the canal. However, Ford was contradicted by the evidence of his own negotiator, Ellsworth Bunker, who admitted in congressional testimony that under the proposed treaty the United States would turn administrative control of the Canal Zone over to Panama in three years, and would yield operational control on the canal itself in twenty-five years at the expiration of the treaty.

The battle was on, and although Reagan narrowly lost his bid for the nomination, he mobilized public sentiment on the Panama issue to the point where Ford delegates joined his supporters in adopting a strongly worded Panama plank in the 1976 presidential party platform:

> The present Panama Canal treaty provides that the United States has jurisdictional rights in the Canal Zone as "if it were sovereign." The United States intends that the Panama Canal be preserved as an international waterway for the ships of all nations. This secure access is enhanced by a relationship which commands the respect of Americans and Panamanians and benefits the people of both countries. In any talks with Panama, however, *the United States negotiators should in no way cede, dilute, forfeit, negotiate or transfer any rights, power, authority, jurisdiction, territory or property that are necessary for the protection and security of the United States and the entire Western Hemisphere.* [Emphasis added.]

There are no two ways about it: the 1976 Republican Party platform clearly repudiated the Kissinger-Tack agreement on principles and bound Gerald Ford to oppose the proposed new treaties if he were elected to a second term.

The Panama Canal Treaty

The preamble to the Panama Canal Treaty of 1977 proclaims that:

> The United States of America and the Republic of Panama, acting in the spirit of the Joint Declaration of April 3, 1964, by the Representatives of the Governments of the United States of America and the Republic of Panama, and the Joint Statement of Principles of February 7, 1974, initialed by the Secretary of State of the United States and the Foreign Minister of the Republic of Panama, and
>> Acknowledging the Republic of Panama's sovereignty over its territory.
>
> Have decided to terminate the prior treaties pertaining to the Panama Canal and to conclude a new treaty to serve as the basis for a new relationship between them and, accordingly, have agreed upon the following. . . .

The text of the treaty in its entirety is published in Appendix 1. Perhaps the most striking thing about it, beyond the initial waiving of all United States claim to sovereignty quoted above, is the fact that, besides surrendering our right to sovereign powers, we pay the Torrijos regime exorbitantly for the "privilege" of doing so. Under the terms of the treaty, the United States agrees to:

—Pay Panama $40 million to $50 million annually from canal toll revenues;

—Pay Panama an annual subsidy of $10 million for the right to continue operating the canal;

—Pay Panama yet another $10 million per year if canal revenues permit;

—Above and beyond all this, give Panama $50 million in military assistance (arms and equipment to keep the Torrijos dictatorship in power) over the next ten years, and;

—Provide Panama with an estimated $300 million in loans and loan guarantees.

Highlights of the fourteen-article agreement include:

1. The concession that "The Republic of Panama shall participate increasingly in the management and protection and de-

fense of the Canal. . . ." (Article I);

2. Replacement of the American-run Panama Canal Company and Canal Zone Government by a Panama Canal Commission "supervised by a Board composed of nine members . . . four of whom shall be Panamanian nationals proposed by the Republic of Panama for appointment by the United States of America. . . ." (Article III);

3. Appointment of a Panamanian national as Deputy Administrator of the Canal Commission through December 31, 1989, and, as of January 1, 1990, appointment of "a Panamanian national . . . as the administrator . . . proposed to the United States of America by the Republic of Panama. . . ." (Article III);

4. Preparation of "contingency plans for the protection and defense of the canal . . . planning and conduct of combined military exercises; and the conduct of United States and Panamanian military operations with respect to the protection and defense of the canal" will be coordinated by "a combined Board comprised of an equal number of senior military representatives of each party [i.e., Panama and the U.S.]." (Article IV);

5. The entire Canal Zone "shall be under the flag of the Republic of Panama, and consequently such flag always shall occupy the position of honor." (Article VII);

6. ". . . the law of the Republic of Panama shall apply" in the Canal Zone. (Article IX);

7. A "system of preference" shall be used to favor hiring of Panamanian nationals for employment by the Panama Canal Commission. (Article X);

8. Canal Commission "employee unions shall have the right to affiliate with international labor organizations." (Article X);

9. Surrender of the United States' right to "negotiate with third states for the right to construct an interoceanic canal on any other route in the Western Hemisphere. . . ." (Article XII);

10. Upon termination of the treaty on December 31, 1999, "the Republic of Panama shall assume *total responsibility* for the management, operation, and maintenance of the Panama Canal, which shall be turned over in operating condition and free of liens and debts. . . ." [Emphasis added] (Article XIII);

11. The United States "transfers, without charge, to the Republic of Panama all right, title and interest . . ." portions of the Panama Railroad, certain housing facilities and other items "upon entry into force of this Treaty. . . ." (Article XII), and;

12. "Upon termination of this Treaty, *all* real property, and non-removable improvements . . . and equipment related to

the management, operation and maintenance of the Canal," become the property of the Government of Panama. (Article XIII).

Reviewing these twelve points we see that, under points 1 through 4, Panama immediately exerts partial and growing responsibility for the running and defense of the canal. Thus we would have already lost the supposedly clear guarantee of American control and use of the canal which, treaty advocates claim, will survive the surrender of American sovereignty. Point 5 formally symbolizes this surrender by placing the entire zone under the Panamanian flag, and point 6 makes the zone subject to Panamanian laws.

Point 7 would lead to a canal work force increasingly dominated by Panamanian nationals (already 70 percent today), hired under the preferential system agreed to in the treaty, and point 8 could ultimately lead to their affiliation with an international labor organization inimical to the United States, and closure of the canal by politically inspired strike.

Meanwhile, under point 9, for the duration of the century we would have surrendered our right to negotiate for—much less construct—any alternative canal in a more friendly Central American country while, under points 10 through 12, we would give the Panamanian government millions of dollars worth of canal property immediately and *all* remaining equipment and property at the expiration of the treaty in the year 2000—all this above and beyond the millions of dollars in subsidies, receipt skimming, military assistance, and loans already mentioned.

In addition, police and fire protection, street lighting, traffic direction, and garbage collection would be provided by the Panamanians which, judging from current squalid conditions in Panama, would be no bargain at the agreed-upon rate of $10 million a year, and would be good news for no one but jaywalkers, arsonists, roadhogs, and burglars.

The Neutrality Treaty

Companion document to the Canal Treaty is the so-called Neutrality Treaty, officially designated as the "Treaty Concerning the Permanent Neutrality and Operation of the Panama Canal." If we could take the word of the State Department on faith, as described in its official publication, *Panama Canal, The New Treaties*, the Neutrality Treaty establishes a "regime of neutrality" under which:

> . . . the canal is to remain open to merchant and naval vessels of all nations indefinitely, without discrimination as to conditions or tolls. It is in Panama's own financial interest . . . that the canal remain open to all, with competitively low tolls so as to encourage maximum use and income.
>
> The neutrality treaty does not give the United States the right to intervene in the internal affairs of Panama, an independent sovereign state. It does, however, give the United States and Panama responsibility to insure that the canal remains open and secure to ships of all nations at all times. Each of the two countries shall have the discretion to take whatever action it deems necessary, in accordance with its constitutional processes, to defend the canal against any threat to the permanent regime of neutrality. They each, therefore, shall have the right to act against any aggression or threat directed against the canal or against the peaceful transit of vessels through it.
>
> The neutrality treaty further provides that U.S. and Panamanian warships and auxiliary vessels shall be entitled to transit the canal expeditiously. This has been interpreted by both governments to mean as quickly as possible and without any impediment, going to the head of the line if necessary.

Very impressive, this, at the first casual reading. But a careful analysis of the working of the Neutrality Treaty itself, and the interpretation given it by Panama's chief negotiator, leftist leader Dr. Romulo Escobar Bethancourt, reveals that this bit of optimistic State Department puffery is, in the words of the poet Dryden:

> Free from all meaning, whether good or bad,
> And in one word, heroically mad.

Even the choice of the advert "indefinitely" in place of the comprehensive phrase "in perpetuity" is open to more than one interpretation. Keeping the canal neutral and open to all nations "indefinitely" could mean forever, or it could, according to Merriam Webster, mean only for a "vague" or "not immediately identifiable" time. Stating that Panama will do so because it is in her own "financial interest" compounds the confusion since Dr. Escobar himself stated, in an August 19, 1977, address to the

Panamanian National Assembly (see Appendix 3 for full text), that Panama has not promised "to maintain the canal permanently open" and that "Panama could not be tied down" to keeping the canal open if it stopped earning a profit. This raises two specters: first, actual Panamanian closure, since the canal, even under today's efficient American control, has only proven marginally profitable at best and in recent years has sometimes operated at a loss. Secondly, the Panamanian government could use the issue of canal profitability as a veiled form of blackmail, shaking down the United States for pay-off after pay-off in return for keeping the waterway open.

In his statement submitted to the Senate Committee on Foreign Relations on October 13, 1977, Gary L. Jarmin, the Legislative Director of the American Conservative Union, touched on this and other key flaws in the treaties. "We believe there are many valid reasons why these treaties should be rejected by the Senate," Mr. Jarmin stated. Chief among them is:

> . . . the problem of the contradictory interpretations by Panamanian and U.S. officials with regard to key provisions guaranteeing: (a) the United States right to intervene to defend the canal; (b) preferential passage for U.S. warships in times of major conflict or war; (c) the neutrality of the canal; and (d) keeping it open under all circumstances (except in cases of natural disasters).

Mr. Jarmin then goes on to quote the speech of Dr. Escobar, adding that:

> In his speech, Dr. Escobar made eleven points about the Neutrality Treaty and its Protocol but, reduced to basics, four items stand out. First, *the U.S. will not have any defense rights* past the year 2000 and will not be the guarantor of the neutrality of the canal. Second, *U.S. warships will not get preferential treatment in terms of transiting the canal*, even in times of war, after the year 2000. Third, the Panamanians think that *it will not be necessary for them to abide by the Neutrality Treaty in cases of foreign attack or internal disorder*. In short, from the Panamanian standpoint, *the U.S. role in canal affairs will be very limited until 1999 and virtually nonexistent thereafter*, which is a far cry from what we have heard about how the canal will be kept open and that adoption of this treaty will make it easier to defend our interests. [Emphasis added.]

On the crucial issue of keeping the canal open, Mr. Jarmin raised two intriguing questions which administration spokesmen and advocates of the treaties have never satisfactorily answered. First, given the pro-Marxist, pro-Cuban stance of the Panamanian government,

> In an international crisis, such as occurred in Cuba in 1962, can we be assured that riotous students, in sympathy to Cuba, would not attempt to disrupt the operation of the canal to prevent passage of U.S. warships? Could not the Panamanian government conveniently declare during such a crisis that the canal was not making money and, therefore, have to close it indefinitely?
>
> In addition, given the heavy communist influence in Panamanian labor unions, could not one day, in a similar crisis, the pilots who move ships through the canal suddenly declare a strike and, thus, paralyze the transit of U.S. warships?

Mr. Jarmin also points out a technical loophole which Ambassador Bunker, an old-fashioned diplomat in his eighties, and Ambassador Linowitz, who was racing against time to complete an agreement before the expiration of his appointment, seem to have missed entirely:

> There is . . . one other provision that would provide for the Panamanians a perfectly legitimate excuse to halt the transit of U.S. warships. Under Article III, Section I, subsection (e), the treaty provides that warships can be "required to certify that they have complied with all applicable health, sanitation and quarantine regulations." Obviously, the Panamanians could, in an international crisis, declare that all U.S. warships transiting the canal be stopped indefinitely to undergo a health and sanitation inspection.

"And what could we do about it," Mr. Jarmin asks, "send in the marines?" After all, one of the main reasons that the administration has given for ratifying the treaties is the argument that, if we do not, we may have to protect the Canal Zone by force. As any soldier knows, it is far more bloody and costly to retake a position than to hold onto it in the first place.

"Use of the canal is more important than ownership," Secretary of Defense Harold Brown stated in his September 27, 1977, testimony supporting the new treaties before the Senate Committee on Foreign Relations. Yet the evidence clearly shows that, besides giving away American *ownership* of the canal, the treaties could be invoked by Panama to deny the United States *actual use* of the canal. In other words, the treaties fail to pass even the meager and questionable standard for acceptance set up by the Carter administration itself. Sensing the weakness of its position, the administration, on October 14, 1977, made a hasty cosmetic attempt to reassure a skeptical American public.

The Misunderstood "Statement of Understanding"

Realizing that the glittering signing ceremony did not, as President Carter had hoped, turn public opinion around, the president called in reinforcements from Panama; General Torrijos flew in for a quick attempt at a salvage mission, the two leaders meeting again at the White House on October 14. Afterwards they issued what they called a "Statement of Understanding" (see Appendix 1, part 7 for text) which purported to clarify the Neutrality Treaty but which only succeeded in further muddying the waters. If truth-in-packaging laws covered diplomatic utterances, one Washington wag remarked at the time, the joint note should have been labeled a "Statement of Misunderstanding," since it was merely a personal agreement—and a vague one at that—between Jimmy Carter and Omar Torrijos, and in no way a legally binding part of the Neutrality Treaty. Even if it were, the statement, by declaring that it "does not mean nor shall it be interpreted as a right of intervention of the United States in the internal affairs of Panama," effectively bans American intervention in the former Canal Zone since, under the terms of the treaties, the zone would become Panamanian territory. Thus, by definition, any American interference in the former zone would be intervention "in the internal affairs of Panama." To paraphrase the late Sir Winston Churchill: Some statement, some understanding.

The staggering strategic and economic cost of America's surrender of both ownership *and* certain access to the canal are the subject of the next chapter. But before concluding discussion of the treaties themselves, an important constitutional point must be considered.

84

Constitutional Barriers to Simple Senate Ratification

As the wording of the new Panama Canal treaty makes clear, the document not only abrogates past diplomatic agreements and arrives at new ones regarding the sovereignty over and operation of the canal; it also disposes of millions of dollars in American property and territory. This is a key point because, whereas the Constitution gives the Senate sole authority to ratify or reject foreign treaties as such, under Article IV, Section 3, Clause 2, the Constitution provides that:

> *Congress* shall have power to dispose of, and make all Rules and Regulations respecting the *Territory or other property belonging to the United States*; and nothing in this Constitution shall be so construed as to prejudice any claims of the United States, or of any particular State. [Emphasis added.]

Testifying before the Senate Subcommittee on Separation of Powers on September 8, 1977, I pointed out the significance of this constitutional delegation of powers vis-à-vis the canal treaties and cited historical precedents:

> . . . on at least three occasions, the House, as well as the Senate, has been involved in relatively minor territorial matters involving the Canal Zone. Admittedly, none of these episodes quite parallels the situation we face today, but if it has been deemed appropriate for the House of Representatives to be involved in relatively minor matters—such as the temporary cession of a small plot of territory to Panama so that the Panamanian government could build a legation—then it stands to reason that it should be involved in what could turn out to be the biggest giveaway in American history.
>
> All rhetoric aside, the facts of the matter are that the United States has spent $163.7 million to acquire rights and title to the canal and Canal Zone, to say nothing of the $366 million in construction costs and the $6.35 billion over the years that went for operation, administration and defense. Just the $163.7 million for title and rights represents more money than it cost the U.S. to acquire all the rest of its territorial additions combined. And now it is proposed that we not only give this entire investment away but that we pay Panama almost $2 billion more between now and the year 2000 for taking it.

Given the fact that the Supreme Court has ruled that the Canal

Zone is United States territory, the need for congressional action to validate the treaties is indisputable. In 1907, in the case of *Wilson v. Shaw*, the Court declared that:

> It is hypercritical to contend that the title of the United States to the Canal Zone is imperfect and that the territory described does not belong to this nation because of the omission of some of the technical terms used in ordinary conveyances of real estate.

Again, as recently as 1972, in *United States v. Husband*, the Court designated the Canal Zone as "unincorporated territory of the United States" over which Congress "has complete and plenary authority." Significantly, the demand that Congress have a voice in approving the treaties has not been taken up by treaty opponents alone. One of the foremost living authorities on the Constitution, Professor Raoul Berger of the Harvard Law School, is a liberal who is in favor of the treaties. However, in a long and studious analysis of the constitutional issues at stake, which he delivered before the Senate Separation of Powers Subcommittee of the Judiciary Committee (for a full text, see Appendix 2), Dr. Berger stated:

> Although I am in favor of the Panama Canal Treaty, I share your solicitude for the preservation of constitutional boundaries and your concern lest the function committed to Congress be diminished. I have long held the conviction that all agents of the United States, be they justices, members of Congress, or the president, must respect these boundaries. No agent of the people may overlap the bounds of delegated power. That is the essence of constitutional government and of our democratic system.

In effect, by attempting to dispose of the Canal Zone (which the Supreme Court has ruled is United States territory) without the consent of the Congress, the president is bypassing the constitutional process. "The effect of these hearings ranges beyond the Panama treaty," Dr. Berger declared:

> The Panama cession will constitute a landmark which, should the State Department prevail, will be cited down the years for "concurrent jurisdiction" of the president in the disposition of United States property. Acquiescence in such claims spells progressive attrition of congressional powers; it emboldens the executive to

make even more extravagant claims. I would remind you that congressional acquiescence encourages solo presidential adventures such as plunged us into the Korean and Vietnam wars. Congressional apathy fostered the expansion of executive secrecy. Then as now, the State Department invoked flimsy "precedents," for example, the pursuit of cattle rustlers across the Mexican border, to justify presidential launching of a full-scale war. If Congress slumbers in the face of such claims it may awaken like Samson shorn of his locks.

Concluding his ringing defense of the constitutional prerogatives of the Congress, Professor Berger stated:

If the president is to fly in the face of the express "power of Congress to dispose" it must be on a sounder basis than the arguments . . . advanced. In my judgment, *the Panama Treaty should contain a provision making it subject to approval of the Congress.* [Emphasis added.]

And both opponents and proponents agree that, if the House of Representatives is given a chance to accept or reject the Panama Canal Treaty, it will be overwhelmingly rejected. Some of the key strategic and economic reasons why both Republican and Democratic members of Congress oppose the treaty are discussed in the following chapter.

Chapter 7:
The Price of Surrender

In the last chapter, we took inventory of some of the things the United States would surrender if the Senate ratifies the Panama Canal Treaty and the Neutrality Treaty. But what would the cost of surrender be? What would it mean, not only to ourselves, our friends and our enemies today, but in the decades ahead? As one anonymous Panamanian bitterly remarked in a quote in the October 18, 1977, issue of the *Panama Star & Herald*, "Instead of the Americans in perpetuity, we now have Omar [Torrijos] in perpetuity." And the strengthened grip of Torrijos on Panama can only mean one thing for the United States in coming years—more and more trouble and a growing Marxist influence in a strategic nerve center of the Americas. Already, as representatives of American citizens in the Canal Zone have testified before the Senate Foreign Relations Committee (October 10, 1977), the pattern of communist subversion and influence is growing alarmingly. Their testimony cited five major examples:

1. Russian planes, seen by the U.S. and Panamanian eyewitnesses alike, on the ground at the Rio Hato airstrip. These planes do more than bring Torrijos his custom-made cigars from Fidel Castro. These planes come in low over coastal water, so as to avoid radar detection.
2. Every six months a fresh group of Panamanian students leaves Panama to study in Cuba. These students are given top priority in the Panamanian visa office. The cumulative effect on the young people of Panama, who will someday be the national leaders, is not hard to imagine.
3. Panamanian students go to Russia for study in five-year tours. A young person who returns after five solid years of Communist Party line at a Russian university is bound to be affected in beliefs about capitalism vs. communism.
4. Panama has requested Cuban advisers to come to Panama to teach the government how to set up neighborhood committees to facilitate the government's control of the people on the local level.

5. The Russians are making plans to build structures in the Colón Free Zone for the sale of Russian-made products. Also in the works are plans for sale of sugar by Panama to Russia, construction by Russia of a hydroelectric plant, and the opening of a Russian bank in Panama.

If President Carter and his advisers do not realize the strategic importance of the canal to American security and the stability of Latin America, there are others who do. In the August issue of the British journal *Intelligence International*, a revealing article was reprinted which originally appeared in *Red Star*, the official Soviet publication of the Red Army. In it, Major Sergei Yunorov wrote that:

> Due to its privileged location as the juncture between South America and the rest of the continent including the canal that permits U.S. warships to operate simultaneously in the Atlantic and the Pacific, the Canal Zone must be considered by the Soviet Union as a priority zone.

Many Panamanians themselves have expressed considerable trepidation about what the future may bring if the treaties are ratified. Writing in the Panamanian journal *La Republica*, columnist Mario Augusto stressed that it is easy to say "out with the gringos" but it is not so easy to replace them. In a condensation of his article carried in the September 14, 1977, issue of the Panama Canal Information Office *Daily Digest*, he recalled that:

> . . . when the U.S. troops evacuated Rio Hato in 1947, they left millions of dollars in installations, which were stolen or vandalized within twenty-four hours. A similar situation existed when the garbage collection was turned over to Panama. It took years to straighten out the system and it still is not operating with the same efficiency. The Canal Zone is different from the rest of the country, not only because it is under foreign domination but because there is order and respect for the natural beauty and protection of public property. The attitude and conduct of Panamanians must be changed and it will take a long process of training.

Doubtless the training will come from Russian and Cuban "advisers" if the Torrijos regime has its way. Concern for the proper managment of the canal itself in Panamanian hands has already spread to other Latin American countries. The threat of massive toll increases is a real one to the many Latin American countries whose fragile economies depend on the canal as their lifeline. Thus, on October 25, 1977, a front-page story in the periodical *Matutino* quoted Peruvian Foreign Minister José de la Puente Radbill as hoping that if canal tolls are raised, the increase will be modest. He pointed out that 80 percent of Peru's foreign trade uses the canal, and that a sharp increase in tolls, coupled with the low prices of Peruvian raw materials, could have a negative effect on his country. Mexico and Brazil, two of the giants of Latin America, were also reportedly concerned; it is no coincidence that neither the Brazilian nor the Mexican chiefs of state bothered to attend the elaborate treaty-signing ceremony in Washington.

At least one Latin American leader was all grins, however. A September 29, 1977, item in *La Llorona* quoted Fidel Castro as having told a French journalist that Panama got the best treaty possible. As for Omar Torrijos himself, typical to his pattern as a spendthrift dictator trying to buy popular support from the peasant masses, he was already boasting of the goodies he would dispense once the treaties were ratified and the American greenbacks started rolling in. In a November 1, 1977, radio address to the nation, summarized in the Canal Information Office's *Daily Digest*, Torrijos:

> . . . promised solutions to such problems as unemployment, housing and education. Free transportation is to be provided for all unemployed people to gather at stadiums in Colón and Panama City, where a census will be taken and emergency income provided to cover basic needs of all families. Lower electric rates are promised when the U.S. Senate ratifies the treaties; private and state printing plants will be made available to produce textbooks (no doubt with a suitable Marxist slant) and other school supplies; 5 million yards of material are being imported for school uniforms; each child will be provided with two pairs of shoes a year at less than cost. . . .

Already, even with the treaties facing serious challenge in the United States Senate, Torrijos was doing exactly what his Panamanian critics had warned us he would: exploiting the treaties and the loot they would bring in if ratified to perpetuate his dictatorial grip on Panama.

Many well-intentioned Americans, including some ordinarily perceptive journalists, are unaware of all of this, perhaps lulled into a false sense of security by misleading State Department briefings. A case in point is venerable editor-reporter Vermont Royster, a respected fixture in American journalism. Presumably on the basis of misinformation provided by treaty proponents, Royster wrote in the pages of the *Wall Street Journal* that the canal was obsolete, since "only secondary navy vessels even use it for transit; it's too small for today's capital ship carriers, and the big submarines," adding that commercial use of the canal has fallen off so sharply that "where it used to operate twenty-four hours a day, transits are now largely confined to daytime."

Unfortunately for the record of an otherwise distinguished journalist, Mr. Royster had been sadly taken in by the Carter-Kissinger axis of treaty salesmen. In fact, there are only thirteen ships in the entire U.S. Navy too large to transit the canal, and the waterway still operates twenty-four hours a day.

Not all Americans were similarly taken in. On October 11, 1977, Representative John M. Murphy, Chairman of the House Committee on Merchant Marines and Fisheries, struck a warning note from the Congress. Testifying before the House Committee on International Relations, the veteran New York Democrat stated that:

> . . . the proposed treaties should be accepted or rejected on the basis of whether they serve the best interests of the United States, not on the basis of who is supporting or opposing them, not on the basis of party or region. The only question to be considered is whether the proposed treaties are good for the United States, or whether they would be better amended, or rejected. . . .
>
> While I agree with President Carter that there is a need for a new treaty relationship, the haste and self-imposed deadline that characterized the most recent phase of the negotiations has resulted in defective treaties which do not achieve the objectives they sought to attain—"an open, safe, efficient, and neutral canal" under a treaty relationship which "protects the national security interests of the United States." Neither will the said treaties help endear us with our Latin American neighbors, nor will they better protect the canal against sabotage.

Representative Murphy cited eight major problem areas with the treaties:

1. The attempt to circumvent the House of Representatives in the matter of disposal of U.S. property and territory;
2. The attempt to circumvent the House in the matter of appropriations;
3. The absence of clear and unequivocal language to allow U.S. action to protect the canal in times of hostility;
4. The absurd prohibition until the year 2000 precluding the U.S. from negotiating for a new sea-level canal with any country other than Panama, a prohibition which places the U.S. in a totally dependent position without any logic or reason;
5. Formulation of an overgenerous economic compensation package which will likely ruin the economic viability of the canal as a self-sustaining operation and result in enormous U.S. subsidies to run the canal in future years;
6. The location of many key items with respect to control of the canal in accompanying executive agreements rather than in the bodies of the treaties, thus allowing for piecemeal erosion of the tenuous and limited rights found in the treaties themselves;
7. The failure of the treaties to address the disposition of other relevant canal agreements, such as the Hay-Pauncefote Treaty of 1901, which set forth the international obligation in connection with the neutral operations of the canal, and the Thomson-Urrutia Treaty of 1914, which gave to Colombia certain privileged rights with respect to transit;
8. The pervasiveness of vague and ambiguous language and, in fact, the absense of language, with respect to many important subject areas, including:
   (a) The U.S. rights of intervention;
   (b) The boundaries of properties being immediately taken over by Panama;
   (c) The taxation of canal properties by Panama;
   (d) The obligation to turn over the canal to Panama in the year 2000 free from debt and in good operating condition;
   (e) The Panamanian takeover and the U.S. use of docks, housing, railroads, etc.;
   (f) The rights of passage for U.S. vessels of war and auxiliary vessels.

Sloppy, hasty, and ill-thought-out negotiations have led to a bad pair of treaties, Representative Murphy concluded, and whereas:

. . . a properly conceived treaty arrangement may serve the U.S. and Panamanian interests . . . I do not believe the treaties should be accepted, at least in their present form. Above all, I think we should be realistic enough to recognize that because of the manner in which these treaties were negotiated, an atmosphere has been created in which violence or stoppage of the canal will probably occur regardless of approval or disapproval. . . .

Violence, and the threat of violence, underlay all of Torrijos's negotiations. It was hinted, and sometimes stated, that if Americans did not go peacefully, and pay a sufficient ransom by way of pennance for our supposed past sins, we would be driven out by force.

The October 11, 1971, edition of *The New York Times* quoted a Torrijos speech in which the dictator swaggered that:

> When all hope is lost of removing this colonial enclave, Omar [already in 1971 Torrijos had picked up the traditional autocratic habit of referring to himself in the third person] will come to this same square to tell you, "Let's advance." Omar will accompany you and the 6000 rifles of the National Guard will be there to defend the integrity and dignity of the people.

Similar rabble-rousing efforts continue to this day; seldom, however, surpassing a particularly bombastic performance delivered at the dedication of a new sugar mill in 1972. In *The Panama Canal Controversy*, Captain Paul B. Ryan described it:

> This was a jingoist appeal entitled "If I Fall, Catch the Flag, Kiss It and Go Forward." . . . he stirred his audience with the prediction that Torrijos would die a violent death as he fought for the canal. He confessed that the prospect of a tragic end was of little concern to him; more important was the thought that the day this tragedy occurred his followers would "catch the flag."

Local skeptics were not long in dubbing this bit of Torrijos rhetoric the "Kiss my Flag" speech. But, absurd as it sounds, it is precisely the kind of incendiary appeal that has sent thousands of Latin American rioters into the streets in the past, and might very well do so again in the future—especially in the face of a passive, docile America that has demonstrated a pattern of yielding to threats instead of dealing from a position of strength.

Annoying as this posturing on Torrijos's part is, it would count for little if the Panama Canal were destined for strategic and economic obsolescence in the years ahead. But, as Representative Murphy demonstrated, this simply is not the case. Because the canal will be of enduring—and in some ways, even *increasing*—

93

importance, the threats and boasts of Torrijos are more than a Latin American echo of Idi Amin: they pose a real menace to world stability.

Representative Murphy illustrated his point with a simple one-page chart which he appended to his testimony:

Data in Support of the Contention of the Continuing Importance of the Panama Canal and Canal Zone

(from testimony of Rep. John M. Murphy before the House Committee on International Relations, October 11, 1977)

Commercially

- The Panama Canal is a U.S.-oriented canal because two-thirds of the vessels transiting have a port in the U.S. as a point of origin or destination.

- The Maritime Administration estimates that by the year 2000, U.S. exports through the canal will have doubled and U.S. exports will be at two-and-a-half times today's levels.

- The percentage of the total dollar value of U.S. ocean foreign trade transiting the Panama Canal has steadily increased in the last generation, and is expected to increase in the future.

- 96 percent of the U.S. fleet and 92 percent of the world's merchant fleet can transit the canal today. The great majority of those supertankers which cannot transit the canal were built for trade routes which do not come near the Isthmus of Panama.

- 70 percent of all the cargo that has transited the canal has done so in the last twenty-five years.

Militarily

- The lack of a true two-ocean navy while the U.S. has commitments in five oceans makes the canal's availability for transit ever more important.

- 96 percent of our naval fleet can transit the canal. Only our Nimitz-class aircraft carriers cannot transit. The trend toward naval ship design is toward a smaller and faster vessel.

- The canal has been a major resource in hostilities and confrontations that occurred in World War II, Korea, the Cuban Missile Crisis, and Vietnam.

- The Canal Zone has the only major ship-repair facilities within 1,600 miles on the Atlantic side and 2,500 miles on the Pacific side.

- The Canal Zone also has the only U.S.-controlled air base within 1,000 miles, and it is a military and communications crossroads of the hemisphere.

- The only existing trans-isthmian pipeline for ship bunker oil and aviation fuel are in the zone.

- The lack of adequate West Coast port facilities for the loading of supplies and ammunition makes the canal crucial to U.S. military efforts, especially those in the Pacific theater.

Latin American Dissatisfaction with the Treaties

Despite the carefully orchestrated State Department attempt to portray Latin American opinion as solidly in favor of the treaties, cracks keep appearing in the façade, warnings that the United States is not the only country that will pay a heavy price for surrender in Panama. On October 11, 1977, the Senate Committee on Foreign Relations heard from Dr. Donald Marquand Dozer, Professor Emeritus of Latin American History and Inter-American Relations at the University of California, Santa Barbara. Besides his long and distinguished academic career, Dr. Dozer served as an intelligence officer for the Office of Strategic Services in Latin America from 1941 to 1943, and from 1944 to 1956 served in the State Department, specializing in policy, intelligence, research, and the history of Latin America. His consultating work in Latin American affairs includes service for the Brookings Institute, the prestigious liberal think-tank, and the respected Center for Strategic Studies at Georgetown University. In 1971 he served as Fulbright lecturer to Argentina, which should clinch his credentials as a respectable "moderate."

Dr. Dozer has written several books on Latin American history and has visited every country in the hemisphere; he is a prominent, well-established Latin American scholar and authority with no political axe to grind. Hence his testimony about the adverse impact of the treaties on other Latin American countries is particularly damning:

> On my recent trip to Latin American countries earlier this year government executives, business leaders, journalists, and other leaders expressed their apprehension about the adverse effects on their national economies of the increased tolls authorized in this new canal treaty for the unjust enrichment of Panama. The Carter-Torrijos Canal Treaty will require a substantial increase in tolls to provide the Torrijos government with an average of $80 million per year to service Panama's debts to a consortium of foreign lending institutions. In the new Canal Treaty Panama assumes no binding obligation, like that which rests upon the United States, to keep the canal free and open at reasonable charges.
>
> Latin American leaders also expressed indignation over the cavalier treatment of Colombia. The Thomson-Urrutia Treaty of 1914 granted Colombia free use of the canal for certain products of its soil and agriculture and also free use of the Panama Railroad under certain conditions. There is no protection of Colombia's treaty rights in either the new Canal Treaty or the new Neutrality Treaty. When Colombia protested this violation of its treaty rights the State Department summarily dismissed the complaint with the statement that Colombia must negotiate with Panama.

As to the long-term implications of the treaties—their potential impact on American power, prestige, and security around the world and in the defense of our own boundaries—Dr. Dozer had this sobering observation to make:

> A pretext advanced by the State Department for renegotiating the treaties with Panama is the international law doctrine of *rebus sic stantibus* which permits the renegotiation of treaties when the conditions of the original negotiation have changed. . . . [However] conditions in international relations are constantly changing, and to seek to renegotiate treaties of territorial cession on this pretext can only lead to international chaos. For example, during the early years of the Eisenhower administration the Soviet government questioned the validity of our Alaska Purchase Treaty of 1867. This question was answered by admission of Alaska to the union as a new state. . . .
>
> Persistent efforts to renegotiate treaties to surrender control over national territory and to let it pass into the hands of foreign

powers only serve to promote international instability and serve the interests of those foreign powers. Claims of the State Department that a new treaty relationship with Panama will protect the vital interest of the United States are only a vain utopian dream.

To restore good relations with Panama and other nations of Latin America, Dr. Dozer concluded, the United States must return to "a Good Neighbor Policy based on self-respect":

> This demands that we retain all our treaty rights in the Canal Zone. We must defend them as indispensable economic, geopolitical, and military assets. . . . There is no substitute for an American canal, on American soil, under American control.

Washington Surrenders Its Last Canal Option

Another prominent scholar to join the Panama debate is William Columbus Davis, former Professor of Latin American history and director of Latin American studies at George Washington University and the National War College. Focusing on Article XII, Section 2 (b) of the new Panama Canal Treaty, Professor Davis pointed out a particularly damaging and constricting part of the price of surrender. The section in question stipulates that:

> During the duration of this Treaty, the United States of America shall not negotiate with third states for the right to construct an interoceanic canal on any other route in the Western Hemisphere, except as the two Parties [Panama and the U.S.] may otherwise agree.

Writing in the December 16, 1977, edition of the *Washington Star*, Professor Davis explained that:

> Arguments by U.S. proponents of the treaty to the effect that the present canal is no longer very important to us because of its limitations, are really arguments for a larger canal. While it is true that there are now some warships and commercial vessels too large to negotiate the canal, it is still a very significant passage, with about 14,000 transits annually. . . .

Several Latin American countries are also dependent on the canal for much of their overseas trade. Voicing traditional opposition to

United States influence, a number of Latin American political leaders have expressed support for Panamanian ownership of the canal. But privately many are worried and would prefer that it remain in U.S. hands.

What is really needed, according to Professor Davis, is a new, larger canal "located across the middle of Panama or any other country." In other words, if Panama doesn't like the idea, there are lots of good fish in the sea—most notably, feasible routes in the extreme northwest of Colombia, near the Panamanian border, and the San Juan River route along the Nicaraguan–Costa Rican border. In both cases, the canal route would be through sparsely populated areas and would not cut the site country in two, thus providing no emotional rallying point for nationalist resentment or communist agitation. American technology could create a model installation guaranteed to meet not only today's needs, but those of the next century and thus solve the canal problem once and for all.

But, no; under the treaties Mssrs. Carter, Bunker, and Linowitz have locked us into an unbreakable embrace with Torrijos's Panama. Not only do the treaties surrender the existing canal to Panama, they prevent us from building a better one elsewhere—one more item in the unacceptable price tag of surrender in Panama.

The Treaties Add to America's Energy Problems

Although President Carter has devoted several fireside chats and countless pages of administration press handouts to the importance of keeping down American energy costs, the new canal treaties he is pushing could also have a substantial negative effect on America's energy problems. As has been pointed out, now that we have finally begun to develop the Alaska oil slope deposits, the canal's importance to America increases rather than decreases.

If, as projected, the flow of Alaska crude creates an oil glut on our West Coast, efficient, economical shipping of vast amounts of it to the East Coast becomes imperative, and this, in turn, makes an open, low-toll canal a vital economic necessity to the United States. The companies developing the Alaska slope recognized this when they planned a building program for medium-sized tankers of 60,000 dead-weight tons designed for transit through the canal.

But at almost the precise moment that the flow of Alaskan oil began pouring into the hulls of the tankers at Valdez, the Carter administration signed the Panama treaties, which guarantee substantial increases in the price of the oil, through higher freight costs—and could even lead to closure of the canal.

Even assuming that the ultimate catastrophe of closure is prevented, we still face the problem of toll increases. Article XIII of the Panama Canal Treaty provides that the government of Panama shall receive 30¢ per ton on all cargo passing through the canal once the treaty comes into force. Thus, for each 60,000-ton oil tanker, we would have to pay an additional political tribute to Torrijos of about $18,000 in increased tolls.

Where will the buck finally stop? With American consumers who will have to pay more at the pump for every gallon of gas flowing from Alaska to the East Coast and energy-hungry communities of the Midwest.

Direct energy shipments through the canal aside, we would suffer enormous energy losses if the canal should ever be closed through Panamanian mismanagement or political chaos. For example, it is estimated that if only American naval vessels that use the canal had to be rerouted around Cape Horn, the cost would run to nearly $10 million a year in extra fuel alone.

The Economic Time Bomb

As of 1975, 40 percent of the cargo moving through the canal was en route between American Atlantic or Gulf ports and the Far East. Canal traffic accounted for $14 billion worth of our gross national product. Thus, while closure of the canal would not (singlehandedly) destroy the American economy, taken in the context of the times—with a new potential oil embargo still hanging over our heads, and America's balance of payments already chronically out of whack—the threat of a canal closure is an economic time bomb that would begin ticking away the moment the Senate ratified the treaties. Captain Ryan's *The Panama Canal Controversy* paints a graphic picture of the impact that such a closure could have on the United States economy:

> . . . grain dealers in the farmlands of Iowa, Nebraska, and Minnesota would face dwindling profits in the short term. Thousands of tons of corn and soybeans normally shipped to the Gulf ports

for transport to the Orient would, instead, be hauled by rail or truck-trailer to the Pacific ports of Seattle and Portland. Even then difficulties would crop up for the reason that ship-loading facilities might be overburdened at West Coast ports to accommodate sudden huge grain shipments. Nor would the obsolescent railroads be prepared to handle such a sharp increase in traffic. . . . Economic experts believe that in time, say five years, these hurdles would be cleared but only at the expense of enormous transport costs and an adverse effect on the U.S. economy.

Yet, critical as these economic problems would be to the United States and the free world, they pale by comparison to the strategic coast of surrender in Panama.

Strategic Cost of the Treaties

On August 20, 1977, Air Force Chief of Staff General David C. Jones transmitted a priority message to all major air force commands. The Jones dispatch is important for two reasons. First, it clearly states the continued strategic importance of the canal to the United States; second, it provides a prime example of the political pressure the Carter administration has put on active-duty military to toe the administration treaty line. The key sections of the Jones five-point message were numbers 2 and 5. Number 2 emphatically stated that:

The Panama Canal is a major defense asset, the use of which enhances United States capability for timely reinforcement of United States forces. Its strategic military advantage lies in the economy and flexibility it provides to accelerate the shift of military forces and logistic support by sea between the Atlantic and Pacific oceans and to overseas areas.

So far, so good, but then General Jones added:

. . . United States military interests in the Panama Canal are in its use, not ownership. The proposed treaties would assure that access to and security of the Panama Canal are protected in time of war and peace.

Here General Jones proved that, while as a military man he understood the vital importance of the canal to U.S. security, as a layman he did not grasp the failure of the treaties to ensure both

100

use of and security of the canal, as has been abundantly illustrated in this text. Evidently, General Jones was taking the State Department's misleading interpretation of the treaties on faith.

In section 5 of the dispatch he issued a thinly disguised gag order to all air force personnel who might have misgivings of their own about the treaties: "It is important that our personnel, particularly our senior people, understand our support for the proposed treaties."

Fortunately, not all of the best military minds in our country are at the mercy of the Carter White House. The impressive testimony of Admirals Moorer, Burke, Anderson, and Carney against the treaties has already been cited, and many other acknowledged authorities on America's strategic interests—men who do not hold their jobs at the whim of President Carter—have put their reputation on the line against the treaties, warning of the staggering strategic cost of surrender in Panama. Thus Hanson Baldwin, veteran military analyst for *The New York Times*, flatly stated in an American Enterprise Institute Study reprinted by the Senate Foreign Relations Committee that:

> The future security and well-being of the United States are threatened by the administration's proposed abandonment of sovereignty over the Panama Canal and the Canal Zone.
>
> Any such action would have global consequences, nowhere more adverse than in the Caribbean Sea–Gulf of Mexico area. The vital interests of a nation can be defined in territorial and regional terms as political, psychological, economic, or military interests. By any and all of these yardsticks, the security of the Caribbean, the ability of the United States to control the Caribbean in war and to be a dominant influence there in peace, is vital to our country.

As Mr. Baldwin points out, the area has been "considered essential to U.S. security since the time of Thomas Jefferson and the enunciation of the Monroe Doctrine." Yet, Mr. Baldwin continues, that capability has already been gravely weakened; the turning point was the communists' seizure of power in Cuba, the Caribbean's most important island, only ninety miles from our shores. Soviet Migs flying in Cuban skies, Soviet submarines calling at Cuban ports, and the hammer and sickle flaunting its red blazon of revolution across the area are both cause and symbol of the deterioration in the past fifteen years of U.S. security on our southern flank.

It is in this broad perspective—the future of the Caribbean–Gulf of Mexico area—that any basic change in the status of the Panama Canal must be judged, for any such change will profoundly affect our interests in the area and hence, ultimately, our political, psychological, economic, and military security. And in an even larger, global sense, any retreat or major concession in Panama in the face of the threats of General Omar Torrijos can only be interpreted around the world as scuttle-and-run, further proof of the weakening of the will and resolution of the United States. Faith in promises made, belief in the power of the nation and its will to use it in defense of its own interests, is the coin of international respect; since Castro, Vietnam, Angola, the credibility of the United States has been severely impaired and our international solvency in doubt.

Panama and the canal are therefore both cause and symbol; the canal is highly important in its own right, but far more so as a symbol of U.S. resolution and as one of the key links in our vital interests in the Caribbean. Looked at in this light, the canal itself, contrary to the claims of its detractors, is in no way obsolete.

What about Torrijos's repeated threats of violence of sabotage if the canal is not surrendered; do they stand up to close scrutiny, or are they mainly the egomaniacal bullying of a tinhorn dictator? In a study prepared for the United States Industrial Council, Egon Tausch, a former U.S. Army officer who served in Vietnam and later taught at West Point, puts the lie to the red herring issue of Panamanian sabotage or insurgency, and makes it clear that the real threat of violence to the canal would crest *after* the departure of American security forces, not while they were in place to protect the zone, as they have successfully done through two world wars, Korea, the Cuban Missile Crisis, and Vietnam. "As long as the zone is controlled by the U.S., few military men fear Panamanian guerrillas," Tausch writes:

> Although large parts of Panama are jungle, the population is concentrated in the two major cities. Panama has never fought a war. The *Guardia Nacional*, which serves as both the army and the police of Panama, is 8,000 strong, but almost all of it is stationed in downtown Panama City, for political uses only. The *Guardia* doesn't like the jungle. The most committed fighters

General Torrijos has are the thousands of leftist professional students, and these do better in romantic street demonstrations than in individual acts of sabotage or concerted struggles. The "martyrs" of the famous riots of 1964 were killed when a department store they were looting caved in. . . .

Panamanians could be trained to fight—the U.S. Army has been trying to do this in jungle warfare schools in the zone for years—but the probability, if war broke out, would be that Cubans would do all the fighting. This is true whether the treaties are rejected, or are ratified with the U.S. retention of military bases but without the zone.

The only safe alternative to continued U.S. control of the canal? Retired Lieutenant General Victor Krulac of the U.S. Marines summed it up in the Winter 1976, issue of *Strategic Review*:

. . . without absolute control of the canal and the essential contiguous land, the United States could not accept the hazard of a one-ocean navy. It would be essential at once to initiate construction of fleets independently able to meet a crisis in either the Atlantic or the Pacific—a massive expenditure which we are now spared only because of our control of the canal.

And an expenditure, General Krulac might well have added, that any Congress that would passively acquiesce to the surrender of the canal would be most unlikely to undertake.

The late author and commentator, Elmer Davis, once wrote that America "will remain the land of the free only so long as it is the home of the brave." The bottom-line cost of surrender in Panama would be the United States' humiliating retreat in the face of blustering threats from the corrupt dictator of a backward banana republic. In such a case, even the construction of a new, two-ocean fleet would not be enough to restore our credibility in the eyes of the world, and our dignity and self-respect in the eyes of our own citizens.

Chapter 8:
Panama and the American Future

"I have faith in the people," Abraham Lincoln stated at the height of our greatest nation ordeal, the Civil War, ". . . the danger is their being misled. Let them know the truth and the country is safe." There is every indication that, as far as our people are concerned, Lincoln's axiom still holds true; given the truth, time and again they have sifted and solved even the most complex national questions. But what about our leaders—those whose responsibility it is to bring the truth to the people? In the case of Panama, too many of them, from President Carter down, have ignited a near-blinding smokescreen of propaganda that has been accepted and passed on by unthinking pundits, vested interest groups, and lesser politicians.

Looking back on the statements of President Carter and other treaty advocates, historians of some future time may well label the late 1970s as the Golden Age of American Guilt. There are times when, listening to the utterances of many of our current national spokesmen, one is tempted to believe that our national motto has been changed from *E Pluribus Unum* to *Mea Culpa*, and that the courageous statesmen of earlier days have been largely replaced by masochists and politicians described once by Senator Goldwater as more possessed of chicken bone than backbone.

Omar Torrijos must have reached some such conclusion during his September 1977 visit to Washington for the treaty-signing ceremony. One of the first things he did on his return home to Panama was gloatingly quote a crow-eating Jimmy Carter in a speech reported in the September 10 issue of the Panamanian periodical *La Estrella*:

"The more I read of the history of Panama," Torrijos quoted President Carter as telling him, "the more ashamed I felt. General Torrijos, you and the Panamanian people have been very patient and in my name, I ask forgiveness from your great people."

Perhaps President Carter was operating with Figaro's maxim in mind: "If you are mediocre and grovel, you shall succeed." If so, he sadly misread the character of the American people. For, whenever the basic canal question is put to the public directly, the response is overwhelmingly against surrender in Panama. Thus, when the Opinion Research Corporation conducted a poll in May 1977 asking the public if it favored keeping the Panama Canal under U.S. control or giving control and ownership to Panama, the response was a massive 78 percent in favor of continued U.S. control. Only 8 percent favored ceding control and ownership to Panama, which is exactly what the treaties would do.

Even a misleadingly phrased Gallup Poll (is described the treaties as only "calling for the U.S. to turn over ownership of the canal to Panama at the end of this century. . . . However, the U.S. will maintain control over the land and installation necessary to operate and defend the canal") found that 54 percent of those expressing an opinion were opposed to the treaties.

The tide of public opinion against the treaties is even more vividly reflected in constituent mail to the United States Senate, the main battleground for ratification or rejection. In August 1977, as chairman of the American Conservative Union, I organized a polling of Senate offices to see just how the grass-roots reaction to the treaty hard-sell was shaping up. Some 66 percent of Senate offices responded and their mail indicated that 93.46 percent of the constituents expressing an opinion were against the treaties and only 6.6 percent were in favor. As of August 1977, the volume of Senate constituent mail on the canal question had already passed the 100,000 mark and, as Chart 4 shows, opposition was overwhelming in every part of the country, transcending traditional party and regional differences:

Chart 4

Senate Constituent Opinion on Panama Treaties as of August 1977:

Senator	Number of Communications	Percentages For Treaty	Against
Abourezk	75 total per week	2%	98%
Allen	no figure	"overwhelmingly against"	
Anderson	188 last week		100%
Baker	1400 against; since 8 for since mid Aug.	1%	99%
Bartlett	2500 against; 3 for	1%	99%
Bayh	2024 against; 11 for	1%	99%
Bellmon	"we don't give out counts"		
Bentsen	1889 total	1%	99%
Biden	100 per week	"no estimate"	
Brooke	6000 against; 10 for	1%	99%
Bumpers	15–20 total per day	"majority against"	
Burdick	no count	"more than 75% against"	
Byrd, H.	50 against per day; 5 for per day	10%	90%
Byrd, R.	"heavy volume"	"majority against"	
Cannon			
Case	several hundred	"majority against"	
Chaffee	no estimate		
Chiles	1000 this week	"majority against"	
Church	"several letters"	"majority against"	
Clark	500–600 against; 5 for	1%	99%
Cranston	no estimate		
Culver	400 per week	20%	80%
Curtis	40–50 per week	1%	99%
Danforth	several hundred	4%	96%
Deconcini	several hundred	1%	99%
Dole	200 against; 10 for	5%	95%
Domenici	"4 years of mail"	2%	98%
Durkin	25 per week	"majority against"	
Eagleton			

Eastland	"heavy volume—only 1 in favor"	1%	99%
Ford	no estimate		
Garn	50 per day	4%	96%
Glenn			
Goldwater	"heavy volume"		
Gravel	25–30 per week	"majority against"	
Griffin	"several hundred in August"	"majority against"	
Hansen	no estimate		
Hart	15–20 per week	10%	90%
Haskell	"hundreds"	1%	99%
Hatch	3000 against; 3 for	1%	99%
Hatfield	several hundred	"majority against"	
Hathaway	5–10 per day	50%	50%
Hayakawa	4000 last week	10%	90%
Heinz			
Helms	500 per month	1%	99%
Hollings			
Huddleston	75 per day	15%	85%
Humphrey			
Inouye	50–100 per week	20%	80%
Jackson	500 against; 9 for	2%	98%
Javits	1500 total	"majority against"	
Johnston	1000 against; 2 for	1%	99%
Kennedy	under 100	"majority against"	
Laxalt	300 against; 0 for		100%
Leahy	no estimate		
Long	"a few hundred"	"majority against"	
Lugar	250 against; 3 for	2%	98%
McClellan	approximately 1000	5%	95%
McClure	2000 against; 1 for	1%	99%
McGovern	30 last week		100%
McIntyre	no estimate		
Magnuson	1000 last month	1%	99%
Mathias	200 per week	5%	95%
Matsunaga	150 total	5%	95%
Melcher	3000 total	10%	90%
Metcalf	300 total	20%	80%
Metzenbaum	2000 total	1%	99%
Morgan	4000 total	10%	90%

Moynihan	1200	2%	98%
Muskie	225 total		100%
Nelson	30 per day	10%	90%
Nunn	no estimate		
Packwood	60 per week	20%	80%
Pearson	160 against; 10 for	7%	93%
Pell	225 total	2%	98%
Percy	2000 total	no estimate	
Proxmire	500 last week		100%
Randolph	130 last week		100%
Ribicoff	300 total	"majority against"	
Riegle	3000 total	1%	99%
Roth	no response		
Sarbanes	100 per day	10%	90%
Sasser	12–15 per day	25%	75%
Schmitt	300 total	20%	80%
Schweiker	450 against; 30 for	7%	93%
Scott	150 total	10%	90%
Sparkman	no figure	"majority against"	
Stafford	15–20 per day	1%	99%
Stennis	100–200 total	"majority against"	
Stevens	25 per day	2%	98%
Stevenson	5600 against; 6	1%	99%
Stone	2000 against; 10	1%	99%
Talmadge	75 per day	10%	90%
Thurmond	300 per day	10%	90%
Tower	1200 this week—10 in favor	1%	99%
Wallop	200 against; 1 for	1%	99%
Weicker	350 this week	1%	99%
Williams	20 per day	33%	66%
Young	15 per day	5%	95%
Zorinsky	500 total	5%	95%

It is clear that the majority of average Americans have instinctively grasped the basic problem, summed up in part by the late General Thomas A. Lane, a veteran strategic analyst with service experience in the Canal Zone. Writing in the Winter 1974 issue of

Strategic Review, General Lane warned that:

> The belief of some officials that U.S. operation and defense of
> the canal under treaty provisions, instead of under sovereign au-
> thority, would eliminate the friction of recent years is a calami-
> tous misjudgment of the present scene. Marxist-Leninist subver-
> sion would be intensified by such a retreat. Friction would mount
> and the U.S. position would become intolerable. The United
> States would be compelled to use force against the Republic of
> Panama, or to withdraw and allow the canal to be operated and
> defended by another [power]. That is a prospect which no presi-
> dent should impose on his successors.

How immediate is the prospect of intensified Marxist-Leninist
subversion in Panama? As we have seen, the present Torrijos regime is already riddled with friends and admirers of Castro and
Moscow—from Omar Torrijos himself down. And when, during a
press conference in Bogotà, Colombia, reported in the August 9,
1977, issue of the *Panama Star & Herald*, radio correspondent
Jaime Arange asked Torrijos outright whether he was a communist,
the following curious exchange took place:

> Arango: General Torrijos, are you a communist?
> [At this point, before Torrijos could respond, his leftist advisor
> and chief treaty negotiator, Romulo Escobar Bethancourt, seized
> the floor and launched into a long, evasive song and dance laced
> with anti-American canards. While Torrijos never answered the
> question, Escobar's harangue is worth reading as a clue to the
> kind of Panamanian officials we would have to deal with when
> using the canal under terms of the new treaties.]
> *Escobar*: Look here, we could answer negatively, but what hap-
> pens is that we do not like to say no because we do not accept
> someone to self-appoint himself into an inquisitor into one's per-
> sonality. It's a feeling very much like someone asks you if you
> are a homosexual. . . .
> The question has been asked of the general and myself for
> many years. Of course, now that he is a general it becomes more
> outstanding, but the question has been asked of me ever since I
> was around fourteen years old, when the Americans were beating
> us because we wanted to free our country; when we were jailed;
> when we were tortured; when we were hanged; when we were
> submitted to all kinds of humiliations the first question asked
> was whether we were communists. And we never answered that
> we were not communists. . . . We never accepted going to a
> confessionary to tell anyone whether we are or we are not com-

munists because we believe that a man's deeds, not what he says, are indicative of what he is.

For a man who claims to have been beaten, jailed, tortured, humiliated, and even "hanged" by the Americans, Dr. Escobar, a plump, boisterous, middle-aged lawyer with extensive Marxist connections, has certainly held up very well, at least in the area of his imagination and vocal chords. In one respect, I happen to agree with him: a man's deeds, not what he says, *are* indicative of what he is. It is precisely because of this that I, and millions of other Americans, believe it would be a criminal blunder to surrender the Canal Zone to a corrupt dictator whose deeds prove that he is a flagrant violator of human rights, surrounded by criminals and Marxists, and an intimate friend of Cuba's Castro, a rabid anti-American, and a seeker after advice, technicians, and aid from the Soviet Union.

The Suez Lesson

As for the much vaunted "guarantees" contained in the Panama treaties, one need only study the experience of Great Britain with the Suez Canal to realize exactly how much the paper guarantees of a treacherous military dictatorship are worth. The situation in Egypt in 1956 was roughly parallel to what the situation in Panama would be *after* ratification of the proposed treaties. In the case of Suez, an officially private company with British government connections and heavy French and British ownership operated under the sovereign authority of the Egyptian government; paper guarantees, theoretical rights to property, and the declaration of the Convention of Constantinople, which supposedly guaranteed the right of passage to vessels of all nations through the Suez Canal, were all to no avail when, in 1956, Colonel Gamal Abdel Nasser nationalized the canal in the name of the Egyptian government and later closed it. The Suez Crisis of 1956 was probably the most damaging single diplomatic confrontation between the United States and two of our oldest allies, France and England, in the entire postwar era. Nor was that the end of the damage. Later, when, as a result of the Arab-Israeli War, the canal was closed for eight years, the rest of the world was powerless to reopen it; millions of dollars in added shipping costs, cargo dislocations and market disruptions were inflicted on the world economy. By surrendering our right to sovereign power in the Canal Zone we would place the government of Panama in approximately the same position as that of Egypt on the eve of the 1956 crisis, with infinite peril to the unobstructed conduct of world trade and the maintenance of free-world security into the indefinite future. And should Torrijos, who if anything is a far more crude, unstable leader than Nasser, act to seize the canal, America would have only two grim options: passive humiliation or war.

Cui Bono?

Who really benefits from these new treaties and from the American surrender that would follow? Perhaps this seminal question was best answered by former ambassador Spruille Braden, a distinguished American diplomat with a lifetime of experience in Latin America. According to Ambassador Braden, only three groups—none of them friends of the U.S. or the free world—would be the major beneficiaries; he listed them in "Panama and the U.S.A.: The Real Story," a statement prepared for and published by the Americanism Educational League. The beneficiaries? in Ambassador Braden's words:

1. A handful of Panamanian politicians, including communists and agitators;
2. The Russian, Chinese, and other communist countries;
3. Communists and guerrillas throughout the Western Hemisphere, who plan to destroy all freedoms everywhere.

"It is to be feared," Ambassador Braden concluded, "that the new treaty with Panama, based on the 'Statement of Principles,' would prove in its effects far more humiliating—not to say disastrous—for the United States than did the so-called Paris Peace Treaty with North Vietnam!"

The Legacy of Surrender

"It is not a field of a few acres of ground, but a cause, that we are defending," Tom Paine wrote in *The American Crisis*. His words, two centuries later, apply to the issue of the Panama Canal. For if we will not stand to defend what is ours today, how can our allies—much less our adversaries—be expected to take our commitments to the rights of others seriously in the years ahead? Writing in England at the same time as Thomas Paine, Edmund Burke warned that, "The concessions of the weak are the concessions of fear." There can be no question but that, in the eyes of a Soviet Union engaged in a massive naval and military build-up, and in the eyes of third-world countries envious of America's affluence, surrender in Panama would appear as not a noble act of magnanimity, but as the cowardly retreat of a tired, toothless paper tiger.

Step by step, beginning with the discovery of the Isthmus of Panama itself, this book has told the story of both the dream and the reality of an isthmian canal. Even before the first ship steamed through its locks in 1914, the canal was recognized by solemn treaties, by the Supreme Court, by international opinion, and by generous repeated payments and subsidies accepted by Panama in return for American sovereignty over an American Canal Zone.

Through facts, figures, and the testimony of military, diplomatic, and economic experts, we have also seen that our continued possession of the zone and the canal are not only in our best national interests, but in the best interests of global economic stability and military security for the entire free world.

The Panama Canal, as Hanson Baldwin has pointed out, is *both* a cause and a symbol, "highly important in its own right, but far more so as a symbol of U.S. resolution." With the present reduced state of the American Navy—and with Russia's massive new fleets plowing the waters of every quarter of the globe—surrender of the canal would be one more nail in the coffin of American sea power, a power of grave historical importance to our posterity and to all the peoples of the world. For, as Admiral Samuel Eliot Morison pointed out in *The Oxford History of the American People*:

> . . . sea power has never lead to despotism. The nations that have enjoyed sea power even for a brief period—Athens, Scandinavia, the Netherlands, England, the United States—are those that have preserved freedom for themselves and have given it to others.

God forbid that our generation of Americans should be the ones to surrender this precious heritage of freedom and replace it with a legacy of shame and surrender. The world is not a Sunday school classroom in Plains, Georgia, much less a glittering hall in the Pan American Union Building. It is a violent, conflict-riven place where peace and freedom only survive when they are protected. If anything, this is even more true today than in Teddy Roosevelt's time, when he remarked in a memorable phrase, "The only safe rule is to promise little and faithfully keep every promise; to 'speak softly and carry a big stick.' "

If President Carter really is as ashamed of America's record in Panama as he reportedly told Omar Torrijos, the problem lies not with our actual historical records but with his own misconceptions, or perhaps with some odd psychological compulsion to confess to sins even where none exist. If anyone should be asking for "forgiveness" it is the corrupt strongman Torrijos, who has persecuted his own people and tried to foment possible violence in his efforts to bluff the United States into a shameful surrender.

In the 1930s another great free-world power lay supine while the forces of tyranny and subversion were on the march around the world, making inroads which ultimately led to war and to the loss of millions of innocent lives. Only a handful of warning voices were heard in England during the early 1930s while fascism, communism and Japanese militarism spread their tentacles ever further, swallowing up more and more territory, and enslaving more and more people. One of the few who did warn was Winston Churchill. His words, recorded in *While England Slept*, should sound an ominous warning to those who are so eager to see America haul down the flag and surrender in Panama in the wake of communist conquest in Indochina and the wavering resolve of even some of our European allies:

> I have watched this famous island descending incontinently, fecklessly, the stairway which leads to a dark gulf. It is a fine, broad stairway at the beginning, but after a bit the carpet ends. A little further on there are only flagstones, and a little further on still these break beneath your feet.

Surrender in Panama would be one more crucial American step in a descent to ignominy—to the end of America's credibility as a world power and a deterrent to aggression. In his inaugural address, John F. Kennedy warned that we must "never negotiate out of fear," and yet it is fear—the foolish fear of a petty dictator's threats, which would be more likely to come to pass *with*, rather than without American surrender—that has been the underlying motivation of the Carters, the Kissingers, the Linowitzes, and the Bunkers who are engineering the surrender of the canal. These men are sincere; they really believe that America has grown too weary, cynical, and self-doubting to stand up for its rights in the world arena.

But they are wrong. Their proposed remedy is no remedy at all; it is a form of temporary escapism that does not even work for ostriches. Peace comes only to the prepared and security only to the strong. In the real world, sackcloth and ashes are no substitute for a strong foreign policy and the moral and physical means of backing it up.

We have nothing to be ashamed of in Panama. We turned a diseased wasteland into a vital international waterway and a viable independent republic for the Panamanian people at the same time. In our hands—bought and paid for—the canal has been an instrument for peaceful commerce and prosperity and a strategic safeguard for the free world. The timid souls and small spirits who advocate surrender would throw all this away and encourage our enemies to further encroachments on American rights and security. They must not prevail.

Appendix 1:
The Treaties

The Hay-Pauncefote Treaty, 1901

Source: Charles I. Bevans, *Treaties and Other International Agreements of the United States of America, 1776–1949.* Washington, U.S. Government Printing Office, 1972, v. 12, pp. 258–260.

Ship Canal (Hay-Pauncefote Treaty)

Treaty sgiigned at Washington November 18, 1901
Senate advice and consent to ratification December 16, 1901
Ratified by the President of the United States December 26, 1901
Ratified by the United Kingdom January 20, 1902
Ratifications exchanged at Washington February 21, 1902
Entered into force February 21, 1902
Proclaimed by the President of the United States February 22, 1902
                              32 Stat. 1903; Treaty Series 401

    The United States of America and His Majesty Edward the Seventh, of the United Kingdom of Great Britain and Ireland, and of the British Dominions beyond the Seas, King, and Emperor of India, being desirous to facilitate the construction of a ship canal to connect the Atlantic and Pacific Oceans, by whatever route may be considered expedient, and to that end to remove any objection which may arise out of the Convention of the 19th April, 1850,[1] commonly called the Clayton-Bulwer Treaty, to the construction of such canal under the auspices of the Government of the United States, without impairing the "general principle" of neutralization established in Article VIII of that Convention, have for that purpose appointed as their Plenipotentiaries: .

[1] TS 122, *anis,* p. 105.

115

The President of the United States, John Hay, Secretary of State of the United States of America;

And His Majesty Edward the Seventh, of the United Kingdom of Great Britain and Ireland, and of the British Dominions beyond the Seas, King, and Emperor of India, the Right Honorable Lord Pauncefote, G. C. B., G. C. M. G., His Majesty's Ambassador Extraordinary and Plenipotentiary to the United States;

Who, having communicated to each other their full powers which were found to be in due and proper form, have agreed upon the following Articles:

Article I

The High Contracting Parties agree that the present Treaty shall supersede the afore-mentioned Convention of the 19th April, 1850.

Article II

It is agreed that the canal may be constructed under the auspices of the Government of the United States, either directly at its own cost, or by gift or loan of money to individuals or Corporations, or through subscription to or purchase of stock or shares, and that, subject to the provisions of the present Treaty, the said Government shall have and enjoy all the rights incident to such construction, as well as the exclusive right of providing for the regulation and management of the canal.

Article III

The United States adopts, as the basis of the neutralization of such ship canal, the following Rules, substantially as embodied in the Convention of Constantinople, signed the 28th [29th] October, 1888,[2] for the free navigation of the Suez Canal, that is to say:

1. The canal shall be free and open to the vessels of commerce and of war of all nations observing these Rules, on terms of entire equality, so that there shall be no discrimination against any such nation, or its citizens or subjects, in respect of the conditions or charges of traffic, or otherwise. Such conditions and charges of traffic shall be just and equitable.

2. The canal shall never be blockaded, nor shall any right of war be exercised nor any act of hostility be committed within it. The United States, however, shall be at liberty to maintain such military police along the canal as may be necessary to protect it against lawlessness and disorder.

3. Vessels of war of a belligerent shall not revictual nor take any stores in the canal except so far as may be strictly necessary; and the transit of such vessels through the canal shall be effected with the least possible delay in accordance with the Regulations in force, and with only such intermission as may result from the necessities of the service.

Prizes shall be in all respects subject to the same Rules as vessels of war of the belligerents.

4. No belligerent shall embark or disembark troops, munitions of war, or warlike materials in the canal, except in case of accidental hindrance of the transit, and in such case the transit shall be resumed with all possible dispatch.

5. The provisions of this Article shall apply to waters adjacent to the canal, within 3 marine miles of either end. Vessels of war of a belligerent shall not remain in such waters longer than twenty-four hours at any one time, except in case of distress, and in such case shall depart as soon as possible; but a vessel of war of one belligerent shall not depart within twenty-four hours from the departure of a vessel of war of the other belligerent.

6. The plant, establishments, buildings, and all works necessary to the construction, maintenance, and operation of the canal shall be deemed to be part thereof, for the purposes of this Treaty, and in time of war, as in time of peace, shall enjoy complete immunity from attack or injury by belligerents, and from acts calculated to impair their usefulness as part of the canal.

²For text, see *British and Foreign State Papers,* vol. 79, p. 18.

Article IV

It is agreed that no change of territorial sovereignty or of the international relations of the country or countries traversed by the before-mentioned canal shall affect the general principle of neutralization or the obligation of the High Contracting Parties under the present Treaty.

Article V

The present Treaty shall be ratified by the President of the United States, by and with the advice and consent of the Senate thereof, and by His Britannic Majesty; and the ratifications shall be exchanged at Washington or at London at the earliest possible time within six months from the date hereof.

IN FAITH WHEREOF the respective Plenipotentiaries have signed this Treaty and thereunto affixed their seals.

DONE in duplicate at Washington, the 18th day of November, in the year of Our Lord one thousand nine hundred and one.

JOHN HAY   [SEAL]

PAUNCEFOTE   [SEAL]

The Hay-Herrán Treaty, 1903

A Convention Between the United States and the Republic of Colombia for the Construction of a Ship Canal, etc., to Connect the Waters of the Atlantic and Pacific Oceans, Signed January 22, 1903.

The United States of America and the Republic of Colombia, being desirous to assure the construction of a ship canal to connect the Atlantic and Pacific Oceans and the Congress of the United States of America having passed an Act approved June 28, 1902, in furtherance of that object, a copy of which is hereunto annexed, the high contracting parties have resolved, for that purpose, to conclude a Convention and have accordingly appointed as their plenipotentiaries,

The President of the United States of America, John Hay, Secretary of State, and

The President of the Republic of Colombia, Thomas Herran, Chargé d'Affaires, thereunto specially empowered by said government,

who, after communicating to each other their respective full powers, found in good and due form, have agreed upon and concluded the following Articles:

Article I

The Government of Colombia authorizes the New Panama Canal Company to sell and transfer to the United States its rights, privileges, properties, and concessions, as well as the Panama Railroad and all the shares or part of the shares of that company; but the public lands situated outside of the zone hereinafter specified, now corresponding to the concessions to both said enterprises shall revert to the Republic of Colombia, except any property now owned by or in the possession of the said companies within Panama or Colon, or the ports and terminals thereof.

But it is understood that Colombia reserves all its rights to the special shares in the capital of the New Panama Canal Company to which reference is made in Article IV of the contract of December 10, 1890, which shares shall be paid their full nominal value at least; but as such right of Colombia exists solely in its character of stockholder in said Company, no obligation under this provision is imposed upon or assumed by the United States.

The Railroad Company (and the United States as owner of the enterprise) shall be free from the obligations imposed by the railroad concession, excepting as to the payment at maturity by the Railroad Company of the outstanding bonds issued by said Railroad Company.

Article II

The United States shall have the exclusive right for the term of one hundred years, renewable at the sole and absolute option of the United States, for periods of similar duration so long as the United States may desire, to excavate, construct, maintain, operate, control, and protect the Maritime Canal with or without locks from the Atlantic to the Pacific Ocean, to and across the territory of Colombia, such canal to be of sufficient depth and capacity for vessels of the largest tonnage and greatest draft now engaged in commerce, and such as may be reasonably anticipated, and also the same rights for the construction, maintenance, operation, control, and protection of the Panama Railroad and of railway, telegraph and telephone lines, canals, dikes, dams, and reservoirs, and such other auxiliary works as may be necessary and convenient for the construction, maintenance, protection, and operation of the canal and railroads.

Article III

To enable the United States to exercise the rights and privileges granted by this Treaty the Republic of Colombia grants to that Government the use and control for the term of one hundred years, renewable at the sole and absolute option of the United States, for periods of similar duration so long as the United States may desire, of a zone of territory along the route of the canal to be constructed five kilometers in width on either side thereof measured from its center line including therein the necessary auxiliary canals not exceeding in any case fifteen miles from the main canal and other works, together with ten fathoms of water in the Bay of Limon in extension of the canal, and at least three marine miles from mean low water mark from each terminus of the canal into the Caribbean Sea and the Pacific Ocean respectively. So far as necessary for the construction, maintenance and operation of the canal, the United States shall have the use and occupation of the group of small islands in the Bay of Panama named Perico, Naos, Culebra and Flamenco, but the same shall not be construed as being within the zone herein defined nor governed by the special provisions applicable to the same.

This grant shall in no manner invalidate the titles or rights of private land owners in the said zone of territory, nor shall it interfere with the rights of way over the public roads of the Department; provided, however, that nothing herein contained shall operate to diminish, impair or restrict the rights elsewhere herein granted to the United States.

This grant shall not include the cities of Panama and Colon, except so far as lands and other property therein are now owned by or in possession of the said Canal Company or the said Railroad Company; but all the stipulations contained in Article 35 of the Treaty of 1846–48 between the contracting parties shall continue

120

and apply in full force to the cities of Panama and Colon and to the accessory community lands and other property within the said zone, and the territory thereon shall be neutral territory, and the United States shall continue to guarantee the neutrality thereof and the sovereignty of Colombia thereover, in conformity with the above-mentioned Article 35 of said Treaty.

In furtherance of this last provision there shall be created a Joint Commission by the Government of Colombia and the United States that shall establish and enforce sanitary and police regulations.

Article IV

The rights and privileges granted to the United States by the terms of this convention shall not affect the sovereignty of the Republic of Colombia over the territory within whose boundaries such rights and privileges are to be exercised.

The United States freely acknowledges and recognizes this sovereignty and disavows any intention to impair it in any way whatever or to increase its territory at the expense of Colombia or of any of the sister republics in Central or South America, but on the contrary, it desires to strengthen the power of the republics on this continent, and to promote, develop and maintain their prosperity and independence.

Article V

The Republic of Colombia authorizes the United States to construct and maintain at each entrance and terminus of the proposed canal a port for vessels using the same, with suitable light houses and other aids to navigation, and the United States is authorized to use and occupy within the limits of the zone fixed by this convention, such parts of the coast line and of the lands and islands adjacent thereto as are necessary for this purpose, including the construction and maintenance of breakwaters, dikes, jetties, embankments, coaling stations, docks and other appropriate works, and the United States undertakes the construction and maintenance of such works and will bear all the expense thereof. The ports when established are declared free, and their demarcations shall be clearly and definitely defined.

To give effect to this Article, the United States will give special attention and care to the maintenance of works for drainage, sanitary and healthful purposes along the line of the canal, and its dependencies, in order to prevent the invasion of epidemics or of securing their prompt suppression should they appear. With this end in view the United States will organize hospitals along the line of the canal, and will suitably supply or cause to be supplied the towns of Panama and Colon with the necessary aqueducts and drainage works, in order to prevent their becoming centers of infection on account of their proximity to the canal.

The Government of Colombia will secure for the United States or its nominees the lands and rights that may be required in the towns of Panama and Colon to effect the improvements above referred to, and the Government of the United States or its nominees shall be authorized to impose and collect equitable water rates, during fifty years for the service rendered; but on the expiration of said term the use of the water shall be free for the inhabitants of Panama and Colon, except to the extent that may be necessary for the operation and maintenance of said water system, including reservoirs, aqueducts, hydrants, supply service, drainage and other works.

Article VI

The Republic of Colombia agrees that it will not cede or lease to any foreign Government any of its islands or harbors within or adjacent to the Bay of Panama, nor on the Atlantic Coast of Colombia, between the Atrato River and the western boundary of the Department of Panama, for the purpose of establishing fortifications, naval or coaling stations, military posts, docks or other works that might interfere with the construction, maintenance, operation, protection, safety, and free use of the canal and auxiliary works. In order to enable Colombia to comply with this stipulation, the Government of the United States agrees to give Colombia the material support that may be required in order to prevent the occupation of said islands and ports, guaranteeing there the sovereignty, independence and integrity of Colombia.

Article VII

The Republic of Colombia includes in the foregoing grant the right without obstacle, cost, or impediment, to such control, consumption and general utilization in any manner found necessary by the United States to the exercise by it of the grants to, and rights conferred upon it by this Treaty, the waters of the Chagres River and other streams, lakes and lagoons, of all non-navigable waters, natural and artificial, and also to navigate all rivers, streams, lakes and other navigable water-ways, within the jurisdiction and under the dominion of the Republic of Colombia, in the Department of Panama, within or without said zone, as may be necessary or desirable for the construction, maintenance and operation of the canal and its auxiliary canals and other works, and without tolls or charges of any kind; and to raise and lower the levels of the waters, and to deflect them, and to impound any such waters and to overflow any lands necessary for the due exercise of such grants and rights to the United States; and to rectify, construct and improve the navigation of any such rivers, streams, lakes and lagoons at the sole cost of the United States; but any such waterways so made by the United States may be used by citizens of Colombia free of tolls or other charges. And the United States shall have the right to use without cost, any water, stone, clay, earth or other minerals belonging to Colombia on the public domain that may be needed by it.

All damages caused to private land owners by inundation or by the deviation of water courses, or in other ways, arising out of the construction or operation of the canal, shall in each case be appraised and settled by a joint commission appointed by the Governments of the United States and Colombia, but the cost of the indemnities so agreed upon shall be borne solely by the United States.

Article VIII

The Government of Colombia declares free for all time the ports at either entrance of the Canal, including Panama and Colon and the waters thereof in such manner that there shall not be collected by the Government of Colombia custom house tolls, tonnage, anchorage, light-house, wharf, pilot, or quarantine dues, nor any other charges or taxes of any kind shall be levied or imposed by the Government of Colombia upon any vessel using or passing through the Canal or belonging to or employed by the United States, directly or indirectly, in connection with the construction, maintenance and operation of the main work or its auxilliaries, or upon the cargo, officers, crew, or passengers of any such vessels; it being the intent of this convention that all vessels and their cargoes, crews, and passengers, shall be permitted to use and pass through the Canal and the ports leading thereto, subject to no other demands or impositions than such tolls and charges as may be imposed by the United States for the use of the Canal and other works. It being understood that such tolls and charges shall be governed by the provisions of Article XVI.

The ports leading to the Canal, including Panama and Colon, also shall be free to the commerce of the world, and no duties or taxes shall be imposed, except upon merchandise destined to be introduced for the consumption of the rest of the Republic of Colombia, or the Department of Panama, and upon vessels touching at the ports of Colon and Panama and which do not cross the Canal.

Though the said ports shall be free and open to all, the Government of Colombia may establish in them such custom houses and guards as Colombia may deem necessary to collect duties on importations destined to other portions of Colombia and to prevent contraband trade. The United States shall have the right to make use of the ports at the two extremities of the Canal including Panama and Colon as places of anchorage, in order to make repairs for loading, unloading, depositing, or transshipping cargoes either in transit or destined for the service of the Canal and other works.

Any concessions or privileges granted by Colombia for the operation of light houses at Colon and Panama shall be subject to expropriation, indemnification and payment in the same manner as is provided by Article XIV in respect to the property therein mentioned; but Colombia shall make no additional grant of any such privilege nor change the status of any existing concession.

Article IX

There shall not be imposed any taxes, national, municipal, de-

124

partmental, or of any other class, upon the canal, the vessels that may use it, tugs and other vessels employed in the service of the canal, the railways and auxiliary works, store houses, work shops, offices, quarters for laborers, factories of all kinds, warehouses, wharves, machinery and other works, property, and effects appertaining to the canal or railroad or that may be necessary for the service of the canal or railroad and their dependencies, whether situated within the cities of Panama and Colon, or any other place authorized by the provisions of this convention.

Nor shall there be imposed contributions or charges of a personal character of whatever species upon officers, employees, laborers, and other individuals in the service of the canal and its dependencies.

Article X

It is agreed that telegraph and telephone lines, when established for canal purposes, may also, under suitable regulations, be used for public and private business in connection with the systems of Colombia and the other American Republics and with the lines of cable companies authorized to enter the ports and territories of these Republics; but the official dispatches of the Government of Colombia and the authorities of the Department of Panama shall not pay for such service higher tolls than those required from the officials in the service of the United States.

Article XI

The Government of Colombia shall permit the immigration and free access to the lands and workshops of the canal and its dependencies of all employees and workmen of whatever nationality under contract to work upon or seeking employment or in any wise connected with the said canal and its dependencies, with their respective families, and all such persons shall be free and exempt from the military service of the Republic of Colombia.

Article XII

The United States may import at any time into the said zone, free of customs duties, imposts, taxes, or other charges, and without any restriction, any and all vessels, dredges, engines, cars, machinery, tools, explosives, materials, supplies, and other articles necessary and convenient in the construction, maintenance and operation of the canal and auxiliary works, also all provisions, medicines, clothing, supplies and other things necessary and convenient for the officers, employees, workmen and laborers in the service and employ of the United States and for their families. If any such articles are disposed of for use without the zone excepting Panama and Colon and within the territory of the Republic, they shall be subject to the same import or other duties as like articles under the laws of Colombia or the ordinances of the Department of Panama.

Article XIII

The United States shall have authority to protect and make secure the canal, as well as railways and other auxiliary works and dependencies, and to preserve order and discipline among the laborers and other persons who may congregate in that region and to make and enforce such police and sanitary regulations as it may deem necessary to preserve order and public health thereon, and to protect navigation and commerce through and over said canal, railways and other works and dependencies from interruption or damage.

I. The Republic of Colombia may establish judicial tribunals within said zone, for the determination, according to its laws and judicial procedure, of certain controversies hereinafter mentioned.

Such judicial tribunal or tribunals so established by the Republic of Colombia shall have exclusive jurisdiction in said zone of all controversies between citizens of the Republic of Colombia, or between citizens of the Republic of Colombia and citizens of any foreign nation other than the United States.

II. Subject to the general sovereignty of Colombia over said zone, the United States may establish judicial tribunals thereon, which shall have jurisdiction of certain controversies hereinafter mentioned to be determined according to the laws and judicial procedure of the United States.

Such judicial tribunal or tribunals so established by the United

States shall have exclusive jurisdiction in said zone of all controversies between citizens of the United States, and between citizens of the United States and citizens of any foreign nation other than the Republic of Colombia; and of all controversies in any wise growing out of or relating to the construction, maintenance or operation of the canal, railway and other properties and works.

III. The United States and Colombia engage jointly to establish and maintain upon said zone, judicial tribunals having civil, criminal and admiralty jurisdiction and to be composed of jurists appointed by the Governments of the United States and Colombia in a manner hereafter to be agreed upon between said Governments, and which tribunals shall have jurisdiction of certain controversies hereinafter mentioned, and of all crimes, felonies and misdemeanors committed within said zone, and of all cases arising in admiralty, according to such laws and procedure as shall be hereafter agreed upon and declared by the two governments.

Such joint judicial tribunal shall have exclusive jurisdiction in said zone of all controversies between citizens of the United States and citizens of Colombia, and between citizens of nations other than Colombia or the United States; and also of all crimes, felonies and misdemeanors committed within said zone, and of all questions of admiralty arising therein.

IV. The two Governments hereafter, and from time to time as occasion arises, shall agree upon and establish the laws and procedures which shall govern such joint judicial tribunal and which shall be applicable to the persons and cases over which such tribunal shall have jurisdiction, and also shall likewise create the requisite officers and employees of such court and establish their powers and duties; and further shall make adequate provision by like agreement for the pursuit, capture, imprisonment, detention and delivery within said zone of persons charged with the commitment of crimes, felonies or misdemenaors without said zone; and for the pursuit, capture, imprisonment, detention and delivery without said zone of persons charged with the commitment of crimes, felonies and misdemeanors within said zone.

Article XIV

The works of the canal, the railways and their auxiliaries are declared of public utility, and in consequence all areas of land and water necessary for the construction, maintenance, and operation of the canal and the other specified works may be expropriated in conformity with the laws of Colombia, except that the indemnity shall be conclusively determined without appeal, by a joint commission appointed by the Government of Colombia and the United States.

The indemnities awarded by the Commission for such expropriation shall be borne by the United States, but the appraisal of such lands and the assessment of damages shall be based upon their value before the commencement of the work upon the canal.

Article XV

The Republic of Colombia grants to the United States the use of all the ports of the Republic open to commerce as places of refuge for any vessels employed in the canal enterprise, and for all vessels in distress having the right to pass through the canal and wishing to anchor in said ports. Such vessels shall be exempt from anchorage and tonnage dues on the part of Colombia.

Article XVI

The canal, when constructed, and the entrance thereto shall be neutral in perpetuity, and shall be opened upon the terms provided for by Section I of Article three of, and in conformity with all the stipulations of, the treaty entered into by the Governments of the United States and Great Britain on November 18, 1901.

Article XVII

The Government of Colombia shall have the right to transport over the canal its vessels, troops, and munitions of war at all times without paying charges of any kind. This exemption is to be extended to the auxiliary railway for the transportation of persons in the service of the Republic of Colombia or of the Department of Panama, or of the police force charged with the preservation of public order outside of said zone, as well as to their baggage, munitions of war and supplies.

128

Article XVIII

The United States shall have full power and authority to establish and enforce regulations for the use of the canal, railways, and the entering ports and auxiliary works, and to fix rates of tolls and charges thereof, subject to the limitations stated in Article XVI.

Article XIX

The rights and privileges granted to the United States by this convention shall not affect the sovereignty of the Republic of Colombia over the real estate that may be acquired by the United States by reason of the transfer of the rights of the New Panama Canal Company and the Panama Railroad Company lying outside of the said canal zone.

Article XX

If by virtue of any existing treaty between the Republic of Colombia and any third power, there may be any privilege or concession relative to an interoceanic means of communication which especially favors such third power, and which in any of its terms may be incompatible with the terms of the present convention, the Republic of Colombia agrees to cancel or modify such treaty in due form, for which purpose it shall give to the said third power the requisite notification within the term of four months from the date of the present convention, and in case the existing treaty contains no clause permitting its modification or annulment, the Republic of Colombia agrees to procure its modification or annulment in such form that there shall not exist any conflict with the stipulations of the present convention.

Article XXI

The rights and privileges granted by the Republic of Colombia to the United States in the preceding Articles are understood to be free of all anterior concessions or privileges to other Governments, corporations, syndicates or individuals, and consequently, if there should arise any claims on account of the present concessions and privileges or otherwise, the claimants shall resort to the Government of Colombia and not to the United States for any indemnity or compromise which may be required.

Article XXII

The Republic of Colombia renounces and grants to the United States the participation to which it might be entitled in the future earnings of the canal under Article XV of the concessionary contract with Lucien N. B. Wyse now owned by the New Panama Canal Company and any and all other rights or claims of a pecuniary nature arising under or relating to said concession, or arising under or relating to the concessions to the Panama Railroad Company or any extension or modification thereof; and it likewise renounces, confirms and grants to the United States, now and hereafter, all the rights and property reserved in the said concessions which otherwise would belong to Colombia at or before the expiration of the terms of ninety-nine years of the concessions granted to or held by the above mentioned party and companies, and all right, title and interest which it now has or may hereafter have, in and to the lands, canal, works, property and rights held by the said companies under said concessions or otherwise, and acquired or to be acquired by the United States from or through the New Panama Canal Company, including any property and rights which might or may in the future either by lapse of time, forfeiture or otherwise, revert to the Republic of Colombia under any contracts of concessions, with said Wyse, the Universal Panama Canal Company, the Panama Railroad Company and the New Panama Canal Company.

The aforesaid rights and property shall be and are free and released from any present or reversionary interest in or claims of Colombia and the title of the United States thereto upon consummation of the contemplated purchase by the United States from the New Panama Canal Company, shall be absolute, so far as concerns the Republic of Colombia, excepting always the rights of Colombia specifically secured under this treaty.

Article XXIII

If it should become necessary at any time to employ armed forces for the safety or protection of the canal, or of the ships that make use of the same, or the railways and other works, the Republic of Colombia agrees to provide the forces necessary for such purpose, according to the circumstances of the case, but if the Government of Colombia cannot effectively comply with this obligation, then, with the consent of or at the request of Colombia, or of her Minister at Washington, or of the local authorities, civil or military, the United Shtates shall employ such force as may be necessary for that sole purpose; and as soon as the necessity shall have ceased will withdraw the forces so employed. Under exceptional circumstances, however, on account of unforeseen or imminent danger to said canal, railways and other works, or to the lives and property of the persons employed upon the canal, railways, and other works, the Government of the United States is authorized to act in the interest of their protection, without the necessity of obtaining the consent beforehand of the Government of Colombia; and it shall give immediate advice of the measures adopted for the purpose stated; and as soon as sufficient Colombian forces shall arrive to attend to the indicated purpose, those of the United States shall retire.

Article XXIV

The Government of the United States agrees to complete the construction of the preliminary works necessary, together with all the auxiliary works, in the shortest time possible; and within two years from the date of the exchange of ratification of this convention the main works of the canal proper shall be commenced, and it shall be opened to the traffic between the two oceans within twelve years after such period of two years. In case, however, that any difficulties or obstacles should arise in the construction of the canal which are at present impossible to foresee, in consideration of the good faith with which the Government of the United States shall have proceeded, and the large amount of money expended so far on the works and the nature of the difficulties which may have arisen, the Government of Colombia will prolong the terms stipulated in this Article up to twelve years more for the completion of the work of the canal.

But in case the United States should, at any time, determine to make such canal practically a sea level canal, then such period shall be extended for ten years further.

Article XXV

As the price or compensation for the right to use the zone granted in this convention by Colombia to the United States for the construction of a canal, together with the proprietary right over the Panama Railroad, and for the annuity of two hundred and fifty thousand dollars gold, which Colombia ceases to receive from the said railroad, as well as in compensation for other rights, privileges and exemptions granted to the United States, and in consideration of the increase in the administrative expenses of the Department of Panama consequent upon the construction of the said canal, the Government of the United States binds itself to pay Colombia the sum of ten million dollars in gold coin of the United States on the exchange of the ratification of this convention after its approval according to the laws of the respective countries, and also an annual payment during the life of this convention of two hundred and fifty thousand dollars in like gold coin, beginning nine years after the date aforesaid.

The provisions of this Article shall be in addition to all other benefits assured to Colombia under this convention.

But no delay nor difference of opinion under this Article shall affect nor interrupt the full operation and effect of this convention in all other respects:

Article XXVI

No change either in the Government or in the laws and treaties of Colombia, shall, without the consent of the United States, affect any right of the United States under the present convention, or under any treaty stipulation between the two countries (that now exist or may hereafter exist) touching the subject-matter of this convention.

If Colombia shall hereafter enter as a constituent into any other

Government or into any union or confederation of States so as to merge her sovereignty or independence in such Government, union, or confederation, the rights of the United States under this convention shall not be in any respect lessened or impaired.

Article XXVII

The joint commission referred to in Articles II, VII and XIV shall be established as follows:

The President of the United States shall nominate two persons and the President of Colombia shall nominate two persons and they shall proceed to a decision; but in case of disagreement of the Commission (by reason of their being equally divided in conclusion) an umpire shall be appointed by the two Governments, who shall render the decision. In the event of death, absence or incapacity of any Commissioner or umpire, or of his omitting, declining or ceasing to act, his place shall be filled by the appointment of another person in the manner above indicated. All decisions by a majority of the Commission or by the umpire shall be final.

Article XXVIII

This convention when signed by the contracting parties, shall be ratified according to the laws of the respective countries and shall be exchanged at Washington within a term of eight months from this date, or earlier if possible.

In faith whereof, the respective plenipotentiaries have signed the present convention in duplicate and have hereunto affixed their respective seals.

Done at the City of Washington, the 22nd day of January in the year of our Lord nineteen hundred and three.

| (Signed) | JOHN HAY | [SEAL.] |
| (Signed) | TOMÁS HERRÁN | [SEAL.] |

The Hay—Bunau-Varilla Treaty, 1903

Convention Between the United States of America and the Republic of Panama for the Construction of a Ship Canal to Connect the Waters of the Atlantic and Pacific Oceans

Signed at Washington, November 18, 1903; ratified by Panama, December 2, 1903; ratification advised by United States Senate, February 23, 1904; ratified by the President, February 25, 1904; ratifications exchanged at Washington, February 26, 1904; proclaimed at Washington, February 26, 1904.

Articles:

Isthmian Canal Convention

The United States of America and the Republic of Panama being desirous to insure the construction of a ship canal across the Isthmus of Panama to connect the Atlantic and Pacific oceans, and the Congress of the United States of America having passed an act approved June 28, 1902, in furtherance of that object, by which the President of the United States is authorized to acquire within a reasonable time the control of the necessary territory of the Republic of Colombia, and the sovereignty of such territory being actually vested in the Republic of Panama, the high contracting parties have resolved for that purpose to conclude a convention and have accordingly appointed as their plenipotentiaries,—

The President of the United States of America, John Hay, Secretary of State, and

The Government of the Republic of Panama, Philippe Bunau-Varilla, Envoy Extraordinary and Minister Plenipotentiary of the Republic of Panama, thereunto specially empowered by said government, who after communicating with each other their respective full powers, found to be in good and due form, have agreed upon and concluded the following articles:

Article I

The United States guarantees and will maintain the independence of the Republic of Panama.

Article II

The Republic of Panama grants to the United States in perpetuity the use, occupation and control of a zone of land and land under water for the construction, maintenance, operation, sanitation and protection of said Canal of the width of ten miles extending to the distance of five miles on each side of the center line of the route of the Canal to be constructed; the said zone beginning in the Caribbean Sea three marine miles from mean low water mark and extending to and across the Isthmus of Panama into the Pacific ocean to a distance of three marine miles from mean low water mark with the proviso that the cities of Panama and Colon and the harbors

135

adjacent to said cities, which are included within the boundaries of the zone above described, shall not be included within this grant. The Republic of Panama further grants to the United States in perpetuity the use, occupation and control of any other lands and waters outside of the zone above described which may be necessary and convenient for the construction, maintenance, operation, sanitation and protection of the said Canal or of any auxiliary canals or other works necessary and convenient for the construction, maintenance, operation, sanitation and protection of the said enterprise.

The Republic of Panama further grants in like manner to the United States in perpetuity all islands within the limits of the zone above described and in addition thereto the group of small islands in the Bay of Panama, named Perioc, Naos, Culebra and Flamenco.

Article III

The Republic of Panama grants to the United States all the rights, power and authority within the zone mentioned and described in Article II of this agreement and within the limits of all auxiliary lands and waters mentioned and described in said Article II which the United States would possess and exercise if it were the sovereign of the territory within which said lands and waters are located to the entire exclusion of the exercise by the Republic of Panama of any such sovereign rights, power or authority.

Article IV

As rights subsidiary to the above grants the Republic of Panama grants in perpetuity to the United States the right to use the rivers, streams, lakes and other bodies of water within its limits for navigation, the supply of water or water-power or other purposes, so far as the use of said rivers, streams, lakes and bodies of water and the waters thereof may be necessary and convenient for the construction, maintenance, operation, sanitation and protection of the said Canal.

Article V

The Republic of Panama grants to the United States in perpetuity a monopoly for the construction, maintenance and operation of any system of communication by means of canal or railroad across its territory between the Caribbean Sea and the Pacific Ocean.

Article VI

The grants herein contained shall in no manner invalidate the titles of rights of private land holders or owners of private property in the said zone or in or to any of the lands or waters granted to the United States by the provisions of any Article of this treaty, nor shall they interfere with the rights of way over the public roads passing through the said zone or over any of the said lands or waters unless said rights of way or private rights shall conflict with rights herein granted to the United States in which case the rights of the United States shall be superior. All damages caused to the owners of private lands or private property of any kind by reason of the grants contained in this treaty or by reason of the operations of the United States, its agents or employees, or by reason of the construction, maintenance, operation, sanitation and protection of the said Canal or of the works of sanitation and protection herein provided for, shall be appraised and settled by a joint Commission appointed by the Governments of the United States and the Republic of Panama, whose decisions as to such damages shall be final and whose awards as to such damages shall be paid solely by the United States. No part of the work on said Canal or the Panama railroad or on any auxiliary works relating thereto and authorized by the terms of this treaty shall be prevented, delayed, or impeded by or pending such proceedings to ascertain such damages. The appraisal of said private lands and private property and the assessment of damages to them shall be based upon their value before the date of this convention.

Article VII

The Republic of Panama grants to the United States within the limits of the cities of Panama and Colon and their adjacent harbors and within the territory adjacent thereto the right to acquire by purchase or by the exercise of the right of eminent domain, any lands, buildings, water rights or other properties necessary and convenient for the construction, maintenance, operation and protection of the Canal and of any works of sanitation, such as the collection and disposition of sewage and the distribution of water in the said cities of Panama and Colon, which, in the discretion of the United States may be necessary and convenient for the construction, maintenance, operation, sanitation and protection of the said Canal and railroad. All such works of sanitation, collection and disposition of sewage and distribution of water in the cities of Panama and Colon shall be made at the expense of the United States, and the Government of the United States, its agents or nominees shall be authorized to impose and collect water rates and sewerage rates which shall be sufficient to provide for the payment of interest and the amortization of the principal of the cost of said works within a period of fifty years and upon the expiration of said term of fifty years the system of sewers and water works shall revert to and become the properties of the cities of Panama and Colon respectively, and the use of the water shall be free to the inhabitants of Panama and Colon, except to the extent that water rates may be necessary for the operation and maintenance of said system of sewers and water.

The Republic of Panama agrees that the cities of Panama and Colon shall comply in perpetuity with the sanitary ordinances whether of a preventive or curative character prescribed by the United States and in case the Government of Panama is unable or fails in its duty to enforce this compliance by the cities of Panama and Colon with the sanitary ordinances of the United States the Republic of Panama grants to the United States the right and authority to enforce the same.

The same right and authority are granted to the United States for the maintenance of public order in the cities of Panama and Colon and the territories and harbors adjacent thereto in case the Republic of Panama should not be, in the judgment of the United States, able to maintain such order.

Article VIII

The Republic of Panama grants to the United States all rights which it now has or hereafter may acquire to the property of the New Panama Canal Company and the Panama Railroad Company as a result of the transfer of sovereignty from the Republic of Colombia to the Republic of Panama over the Isthmus of Panama and authorizes the New Panama Canal Company to sell and transfer to the United States its rights, privileges, properties and concessions as well as the Panama Railroad and all the shares or part of the shares of that company; but the public lands situated outside of·the zone described in Article II of this treaty now included in the concessions to both said enterprises and not required in the construction or operation of the Canal shall revert to the Republic of Panama except any property now owned by or in the possession of said companies within Panama or Colon or the ports or terminals thereof.

Article IX

The United States agrees that the ports at either entrance of the Canal and the waters thereof, and the Republic of Panama agrees that the towns of Panama and Colon shall be free for all time so that there shall not be imposed or collected custom house tolls, tonnage, anchorage, lighthouse, wharf, pilot, or quarantine dues or any other charges or taxes of any kind upon any vessel using or passing through the Canal or belonging to or employed by the United States, directly or indirectly, in connection with the construction, maintenance, operation, sanitation and protection of the main Canal, or auxiliary works, or upon the cargo, officers, crew, or passengers of any such vessels, except such tolls and charges as may be imposed by the United States for the use of the Canal and other works, and except tolls and charges imposed by the Republic of Panama upon merchandise destined to be introduced for the consumption of the rest of the Republic of Panama, and upon vessels touching at the ports of Colon and Panama and which do not cross the Canal.

The Government of the Republic of Panama shall have the right to establish in such ports and in the towns of Panama and Colon such houses and guards as it may deem necessary to collect duties on importations destined to other portions of Panama and to prevent contraband trade. The United States shall have the right to make use of the towns and harbors of Panama and Colon as places of anchorage, and for making repairs, for loading, unloading, depositing, or transshipping cargoes either in transit or destined for the service of the Canal and for other works pertaining to the Canal.

Article X

The Republic of Panama agrees that there shall not be imposed any taxes, national, municipal, departmental, or of any other class, upon the Canal, the railways and auxiliary works, tugs and other vessels employed in the service of the Canal, store houses, work shops, offices, quarters for laborers, factories of all kinds, warehouses, wharves, machinery and other works, property, and effects appertaining to the Canal or railroad and auxiliary works, or their officers or employees, situated within the cities of Panama and Colon, and that there shall not be imposed contributions or charges of a personal character of any kind upon officers, employees, laborers, and other individuals in the service of the Canal and railroad and auxiliary works.

Article XI

The United States agrees that the official dispatches of the Government of the Republic of Panama shall be transmitted over any telegraph and telephone lines established for canal purposes and used for public and private business at rates not higher than those required from officials in the service of the United States.

Article XII

The Government of the Republic of Panama shall permit the immigration and free access to the lands and workshops of the Canal and its auxiliary works of all employees and workmen of whatever nationality under contract to work upon or seeking employment upon or in any wise connected with the said Cdanal and its auxiliary works, with their respective families, and all such persons shall be free and exempt from the military service of the Republic of Panama.

Article XIII

The United States may import at any time into the said zone and auxiliary lands, free of custom duties, imposts, taxes, or other charges, and without any restrictions, any and all vessels, dredges, engines, cars, machinery, tools, explosives, materials, supplies and other articles necessary and convenient in the construction, maintenance, operation, sanitation and protection of the Canal and auxiliary works, and all provisions, medicines, clothing, supplies and other things necessary and convenient for the officers, employees, workmen and laborers in the service and employ of the United States and for their families. If any such articles are disposed of for use outside of the zone and auxiliary lands granted to the United States and within the territory of the Republic, they shall be subject to the same import or other duties as like articles imported under the laws of the Republic of Panama.

Article XIV

As the price of compensation for the rights, powers and privileges granted in this convention by the Republic of Panama to the United States, the Government of the United States agrees to pay to the Republic of Panama the sum of ten million dollars ($10,000,000) in gold coin of the United States on the exchange of the ratification of this convention and also an annual payment during the life of this convention of two hundred and fifty thousand dollars ($250,000) in like gold coin, beginning nine years after the date aforesaid.

The provisions of this Article shall be in addition to all other benefits assured to the Republic of Panama under this convention.

But no delay or different of opinion under this Article or any other provisions of this treaty shall affect or interrupt the full operation and effect of this convention in all other respects.

Article XV

The joint commission referred to in Article VI shall be established as follows:

The President of the United States shall nominate two persons and the President of the Republic of Panama shall nominate two persons and they shall proceed to a decision; but in case of disagreement of the Commission (by reason of their being equally divided in conclusion) an umpire shall be appointed by the two Governments who shall render the decision. In the event of the death, absence, or incapacity of a Commissioner or Umpire, or of his omitting, declining or ceasing to act, his place shall be filled by the appointment of another person in the manner above indicated. All decisions by a majority of the Commission or by the umpire shall be final.

Article XVI

The two Governments shall make adequate provision by future agreement for the pursuit, capture, imprisonment, detention and delivery within said zone and auxiliary lands to the authorities of the Republic of Panama of persons charged with the commitment of crimes, felonies or misdemeanors without said zone and for the pursuit, capture, imprisonment, detention and delivery without said zone to the authorities to the United States of persons charged with the commitment of crimes, felonies and misdemeanors within said zone and auxiliary lands.

Article XVII

The Republic of Panama grants to the United States the use of all the ports of the Republic open to commerce as places of refuge for any vessels employed in the Canal enterprise, and for all vessels passing or bound to pass through the Canal which may be in distress and be driven to seek refuge in said ports. Such vessels shall be exempt from anchorage and tonnage dues on the part of the Republic of Panama.

Article XVIII

The Canal, when constructed, and the entrances thereto shall be neutral in perpetuity, and shall be opened upon the terms provided for by Section I of Article three of, and in conformity with all the stipulations of, the treaty entered into by the Governments of the United States and Great Britain on November 18, 1901.

Article XIX

The Government of the Republic of Panama shall have the right to transport over the Canal its vessels and its troops and munitions of war in such vessels at all times without paying charges of any kind. The exemption is to be extended to the auxiliary railway for the transportation of persons in the service of the Republic of Panama, or of the police force charged with the preservation of public order outside of said zone, as well as to their baggage, munitions of war and supplies.

Article XX

If by virtue of any existing treaty in relation to the territory of the Isthmus of Panama, whereof the obligations shall descend or be assumed by the Republic of Panama, there may be any privilege or concession in favor of the Government or the citizens and subjects of a third power relative to an interoceanic means of communication which in any of its terms may be incompatible with the terms of the present convention, the Republic of Panama agrees to cancel or modify such treaty in due form, for which purpose it shall give to the said third power the requisite notification within the term of four months from the date of the present convention, and in case the existing treaty contains no clause permitting its modifications or annulment, the Republic of Panama agrees to procure its modification or annulment in such form that there shall not exist any conflict with the stipulations of the present convention.

Article XXI

The rights and privileges granted by the Republic of Panama to the United States in the preceding Articles are understood to be free of all anterior debts, liens, trusts, or liabilities, or concessions or privileges to other Governments, corporations, syndicates or individuals, and consequently, if there should arise any claims on account of the present concessions and privileges or otherwise, the claimants shall resort to the Government of the Republic of Panama and not to the United States for any indemnity or compromise which may be required.

Article XXII

The Republic of Panama renounces and grants to the United States the participation to which it might be entitled in the future earnings of the Canal under Article XV of the concessionary contract with Lucien N. B. Wyse now owned by the New Panama Canal Company and any and all other rights or claims of a pecuniary nature arising under or relating to said concession, or arising under or relating to the concessions to the Panama Railroad Company or any extension or modification thereof; and it likewise renounces, confirms and grants to the United States, now and hereafter, all the rights and property reserved in the said concessions which otherwise would belong to Panama at or before the expiration of the terms of ninety-nine years of the concessions granted to or held by the above mentioned party and companies, and all right, title and interest which it now has or may hereafter have, in and to the lands, canal, works, property and rights held by the said companies under said concessions or otherwise, and acquired or to be acquired by the United States from or through The New Panama Canal Company, including any property and rights which might or may in the future either by lapse of time, forfeiture or otherwise, revert to the Republic of Panama under any contracts or concessions, with said Wyse, the Universal Panama Canal Company, the Panama Railroad Company and the New Panama Canal Company.

The aforesaid rights and property shall be and are free and released from any present or reversionary interest in or claims of

Panama and the title of the United States thereto upon consummation of the contemplated purchase by the United States from the New Panama Canal Company, shall be absolute, so far as concerns the Republic of Panama, excepting always the rights of the Republic specifically secured under this treaty.

Article XXIII

If it should become necessary at any time to employ armed forces for the safety or protection of the Canal, or of the ships that make use of the same, or the railways and auxiliary works, the United States shall have the right, at all times and in its discretion, to use its police and its land and naval forces or to establish fortifications for these purposes.

Article XXIV

No change either in the Government or in the laws and treaties of the Republic of Panama shall, without the consent of the United States, affect any right of the United States under the present convention, or under any treaty stipulation between the two countries that now exists or may hereafter exist touching the subject matter of this convention.

If the Republic of Panama shall hereafter enter as a constituent into any other Government or into any union or confederation of states, so as to merge her sovereignty or independence in such Government, union or confederation, the rights of the United States under this convention shall not be in any respect lessened or impaired.

Article XXV

For the better performance of the engagements of this convention and to the end of the efficient protection of the Canal and the preservation of its neutrality, the Government of the Republic of Panama will sell or lease to the United States lands adequate and necessary for naval or coaling stations on the Pacific coast and on the western Caribbean coast of the Republic at certain points to be agreed upon with the President of the United States.

Article XXVI

This convention when signed by the Plenipotentiaries of the Contracting Parties shall be ratified by the respective Governments and the ratifications shall be exchanged at Washington at the earliest date possible.

IN FAITH WHEREOF the respective Plenipotentiaries have signed the present convention in duplicate and have hereunto affixed their respective seals.

DONE at the City of Washington the 18th day of November in the year of our Lord nineteen hundred and three.

JOHN HAY   [*Seal*]

P. BUNAU VARILLA   [*Seal*]

General Treaty of Friendship and Cooperation Between the United States of America and Panama, 1936

Signed at Washington, March 2, 1936; ratification advised by the Senate of the United States, July 25, 1939; ratified by the President of the United States, July 26, 1939; ratified by Panama, July 17, 1939; ratifications exchanged at Washington, July 27, 1939; proclaimed by the President of the United States, July 27, 1939.

BY THE PRESIDENT OF THE UNITED STATES OF AMERICA
A Proclamation

Whereas a Treaty between the United States of America and the Republic of Panama to strengthen further the bonds of friendship and cooperation between the two countries and to regulate on a stable and mutually satisfactory basis certain questions which have arisen as a result of the construction of the interoceanic canal across the Isthmus of Panama was concluded and signed by their respective Plenipotentiaries at Washington on the second day of March, one thousand nine hundred and thirty-six, the original of which Treaty, being in the English and Spanish languages, is word for word as follows:

The United States of America and the Republic of Panama, animated by the desire to strengthen further the bonds of friendship and cooperation between the two countries and to regulate on a stable and mutually satisfactory basis certain questions which have arisen as a result of the construction of the interoceanic canal across the Isthmus of Panama, have decided to conclude a treaty, and have designated for this purpose as their Plenipotentiaries:

The President of the United States of America:

Mr. Cordell Hull, Secretary of State of the United States of America, and Mr. Sumner Welles, Assistant Secretary of State of the United States of America; and

The President of the Republic of Panama:

The Honorable Doctor Ricardo J. Alfaro, Envoy Extraordinary and Minister Plenipotentiary of Panama to the United States of America, and The Honorable Doctor Narciso Garay, Envoy Extraordinary and Minister Plenipotentiary of Panama on special mission;

Who, having communicated their respective full powers to each other, which have been found to be in good and due form, have agreed upon the following:

Article I

Article I of the Convention of November 18, 1903, is hereby superseded.

There shall be a perfect, firm and inviolable peace and sincere friendship between the United States of America and the Republic of Panama and between their citizens.

In view of the official and formal opening of the Panama Canal on July 12, 1920, the United States of America and the Republic of Panama declare that the provisions of the Convention of November 18, 1903, contemplate the use, occupation and control by the United States of America of the Canal Zone and of the additional lands and waters under the jurisdiction of the United States of America for the purposes of the efficient maintenance, operation, sanitation and protection of the Canal and of its auxiliary works.

The United States of America will continue the maintenance of the Panama Canal for the encouragement and use of interoceanic commerce, and the two Governments declare their willingness to cooperate, as far as it is feasible for them to do so, for the purpose of insuring the full and perpetual enjoyment of the benefits of all kinds which the Canal should afford the two nations that made possible its construction as well as all nations interested in world trade.

Article II

The United States of America declares that the Republic of Panama has loyally and satisfactorily complied with the obligations which it entered into under Article II of the Convention of November 18, 1903, by which it granted in perpetuity to the United States the use, occupation and control of the zone of land and land under water as described in the said Article, of the islands within the limits of said zone, of the group of small islands in the Bay of Panama, named Perioc, Naos, Bulebra and Flamenco, and of any other lands and waters outside of said zone necessary and convenient for the construction, maintenance, operation, sanitation and protection of the Panama Canal or of any auxiliary canals or other works, and in recognition thereof the United States of America hereby renounces the grant made to it in perpetuity by the Republic of Panama of the use, occupation and control of lands and waters, in addition to those now under the jurisdiction of the United States of America outside of the zone as described in Article II of the aforesaid Convention, which may be necessary and convenient for the construction, maintenance, operation, sanitation and protection of the Panama Canal or of any auxiliary canals or other works necessary and convenient for the construction, maintenance, operation, sanitation and protection of the said enterprise.

While both Governments agree that the requirement of further lands and waters for the enlargement of the existing facilities of the Canal appears to be improbable, they nevertheless recognize, subject to the provisions of Articles I and X of this Treaty, their joint obligation to insure the effective and continuous operation of the Canal and the preservation of its neutrality, and consequently, if, in the event of some now unforeseen contingency, the utilization of lands or waters additional to those already employed should be in fact necessary for the maintenance, sanitation, or efficient operation of the Canal, or for its effective protection, the Governments of the United States of America and the Republic of Panama will agree upon such measures as it may be necessary to take in order to insure the maintenance, sanitation, efficient operation and effective protection of the Canal, in which the two countries are jointly and vitally interested.

Article III

In order to enable the Republic of Panama to take advantage of the commercial opportunities inherent in its geographical situation, the United States of America agrees as follows:

1) The sale to individuals of goods imported into the Canal Zone or purchased, produced or manufactured therein by the Government of the United States of America shall be limited by it to the persons included in classes (a) and (b) of Section 2 of this Article; and with regard to the persons included in classes (c), (d) and (e) of the said Section and members of their families, the sales above mentioned shall be made only when such persons actually reside in the Canal Zone.

2) No person who is not comprised within the following classes shall be entitled to reside within the Canal Zone:

(a) Officers, employees, workmen or laborers in the service or employ of the United States of America, the Panama Canal or the Panama Railroad Company, and members of their families actually residing with them;

(b) Members of the armed forces of the United States of America and members of their families actually residing with them;

(c) Contractors opening in the Canal Zone and their employees, workmen and laborers during the performance of contracts;

(d) Officers, employees or workmen of companies entitled under Section 5 of this Article to conduct operations in the Canal Zone;

(e) Persons engaged in religious, welfare, charitable, educational, recreational and scientific work exclusively in the Canal Zone;

(f) Domestic servants of all the beforementioned persons and members of the families of the persons in classes (c), (d) and (e) actually residing with them.

3) No dwellings belonging to the Government of the United States of America or to the Panama Railroad Company and situated within the Canal Zone shall be rented, leased or sublet except to persons within classes (a) to (e), inclusive of Section 2

149

hereinabove.

4) The Government of the United States of America will continue to cooperate in all proper ways with the Government of the Republic of Panama to prevent violations of the immigration and customs laws of the Republic of Panama, including the smuggling into territory under the jurisdiction of the Republic of goods imported into the Canal Zone or purchased, produced or manufactured therein by the Government of the United States of America.

5) With the exception of concerns having a direct relation to the operation, maintenance, sanitation or protection of the Canal, such as those engaged in the operation of cables, shipping, or dealing in oil or fuel, the Government of the United States of America will not permit the establishment in the Canal Zone of private business enterprises other than those existing therein at the time of the signature of this Treaty.

6) In view of the proximity of the port of Balboa to the city of Panama and of the port of Cristobal to the city of Colón, the United States of America will continue to permit, under suitable regulations and upon the payment of proper charges, vessels entering at or clearing from the ports of the Canal Zone to use and enjoy the dockage and other facilities of the said ports for the purpose of loading and unloading cargoes and receiving or disembarking passengers to or from the territory under the jurisdiction of the Republic of Panama.

The Republic of Panama will permit vessels entering at or clearing from the ports of Panamá or Colón, in case of emergency and also under suitable regulations and upon the payment of proper charges, to use and enjoy the dockage and other facilities of said ports for the purpose of receiving or disembarking passengers to or from the territory of the Republic of Panama under the jurisdiction of the United States of America, and of loading and unloading cargoes either in transit or destined for the service of the Canal or of works pertaining to the Canal.

7) The Government of the United States of America will extend to private merchants residing in the Republic of Panama full opportunity for making sales to vessels arriving at terminal ports of the Canal or transiting the Canal, subject always to appropriate administrative regulations of the Canal Zone.

150

Article IV

The Government of the Republic of Panama shall not impose import duties or taxes of any kind on goods destined for or consigned to the agencies of the Government of the United States of America in the Republic of Panama when the goods are intended for the official use of such agencies, or upon goods destined for or consigned to persons included in classes (a) and (b) in Section 2 of Article III of this Treaty, who reside or sojourn in territory under the jurisdiction of the Republic of Panama during the performance of their service with the United States of America, the Panama Canal or the Panama Railroad Company, when the goods are intended for their own use and benefit.

The United States of America shall not impose import duties or taxes of any kind on goods, wares and merchandise passing from territory under the jurisdiction of the Republic of Panama into the Canal Zone.

No charges of any kind shall be imposed by the authorities of the United States of America upon persons residing in territory under the jurisdiction of the Republic of Panama passing from the said territory into the Canal Zone, and no charges of any kind shall be imposed by the authorities of the Republic of Panama upon persons in the service of the United States of America or residing in the Canal Zone passing from the Canal Zone into territory under the jurisdiction of the Republic of Panama, all other persons passing from the Canal Zone into territory under the jurisdiction of the Republic of Panama being subject to the full effects of the immigration laws of the Republic.

In view of the fact that the Canal Zone divides the territory under the jurisdiction of the Republic of Panama, the United States of America agrees that, subject to such police regulations as circumstances may require, Panamanian citizens who may occasionally be deported from the Canal Zone shall be assured transit through the said Zone, in order to pass from one part to another of the territory under the jurisdiction of the Republic of Panama.

Article V

Article IX of the Convention of November 18, 1903, is hereby superseded.

The Republic of Panama has the right to impose upon merchandise destined to be introduced for use or consumption in territory under the jurisdiction of the Republic of Panama, and upon vessels touching at Panamanian ports and upon the officers, crew or passengers of such vessels, the taxes or charges provided by the laws of the Republic of Panama; it being understood that the Republic of Panama will continue directly and exclusively to exercise its jurisdiction over the ports of Panamá and Colón and to operate exclusively with Panamanian personnel such facilities as are or may be established therein by the Republic or by its authority. However, the Republic of Panama shall not impose or collect any charges or taxes upon any vessel using or passing through the Canal which does not touch at a port under Panamanian jurisdiction or upon the officers, crew or passengers of such vessels, unless they enter the Republic; it being also understood that taxes and charges imposed by the Republic of Panama upon vessels using or passing through the Canal which touch at ports under Panamanian jurisdiction, or upon their cargo, officers, crew or passengers, shall not be higher than those imposed upon vessels which touch only at ports under Panamanian jurisdiction and do not transit the Canal, or upon their cargo, officers, crew or passengers.

The Republic of Panama also has the right to determine what persons or classes of persons arriving at ports of the Canal Zone shall be admitted to the Republic of Panama and to determine likewise what persons or classes of persons arriving at such ports shall be excluded from admission to the Republic of Panama.

The United States of America will furnish to the Republic of Panama free of charge the necessary sites for the establishment of customhouses in the ports of the Canal Zone for the collection of duties on importations destined to the Republic and for the examination of merchandise, baggage and passengers consigned to or bound for the Republic of Panama, and for the prevention of contraband trade, it being understood that the collection of duties and the examination of merchandise and passengers by the agents of the Government of the Republic of Panama, in accordance with this provision, shall take place only in the customhouses to be established by the Government of the Republic of Panama as herein provided, and that the Republic of Panama will exercise exclusive jurisdiction within the sites on which the customhouses are located so far as concerns the enforcement of immigration or customs laws of the Republic of Panama, and over all property therein contained and the personnel therein employed.

To further the effective enforcement of the rights hereinbefore recognized, the Government of the United States of America agrees that, for the purpose of obtaining information useful in determining whether persons arriving at ports of the Canal Zone and destined to points within the jurisdiction of the Republic of Panama should be admitted or excluded from admission into the Republic, the immigration officers of the Republic of Panama shall have the right of free access to vessels upon their arrival at the Balboa or Cristobal piers or wharves with passengers destined for the Republic; and that the appropriate authorities of the Panama Canal will adopt such administrative regulations regarding persons entering ports of the Canal Zone and destined to points within the jurisdiction of the Republic of Panama as will facilitate the exercise by the authorities of Panama of their jurisdiction in the manner provided in Paragraph 4 of this Article for the purposes stated in Paragraph 3 thereof.

Article VI

The first sentence of Article VII of the Convention of November 18, 1903, is hereby amended so as to omit the following phrase: "or by the exercise of the right of eminent domain".

The third paragraph of article VII of the Convention of November 18, 1903, is hereby abrogated.

Article VII

Beginning with the annuity payable in 1934 the payments under Article XIV of the Convention of November 18, 1903, between the United States of America and the Republic of Panama, shall be four hundred and thirty thousand Balboas (B/430,000.00) as defined by the agreement embodied in an exchange of notes of this date. The United States of America may discharge its obligation with respect to any such payment, upon payment in any coin or currency, provided the amount so paid is the equivalent of four hundred and thirty thousand Balboas (B/430,000,00) as so defined.

Article VIII

In order that the city of Colón may enjoy direct means of land communication under Panamanian jurisdiction with other territory under jurisdiction of the Republic of Panama, the United States of America hereby transfers to the Republic of Panama jurisdiction over a corridor, the exact limits of which shall be agreed upon and demarcated by the two Governments pursuant to the following description:

(a) The end at Colón connects with the southern end of the east half of the Paseo del Centenario at Sixteenth Street, Colón; thence the corridor proceeds in a general southerly direction, parallel to and east of Bolivar Highway to the vicinity of the northern edge of Silver City; thence eastward near the shore line of Folks River, around the northeast corner of Silver City; thence in a general southeasterly direction and generally parallel to the Randolph Road to a crossing of said Randolph Road, about 1200 feet east of the East Diversion; thence in a general northeasterly direction to the eastern boundary line of the Canal Zone near the southeastern corner of the Fort Randolph Reservation, southwest of Cativá. The approximate route of the corridor is shown on the map which accompanies this Treaty, signed by the Plenipotentiaries of the two countries and marked "Exhibit A".

(b) The width of the corridor shall be as follows: 25 feet in width from the Colón end to a point east of the southern line of Silver City; thence 100 feet in width to Randolph Road, except that, at any elevated crossing which may be built over Randolph Road and the railroad, the corridor will be no wider than is necessary to include the viaduct and will not include any part of Randolph Road proper, or of the railroad right of way, and except that, in case of a grade crossing over Randolph Road and the railroad, the corridor will be interrupted by that highway and railroad; thence 200 feet in width to the boundary line of the Canal Zone.

The Government of the United States of America will extinguish any private titles existing or which may exist in and to the land included in the above-described corridor.

The stream and drainage crossing of any highway built in the corridor shall not restrict the water passage to less than the capacity of the existing streams and drainage.

No other construction will take place within the corridor than that relating to the construction of a highway and to the installation of electric power, telephone and telegraph lines; and the only activities which will be conducted within the said corridor will be those pertaining to the construction, maintenance and common uses of a highway and of power and communication lines.

The United States of America shall enjoy at all times the right of unimpeded transit across said corridor at any point, and of travel along the corridor, subject to such traffic regulations as may be established by the Government of the Republic of Panama; and the Government of the United States of America shall have the right to such use of the corridor as would be involved in the construction of connecting or intersecting highways or railroads, overhead and underground power, telephone, telegraph and pipe lines, and additional drainage channels, on condition that these structures and their use shall not interfere with the purpose of the corridor as provided hereinabove.

Article IX

In order that direct means of land communication, together with accommodation for the high tension power transmission lines, may be provided under jurisdiction of the United States of America from the Madden Dam to the Canal Zone, the Republic of Panama hereby transfers to the United States of America jurisdiction over a corridor, the limits of which shall be demarcated by the two Governments pursuant to the following descriptions:

A strip of land 200 ft. in width, extending 62.5 ft. from the center line of the Madden Road on its eastern boundary and 137.5 ft. from the center line of the Madden Road on its western boundary, containing an area of 105.8 acres of 42.81 hectares, as shown on the map which accompanies this Treaty, signed by the Plenipotentiaries of the two countries and marked "Exhibit B".

Beginning at the intersection of the located center line of the Madden Road and the Canal Zone-Republic of Panama 5-mile boundary line, said point being located N. 29°20' W. a distance of 168.04 ft. along said boundary line from boundary monument No. 65, the geodetic position of boundary monument No. 65 being latitude N. 9°07' plus 3,948.8 ft. and longitude 79°37' plus 1,174.6 ft.;

155

thence N. 43°10′ E. a distance of 541.1 ft. to station 324 plus 06.65 ft.;

thence on a 3° curve to the left, a distance of 347.2 ft. to station 327 plus 53.9 ft.;

thence N. 32°45′ E. a distance of 656.8 ft. to station 334 plus 10.7 ft.;

thence on a 3° curve to the left a distance of 455.55 ft. to station 338 plus 66.25 ft.;

thence N. 19°05′ E. a distance of 1,135.70 ft. to station 350 plus 01.95 ft.;

thence on an 8° curve to the left a distance of 650.7 ft. to station 356 plus 52.7 ft.;

thence N. 32°58′ W. a distance of 636.0 ft. to station 362 plus 88.7 ft.;

thence on a 10° cruve to the right a distance of 227.3 ft. to station 365 plus 16.0 ft.;

thence N. 10°14′ W. a distance of 314.5 ft. to station 368 plus 30.5 ft.;

thence on a 5° curve to the left a distance of 178.7 ft. to station 370 plus 09.2 ft.;

thence N. 19°10′ W. a distance of 4,250.1 ft. to station 412 plus 59.3 ft.;

thence on a 5° curve to the right a distance of 720.7 ft. to station 419 plus 80.0 ft.;

thence N. 16°52′ E. a distance of 1,664.3 ft. to station 436 plus 44.3 ft.;

thence on a 5° curve to the left a distance of 597.7 ft. to station 442 plus 42.0 ft.;

thence N. 13°01′ W. a distance of 543.8 ft. to station 447 plus 85.8 ft.;

thence on a 5° curve to the right a distance of 770.7 ft. to station 455 plus 56.5 ft.;

thence N. 25°31′ E. a distance of 1,492.2 ft. to station 470 plus 48.7 ft.;

thence on a 5° curve to the right a distance of 808.0 ft. to station 478 plus 56.7 ft.;

thence N. 65°55′ E. a distance of 281.8 ft. to station 481 plus 38.5 ft.;

thence on an 8° curve to the left a distance of 446.4 ft. to station 485 plus 84.9 ft.;

thence N. 30°12′ E. a distance of 479.6 ft. to station 490 plus 64.5 ft.;

thence on a 5° curve to the left a distance of 329.4 ft. to station 493 plus 93.9 ft.;

thence N. 13°44′ E. a distance of 1,639.9 ft. to station 510 plus 33.8 ft.;

thence on a 5° curve to the left a distance of 832.3 ft. to station 518 plus 66.1 ft.;

thence N. 27°53' W. a distance of 483.9 ft. to station 523 plus 50.0 ft.;

thence on an 8° curve to the right a distance of 469.6 ft. to station 528 plus 19.6 ft.;

thence N. 9°41' E. a distance of 1,697.6 ft. to station 545 plus 17.2 ft.;

thence on a 10° curve to the left a distance of 451.7 ft. to station 549 plus 68.9 ft., which is the point marked Point Z on the above-mentioned map known as "Exhibit B".

(All bearings are true bearings)

The Government of the Republic of Panama will extinguish any private titles existing or which may exist in and to the land included in the above-described corridor.

The stream and drainage crossings of any highway built in the corridor shall not restrict the water passage to less than the capacity of the existing streams and drainage.

No other construction will take plae within the corridor than that relating to the construction of a highway and to the installation of electric power, telephone and telegraph lines; and the only activities which will be conducted within the said corridor will be those pertaining to the construction, maintenance and common uses of a highway, and of power and communication lines, and auxiliary works thereof.

The Republic of Panama shall enjoy at all times the right of unimpeded transit across the said corridor at any point, and of travel along the corridor, subject to such traffic regulations as may be established by the authorities of the Panama Canal; and the Government of the Republic of Panama shall have the right to such use of the corridor as would be involved in the construction of connecting or intersecting highways or railroads, overhead and underground power, telephone, telegraph and pipe lines, and additional drainage channels, on condition that these structures and their use shall not interfere with the purpose of the corridor as provided hereinabove.

Article X

In case of an international conflagration or the existence of any threat of aggression which would endanger the security of the Republic of Panama or the neutrality or security of the Panama Canal, the Governments of the United States of America and the Republic of Panama will take such measures of prevention and defense as they may consider necessary for the protection of their common interests. Any measures, in safeguarding such interests, which it shall appear essential to one Government to take, and which may affect the territory under the jurisdiction of the other Government, will be the subject of consultation between the two Governments.

Article XI

The provisions of this Treaty shall not affect the rights and obligations of either of the two High Contracting Parties under the treaties now in force between the two countries, nor be considered as a limitation, definition, restriction or restrictive interpretation of such rights and obligations, but without prejudice to the full force and effect of any provisions of this Treaty which constitute addition to, modification or abrogation of, or substitution for the provisions of previous treaties.

Article XII

The present Treaty shall be ratified in accordance with the constitutional methods of the High Contracting Parties and shall take effect immediately on the exchange of ratifications which shall take place at Washington.

IN WITNESS WHEREOF, the Plenipotentiaries have signed this Treaty in duplicate, in the English and Spanish languages, both texts being authentic, and have hereunto affixed their seals.

DONE at the city of Washington the second day of March, 1936.

	CORDELL HULL	[SEAL]
SUMNER WELLES		[SEAL]
	SUMNER WELLES	[SEAL]
	R. J. ALFARO	[SEAL]
	NARCISO GARAY	[SEAL]

AND WHEREAS the said Treaty has been duly ratified on both parts, and the ratifications of the two Governments were exchanged in the city of Washington on the twenty-seventh day of July one thousand nine hundred and thirty-nine;

Now, THEREFORE, be it known that I, Franklin D. Roosevelt, President of the United States of America, have caused the said Treaty to be made public, to the end that the same and every article and clause thereof may be observed and fulfilled with good faith by the United States of America and the citizens thereof.

IN TESTIMONY WHEREOF, I have hereunto set my hand and caused the Seal of the United States of America to be affixed.

DONE at the city of Washington this twenty-seventh day of July in the year of our Lord one thousand nine hundred and thirty-nine and of the Independence of the United States of America the one hundred and sixty-fourth.

[SEAL]

By the President:
    CORDELL HULL
       Secretary of State.

                        FRANKLIN D. ROOSEVELT

Treaty of Mutual Understanding and Cooperation, 1955

Treaty, with memorandum of understandings reached; signed at Panama, January 25, 1955; ratification advised by the Senate of the United States of America, July 29, 1955; ratified by the President of the United States of America, August 17, 1955; ratified by Panama, August 15, 1955; ratifications exchanged at Washington, August 23, 1955; proclaimed by the President of the United States of America, August 26, 1955; entered into force, August 23, 1955.

BY THE PRESIDENT OF THE UNITED STATES OF AMERICA

A Proclamation

WHEREAS a Treaty of Mutual Understanding and Cooperation between the United States of America and the Republic of Panama, together with a related Memorandum of Understandings Reached, was signed at Panamá on January 25, 1955;

WHEREAS the texts of the sait Treaty and related Memorandum of Understandings Reached, in the English and Spanish languages, are word for word as follows:

Treaty of Mutual Understanding and Cooperation Between
the United States of America and the Republic of Panama

The President of the United States of America and the President of the Republic of Panama, desirous of concluding a treaty further to demonstrate the mutual understanding and cooperation of the two countries and to strengthen the bonds of understanding and friendship between their respective peoples, have appointed for that purpose as their respective Plenipotentiaries:

The President of the United States of America:

Selden Chapin, Ambassador Extraordinary and Plenipotentiary of the United States of America to the Republic of Panama,

The President of the Republic of Panama:

Octavio Fábrega, Minister of Foreign Relations of the Republic of Panama,

who, having communicated to one another their respective full powers, found in good and due form, and recognizing that neither the provisions of the Convention signed November 18, 1903, nor the General Treaty signed March 2, 1936, nor the present Treaty may be modified except by mutual consent, agree upon the following articles:

Article I

Beginning with the first annuity payable after the exchange of ratifications of the present Treaty, the payments under Article XIV of the Convention for the Construction of a Ship Canal between the United States of America and the Republic of Panama, signed November 18, 1903, as amended by Article VII of the General Treaty of Friendship and Cooperation, signed March 2, 1936, shall be One Million Nine Hundred Thirty Thousand and no/100 Balboas (B/1,930,000) as defined by the agreement embodied in the exchange of notes of March 2, 1936, between the Secretary of State of the United States of America and the Members of the Panamanian Treaty Commission. The United States of America may discharge its obligation with respect to any such payment in any coin or currency, provided the amount so paid is the equivalent of One Million Nine Hundred Thirty Thousand and no/100 Balboas (B/1,930,000) as so defined.

On the date of the first payment under the present Treaty, the provisions of this Article shall supersede the provisions of Article VII of the General Treaty signed March 2, 1936.

Notwithstanding the provisions of this Article, the High Contracting Parties recognize the absence of any obligation on the part of either Party to alter the amount of the annuity.

Article II

(1) Notwithstanding the provisions of Article X of the Convention signed November 18, 1903, between the United States of America and the Republic of Panama, the United States of America agrees that the Republic of Panama may, subject to the provisions of paragraphs (2) and (3) of this Article, impose taxes upon the income (including income from sources within the Canal Zone) of all persons who are employed in the service of the Canal, the railroad, or auxiliary works, whether resident within or outside the Canal Zone, except—

> (a) members of the Armed Forces of the United States of America.
> (b) citizens of the United States of America, including those who have dual nationality, and
> (c) other individuals who are not citizens of the Republic of Panama and who reside within the Canal Zone.

(2) It is understood that any tax levied pursuant to paragraph (1) of this Article shall be imposed on a non-discriminatory basis and shall in no case be imposed at a rate higher or more burdensome than that applicable to income of citizens of the Republic of Panama generally.

(3) The Republic of Panama agrees not to impose taxes on pensions, annuities, relief payments, or other similar payments, or payments by way of compensation for injuries or death occurring in connection with, or incident to, service on the Canal, the railroad,

or auxiliary works paid to or for the benefit of members of the Armed Forces or citizens of the United States of America or the lawful beneficiaries of such members or citizens who reside in territory under the jurisdiction of the Republic of Panama.

The provisions of this Article shall be operative for the taxable years beginning on or after the first day of January following the year in which the present Treaty enters into force.

Article III

Subject to the provisions of the succeeding paragraphs of this Article, the United States of America agrees that the monopoly granted in perpetuity by the Republic of Panama to the United States for the construction, maintenance and operation of any system of communication by means of canal or railroad across its territory between the Caribbean Sea and the Pacific Ocean, by Article V of the Convention signed November 18, 1903, shall be abrogated as of the effective date of this Treaty in so far as it pertains to the construction, maintenance and operation of any system of trans-Isthmian communication by railroad within the territory under the jurisdiction of the Republic of Panama.

Subject to the provisions of the succeeding paragraphs of this Article, the United States further agrees that the exclusive right to establish roads across the Isthmus of Panama acquired by the United States as a result of a concessionary contract granted to the Panama Railroad Company shall be abrogated as of the date of the entry into force of this Treaty, in so far as the right pertains to the establishment of roads within the territory under the jurisdiction of the Republic of Panama.

In view of the vital interest of both countries in the effective protection of the Canal, the High Contracting Parties further agree that such abrogation is subject to the understanding that no system of inter-oceanic communication within the territory under the jurisdiction of the Republic of Panama by means of railroad or highway may be financed, constructed, maintained, or operated directly or indirectly by a third country or nationals thereof, unless in the opinion of both High Contracting Parties such financing, construction, maintenance, or operation would not affect the security of the Canal.

The High Contracting Parties also agree that such abrogation as is contemplated by this Article shall in no wise affect the maintenance and operation of the present Panama Railroad in the Canal Zone and in territory subject to the jurisdiction of the Republic of Panama.

Article IV

The second paragraph of Article VII of the Convention signed November 18, 1903, having to do with the issuance of, compliance with, and enforcement of, sanitary ordinances in the Cities of Panamá and Colón, shall be abrogated in its entirety as of the date of entry into force of this Treaty.

Article V

The United States of America agrees that, subject to the enactment of legislation by the Congress, there shall be conveyed to the Republic of Panama free of cost all the right, title and interest held by the United States of America or its agencies in and to certain lands and improvements in territory under the jurisdiction of the Republic of Panama when and as determined by the United States to be no longer needed for the operation, maintenance, sanitation or protection of the Panama Canal or of its auxiliary works, or for other authorized purposes of the United States in the Republic of Panama. The lands and improvements referred to in the preceding sentence and the determinations by the United States of America respecting the same, subject to the enactment of legislation by the Congress, are designated and set forth in Item 2 of the Memorandum of Understandings Reached which bears the same date as this Treaty. The United States of America also agrees that, subject to the enactment of legislation by the Congress, there shall be conveyed to the Republic of Panama free of cost all its right, title and interest to the land and improvements in the area known as Paitilla Point and that effective with such conveyance the United States of America shall relinquish all the rights, power and authority granted to it in such area under the Convention signed November 18, 1903. The Republic of Panama agrees to save the Government of the United States harmless from any and all claims which may arise

163

incident to the conveyance of the area known as Paitilla Point to the Republic of Panama.

Article VI

Article V of the Boundary Convention, signed September 2, 1914, between the United States of America and the Republic of Panama, shall be replaced by the following provisions:

"It is agreed that the permanent boundary line between the City of Colón (including the Harbor of Colón, as defined in Article VI of the Boundary Convention of 1914, and other waters adjacent to the shores of Colón, and the Canal Zone shall be as follows:

Beginning at an unmarked point called "E", located on the northeasterly boundary of the Colón Corridor (at its Colón extremity), the geodetic position of which, referred to the Panamá-Colón datum of the Canal Zone triangulation system, is in latitude 9° 21' N. plus 0.00 feet (0.000 meters) and longitude 79° 54' W. plus 356.09 feet (108.536 meters).

Thence from said initial point by metes and bounds:

Due East, 2662.83 feet (811.632 meters), along North latitude 9° 21' plus 0.00 feet (0.000 meters); to an unmarked point in Folks River, called "F", located at longitude 79° 53' W. plus 3700.00 feet (1127.762 meters);

N. 36° 36' 30" E., 2616.00 feet (797.358 meters), to an unmarked point in Manzanillo Bay, called "G";

N. 22° 41' 30" W., 1192.00 feet (363.322 meters), to an unmarked point in Manzanillo Bay, called "H";

N. 56° 49' 00" W., 777.00 feet (236.830 meters), to an unmarked point in Manzanillo Bay, called "I";

N. 29° 51' 00" W., 2793.00 feet (851.308 meters), to an unmarked point in Manzanillo Bay, called "J";

N. 50' 56" 00" W., 3292.00 feet (1003.404 meters), to an unmarked point in Limon Bay, called "K";

S. 56° 06' 11" W., 4258.85 feet (1298.100 meters), to an unmarked point in Limon Bay, called "L", which is located on the northerly boundary of the Harbor of Colón.

Thence following the boundary of the Harbor of Colón, as described in Article VI of the Boundary Convention signed September 2, 1914, to monument "D'", as follows:

N. 78° 30" 30" W., 2104.73 feet (641.523 meters), on a line to the light house on Toro Point, to an unmarked point in Limon Bay, called "M", located 330 meters or 1082.67 feet easterly and at right angles from the centerline of the Panama Canal;

164

S. 00° 14' 50" W., 3074.46 feet (937.097 meters), parallel to and 330 meters or 1082.67 feet easterly from the centerline of the Panama Canal, to an unmarked point in Limon Bay, called "N";

S. 78° 30' 30" E., 3952.97 feet (1204.868 meters), to monument "D", which is a concrete monument, located on the easterly shore of Limon Bay.

Thence following the boundary between the City of Colón and the Canal Zone, as described in Article V of the Boundary Convention signed September 2, 1914, to monument "B" as follows:

S. 78° 30' 30" E., 258.65 feet (78.837 meters) through monuments Nos. 28 and 27 which are brass plugs in pavement, to monument "D", which is a concrete monument, the distances being 159.96 feet (48.756 meters), 28.26 feet (8.614 meters), and 70.43 feet (21.467 meters), successively, from beginning of the course;

N. 74° 17' 35" E., 533.60 feet (169.642 meters), along the centerline of Eleventh Street, through monuments Nos. 26, 25, 24 and 23, which are brass plugs in the pavement, to "C", which is an unmarked point beneath the clock pedestal on the centerline of Bolivar Avenue, the distances being 95.16 feet (29.005 meters), 91.02 feet (27.743 meters), 166.71 feet (50.813 meters), 158.66 feet (48.360 meters) and 22.05 feet (6.721 meters), successively, from beginning of the course;

S. 15° 58' 00" E., 965.59 feet (294.312 meters), along the centerline of Bolivar Avenue, through monuments Nos. 22, 21, 20 and 19, which are brass plugs in the pavement, to monument "B", which is a brass plug, the distances being 14.35 feet (4.374 meters), 143.13 feet (43.626 meters), 238.77 feet (72.777 meters), 326.77 feet (99.600 meters) and 242.57 feet (73,935 meters), successively from beginning of the course. (Monument "B" is the point of beginning referred to in Article I of the Convention between the United States of America and the Republic of Panama regarding the Colón Corridor and certain other Corridors through the Canal Zone, signed at Panamá on May 24, 1950.)

Thence following the boundary between the City of Colón and the Canal Zone, to monument "A", as described in Article I of the Corridor Convention referred to in the next-preceding paragraph:

S. 15° 57' 40" E., 117.10 feet (35.692 meters) along the centerline of Bolivar Avenue to Monument No. A—8, which is a brass plug located at the intersection with the centerline of 14th Street projected westerly, in North latitude 9° 21' plus 1356.18 feet (413.364 meters) and West longitude 79° 54' plus 1862.57 feet (567.712 meters);

N. 73° 59' 35" E., 172.12 feet (52.462 meters) along the centerline of 14th Street to Monument No. A—7, which is a brass plug located at the intersection with the line of the west curb of Boundary Street projected northerly in North latitude 9° 21' plus 1403.64 feet (427.830 meters) and West longitude 79° 54' plus 1697.12 feet (517.283 meters);

Southerly along the westerly curb of Boundary Street and its prolongation to Monument No. A—4, which is a brass plug located at the intersection of two curves, in North latitude 9° 21' plus 833.47 feet (254.042 meters) and West longitude 79° 54' plus 980.94 feet (298.991 meters) (this last mentioned course passes through a curve to the left with a radius of 40.8 feet (12.436 meters) and the intersection of its tangents at point A—6 in North latitude 9° 21' plus 1306.23 feet (398.140 meters) and West longitude 79° 54' plus 1669.37 feet (508.825 meters), and a curve to the right with a radius of 1522 feet (436.907 meters) with the point of intersection of its tangents at point A—5 in North latitude 9° 21' plus 958.14 feet (292.042 meters) and West longitude 79° 54' plus 1105.89 feet (337.076 meters));

Through a curve to the left with a radius of 262.2 feet (79.919 meters) and the intersection of its tangents at point A—3 in North latitude 9° 21' plus 769.07 feet (234.413 meters) and West longitude 79° 54' plus 955.43 feet (291.216 meters); a curve to the right with a radius of 320.0 feet (97.536 meters) and the intersection of its tangents at point A—2 in North latitude 9° 21' plus 673.38 feet (205.247 meters) and West longitude 79° 54' plus 836.40 feet (254.935 meters); and a curve to the left with a radius of 2571.5 feet (783.795 meters) and the intersection of its tangents at point A—1 in North latitude 9° 21' plus 302.15 feet (92.096 meters) and West longitude 79° 54' plus 680.96 feet (207.557 meters) to Monument No. "A", which is a 1½ inch brass plug located in the old sea wall, in North latitude 79° 21' plus 45.60 feet (13.899 meters) and West longitude 79° 54' plus 487.65 feet (148.636 meters);

S. 21° 34' 50" W., 29.19 feet (8.897 meters), to an unmarked point called #1;

Southeasterly, 23.26 feet (7.090 meters), along a curve to the left with a radius of 2596.48 feet (791.409 meters) (the chord of which bears S. 37° 28' 20" E., 23.26 feet (7.090 meters) to an unmarked point called #2, located on the southwesterly boundary of the Colón Corridor at North latitude 9° 21' plus 0.00 feet (0.000 meters).

The directions of the lines refer to the true meridian.

The above-described boundary is as shown on Panama Canal Company drawing No. 6117—22, entitled "Boundary Line Between the City of Colón and the Canal Zone", scale 1 inch to 600 feet, dated December 23, 1954, prepared for the Canal Zone

Government, attrached as an annex hereto and forming a part hereof.

Article VIII of the General Treaty signed March 2, 1936, as amended by Article III of the Convention between the United States of America and the Republic of Panama regarding the Colón Corridor and certain other corridors through the Canal Zone, signed May 24, 1950, is hereby modified by removing from the Colón, or westerly, end of the Colón Corridor the portion thereof lying north of North latitude 9° 21' and incorporating such portion within the boundary of the City of Colón as described above.

This Article shall become effective upon completion of the withdrawal by the United States of America from the sections of the city of Colón known as New Cristobal, Colón Beach and the de Lesseps Area, with the exception of the lots retained for consulate purposes, except that it shall in no case become effective prior to the exchange of the instruments of ratification of this Treaty and the exchange of instruments of ratification of the Convention signed May 24, 1950, referred to in the preceding paragraph.

Article VII

The second paragraph of Article VII of the Boundary Convention signed September 2, 1914, between the United States of America and the Republic of Panama, shall be abrogated in its entirety as of the date of entry into force of the present Treaty.

The landing pier situated in the small cove on the southerly side of Manzanillo Island, constructed pursuant to provisions contained in the second paragraph of Article VII of the Boundary Convention of 1914 between the two countries, shall become the property of the Government of the Republic of Panama as of the date of entry into force of the present Treaty.

Article VIII

(a) The Republic of Panama will reserve exclusively for the purpose of maneuvers and military training the area described in the maps (Nos. SGN—7—54 and SGN—8—54, each dated November 17, 1954) and accompanying descriptions prepared by the Comisión Catastral of the Republic of Panama, attached as the Annex hereto, and will permit the United States of America, without cost and free of all encumbrances, exclusively to utilize said area for the indicated purpose for a period of fifteen (15) years, subject to extension thereafter as agreed by the two Governments. This authorization includes the free access to, egress from, and movements within and over, said area. This utilization will not affect the sovereignty of the Republic of Panama, or the operation of the Constitution and the laws of the Republic over the mentioned area.

(b) The United States Armed Forces, the members thereof and their families actually residing with them, and United States nationals who, in an official capacity, are serving with or accompanying the Armed Forces of the United States and members of their families actually residing with them will be exempted within the said area from all taxation by the Republic of Panama or any of its political subdivisions.

(c) Prior to the expiration of the period envisaged in this Article and within a reasonable time thereafter the United States shall have the right to remove from this training and maneuver area, or otherwise to dispose of, without limitation or restriction all structures, installations, facilities, equipment and supplies brought into, or constructed or erected within this training and maneuver area by or on behalf of the United States. The Republic of Panama will not be required to reimburse the United States for any structures, installations, facilities, equipment and supplies not removed or otherwise disposed of as provided herein.

(d) The United States shall be under no obligation to restore this training and meneuver area or the facilities and installations thereon to their original condition upon the termination of this Article, except for the landing strip which will be returned in at least as good condition as that obtaining at the time of coming into effect of this Article.

(e) The provisions of this Article shall in no manner terminate or modify the provisions concerning the holding of military maneuvers in the Republic of Panama established by the Notes ancillary to the General Treaty signed March 2, 1936 other than as provided herein for this training and maneuver area.

Article IX

The Republic of Panama hereby waives the right under Article XIX of the Convention signed November 18, 1903, to transportation by railway within the Zone, without paying charges of any kind, of persons in the service of the Republic of Panama, or of the police force charged with the preservation of public order outside of the Canal Zone, as well as of their baggage, munitions of war and supplies.

Article X

The High Contracting Parties agree that, in the event of the discontinuance of the Panama Railroad, and of the construction or completion by the United States of a strategic highway across the Isthmus lying wholly within the Canal Zone intended primarily for serving the operation, maintenance, civil government, sanitation and protection of the Panama Canal and Canal Zone, and notwithstanding anything to the contrary in Article VI of the Convention signed November 18, 1903, the United States of America may in its discretion either prohibit or restrict the use, by busses or trucks not at the time engaged exclusively in the servicing of, or the transportation of supplies to, installations, facilities or residents of the Canal Zone, of that portion of such highway which lies between Mount Hope, Canal Zone and the intersection of such highway with the Canal Zone section of the Trans-Isthmian Highway referred to in the Trans-Isthmian Highway Convention between the United States of America and the Republic of Panama, signed March 2, 1936.

Article XI

The Republic of Panama agrees, notwithstanding the provisions of Article III of the General Treaty signed March 2, 1936, that the United States of America may extend the privilege of purchasing at post exchanges small items of personal convenience and items necessary for professional use, to military personnel of friendly third countries present in the Zone under auspices of the United States.

Article XII

The United States of America agrees that, effective December 31, 1956, there will be excluded from the privilege of making purchases in the commissaries and other sales stores in the Canal Zone as well as the privilege of making importations into the Canal Zone all those persons who are not citizens of the United States of America, except members of the Armed Forces of the United States, and who do not actually reside in the Canal Zone but who are included in the categories, of persons authorized to reside in said Zone; it being understood nevertheless that all personnel of the agencies of the United States of America will be permitted under adequate controls to purchase small articles such as meals, sweets, chewing gum, tobacco and similar articles near the sites of their jobs.

The United States of America further agrees that, effective December 31, 1956, and notwithstanding the provisions of the first paragraph of Article IV of the General Treaty signed March 2, 1936, the Government of the Republic of Panama may impose import duties and other charges upon goods destined or consigned to persons, other than citizens of the United States of America, included in class (a) in Section 2 of Article III of said Treaty, who reside or sojourn in territory under the jurisdiction of the Republic of Panama during the performance of their service with the United States of America or its agencies, even though such goods are intended for their own use and benefit.

Article XIII

The present Treaty shall be subject to ratification and the instruments of ratification shall be exchanged at Washington. It shall enter into force on the date of the exchange of the instruments of ratification.

Memorandum of Understandings Reached

In connection with the 1953—1954 negotiations between representatives of the United States of America and the Republic of Panama, which have resulted in the signature of a Treaty between the two countries, the following understandings have been reached:

On the part of the United States of America:

1. Legislation will be sought which will authorize each agency of the United States Government in the Canal Zone to conform its existing wage practices in the Zone to the following principles:

(a) The basic wage for any given grade level will be the same for any employee eligible for appointment to the position without regard to whether he is a citizen of the United States or of the Republic of Panama.

(b) In the case of an employee who is a citizen of the United States, there may be added to the base pay an increment representing an overseas differential plus an allowance for those elements, such as taxes, which operate to reduce the disposable income of such an employee as compared with an employee who is a resident of the area.

(c) The employee who is a citizen of the United States will also be eligible for greater annual leave benefits and travel allowances because of the necessity for periodic vacations in the United States for recuperation purposes and to maintain contact with the employee's home environment.

Legislation will be sought to make the Civil Service Retirement Act uniformly applicable to citizens of the United States and of the Republic of Panama employed by the Government of the United States in the Canal Zone.

The United States will afford equality of opportunity to citizens of Panama for employment in all United States Government positions in the Canal Zone for which they are qualified and in which the employment of United States citizens is not required, in the judgement of the United States, for security reasons.

The agencies of the United States Government will evaluate, classify and title all positions in the Canal Zone without regard to the nationality of the incumbent or proposed incumbent.

Citizens of Panama will be afforded opportunity to participate in such training programs as may be conducted for employees by United States agencies in the Canal Zone.

2. With reference to that part of Article V of the Treaty signed today which deals with the conveyance to the Republic of Panama free of cost of all the right, title and interest held by the United States of America or its agencies in and to certain lands and improvements situated in territory under the jurisdiction of the Republic of Panama, steps will be taken as provided in this Item.

(a) Legislation will be sought to authorize and direct the transfer

171

to the Republic of Panama of all the right, title and interest held by the United States or its agencies in or to the following real property:

1. The J. N. Vialette and Huerta de San Doval tracts in the city of Panamá and the Aspinwall tract on the Island of Taboga.

2. Las Isletas and Santa Catalina Military Reservations on the Island of Taboga. This transfer will include the cable rights-of-way which have a width of 20 feet (6.10 meters) and extend between the Ancon Cove Military Reservation and the Santa Catalina Military Reservation, and between the El Vigia Military Reservation and the Las Isletas Military Reservation.

3. The lot in Colón now reserved for consulate purposes.

4. Certain lands on the westerly shores of the city of Colón described roughly as extending from the southerly boundary of the de Lesseps area (4th Street extended) to the Colón-Canal Zone boundary and bounded on the east by the east wall of the old freight house and, below that structure, by a line 25 feet (7.622 meters) west of the center line of the most westerly railroad track. This transfer will include the certain improvements consisting of the old freight house and Colón Pier Number 3.

(b) Legislation will be sought to authorize and direct the Panama Canal Company to remove its railway terminal operations from the city of Panamá and to transfer to the Republic of Panama free of coast all of the right, title and interest of the Panama Canal Company in and to the lands known as the Panama Railroad Yard, including the improvements thereon and specifically including the railway passenger station. This action will also relieve the Government of the Republic of Panama of its obligation under Point 10 of the General Relations Agreement between the United States of America and the Republic of Panama signed May 18, 1942 to make available without cost to the Government of the United States of America a suitable new site for such terminal facilities.

(c) With respect to those areas in the city of Colón known as de Lesseps, Colón Beach and New Cristobal (with the exception of two lots in the de Lesseps area which the United States intends to use for consulate purposes), legislation will be sought to authorize and direct the gradual withdrawal from these areas and the conveyance or transfer to the the Republic of Panama free of cost of all the right, title and interest of the United States and of its agency, the Panama Canal Company, in and to the lands and improvements thereon. Under this process of gradual withdrawal the United States Government, and/or its agencies, will not be obligated to install any new structure in such areas and, as severable parts of the areas cease to be needed, the lands and improvements would be conveyed or transferred. The severability of parts of the areas depends upon a number of practical considerations including those having to do with the present obligations of the United States, with respect to the subject areas, concerning water and sewerage facilities, street cleaning and pavaing, water supply, et cetera, as stipulated in the Instrument of Transfer of Water and Sewerage Systems, executed between the Governor of the Panama Canal and the Foreign Minister of Panama on December 28, 1945.

(d) With respect to the railroad passenger station and site in the city of Colón, legislation will be sought to authorize and direct the withdrawal from such site and structure at such time as the withdrawal from the areas known as de Lesseps, Colón Beach and New Cristobal, contemplated by the next preceding subparagraph, shall have been fully completed, and the conveyance to the Republic of Panama free of cost of all the right, title and interest of the United States and of its agency, the Panama Canal Company, in and to such site and structure. However, the railroad tracks and trackage area in Colón, being required for switching purposes serving the Cristobal piers, will be retained for such purposes.

(e) All transfers or conveyances of lands and improvements contemplated by this Item, subject to legislative authorization and direction, will necessarily be made subject to any leases which may be outstanding in the respective areas. and will also contain provisions fully protecting the Government of the United States of America against any claims by lessees for damages or losses which may arise as a result of such transfers or conveyances.

(f) The transfers or conveyances contemplated by this Item, subject to legislative authorization, are in addition to the conveyance of Paitilla Point as specifically covered by Article V of the Treaty signed today, and to the transfer of real property effected by Article VI of said Treaty.

3. Articles, materials, and supplies that are mined, produced or manufactured in the Republic of Panama, when purchased for use in the Canal Zone, will be exempted from the provisions of the Buy American Act.

4. Referring to the exchange of notes dated March 2, 1936, accessory to the General Treaty between the United States of America

and the Republic of Panama signed on that date, relative to the sale to ships of goods imported into the Canal Zone by the Government of the United States of America, the United States of America agrees, effective December 31, 1956, and in benefit of Panamanian commerce, to withdraw wholly from, and thereafter to refrain from, any such sales to ships, provided that nothing in this Item shall apply—

(a) to sales to ships operated by or for the account of the Government of the United States of America,

(b) to the sale of fuel or lubricants, or

(c) to any sale or furnishing of ships stores which is incidental to the performance of ship repair operations by any agency of the Government of the United States of America.

5. Legislative authorization and the necessary appropriations will be sought for the construction of a bridge at Balboa referred to in Point 4 of the General Relations Agreement of 1942.

6. The United States of America agrees, effective December 31, 1956, to withdraw from persons employed by agencies of the Government of the United States of America in the Canal Zone who are not citizens of the United States of America and who do not actually reside in said Zone the privilege of availing themselves of services which are offered within said Zone except those which are essential to health or necessary to permit them to perform their duties.

7. It is and will continue to be the policy of the Panama Canal agencies and of the Armed Forces in the Canal Zone in making purchases of supplies, materials and equipment, so far as permitted under United States legislation, to afford to the economy of the Republic of Panama full opportunity to compete for such business.

8. In general connection with the matter of the importation of items of merchandise for resale in the sales stores in the Canal Zone, it will be the practice of the agencies concerned to acquire such items either from United States sources or Panamanian sources unless, in certain instances, it is not feasible to do so.

9. With respect to the manufacture and processing of goods for sale to or consumption by individuals, now carried on by the Panama Canal Company, it will be the policy of the United States of America to terminate such activities whenever and for so long as such goods, or particular classes thereof, are determined by the United States of America to be available in the Republic of Panama

on a continuing basis, in satisfactory qualities and quantities, and at reasonable prices. The United States of America will give prompt consideration to a request in writing on the part of the Government of Panama concerning the termination of the manufacture or processing of any goods covered in this Item as to which the Government of Panama may consider the criteria specified in this Item to have been met.

10. Prompt consideration will be given to withdrawing from the handling of commercial cargo for transshipment on Canal Zone piers so soon as Panamanian port facilities are in satisfactory operation in Colón.

11. The United States agrees that the term "auxiliary works" as used in the Treaty includes the Armed Forces of the United States of America.

On the part of the Republic of Panama:

1. The Republic of Panama will lease to the United States of America, free of all cost save for the recited consideration of one Balboa, for a period of 99 years, two parcels of land contiguous to the present United States Embassy residence site, as designated on the sketch (No. SGN—9—54, dated November 19, 1954) and accompanying descriptions prepared by the Comisón Catastral of the Republic of Panama, attached hereto.

2. The Republic of Panama assures the United States of America that the property, shown and described on the attached map (No. SGN—6—54, dated October 1954) and accompanying description prepared by the Comisión Catastral of the Republic of Panama, in front of the United States Embassy office building site and between the Bay of Panama and Avenida Balboa as it may be extended between 37th and 39th Streets, will be preserved permanently as a park and not developed for commercial or residential purposes.

3. So long as the United States of America maintains in effect those provisions of Executive Order No. 6997 of March 25, 1935 governing the importation of alcoholic beverages into the Canal Zone, the Republic of Panama will grant a reduction of 75 percent in the import duty on alcoholic beverages which are sold in Panama for importation into the Canal Zone pursuant to such Executive Order.

4. In connection with the authorization granted to the United States of America in Article VIII of the Treaty, the United States

shall have free access to the beach areas contiguous to the maneuver area described in said Article VIII for purposes connected with training and maneuvers, subject to the public use of said beach as provided under the Constitution of Panama.

The provisions of this Memorandum of Understandings Reached shall enter into force upon the exchange of instruments of ratification of the Treaty signed this day by the United States of America and the Republic of Panama.

Comparison of the Rights and Obligations of the United States Under the Terms of the Three Basic Treaties with Panama

Hay–Bunau-Varilla Treaty, 1903

Rights Received

(1) In perpetuity, to a zone of land and land under water 10 miles in width and extending 3 miles into the Caribbean sea and 3 miles into the Pacific ocean, plus certain small islands in the Bay of Panama, for the maintenance, operation, sanitation, and protection of a canal across the Isthmus of Panama.

(2) In perpetuity, the use, occupation, and control of any other lands and waters outside of the zone which may be necessary and convenient for the construction, maintenance, operation, sanitation, and protection of the canal.

(3) All the power and authority within the zone and within the limits of all auxiliary lands and waters which the United States would possess and exercise if it were sovereign, to the entire exclusion of the exercise by the Republic of Panama of any such sovereign rights, power, or authority.

(4) All the rights of the New Panama Canal Company and the Panama Railroad upon purchase of the Company's rights, privileges, properties, and concessions.

(5) At all times and at its discretion to use its police and its land and naval forces or to establish fortifications for the safety or protection of the canal, or of the ships that transit it, or the railways and auxiliary works.

(6) To use the rivers, streams, lakes, and other bodies of water in the Republic of Panama for navigation, the supply of water, or water power or other purposes as may be necessary and convenient for the construction, maintenance, operation, sanitation, and protection of the canal.

(7) A monopoly in perpetuity for the construction, maintenance, and operation of any system of communication by means of canal or railroad connecting the Caribbean Sea and the Pacific Ocean across Panamanian territory.

(8) To acquire in the cities of Panama and Colon, by purchase or by the exercise of the right of eminent domain, any lands, buildings, water rights, or other properties necessary and convenient for the construction, maintenance, operation, and protection of the canal and of any works of sanitation, such as the collection and disposition of sewage and the distribution of water in the said cities of Panama and Colon, at the discretion of the United States.

(9) To impose and collect water rates and sewerage rates which shall be sufficient to provide for the payment of interest and the amortization of the principal of the cost of such works within a period of fifty years, upon which time the system of sewers and water works shall revert to and become the properties of the cities of Panama and Colon.

(10) To enforce in perpetuity sanitary ordinances prescribed by the United States in the cities of Panama and Colon and the territories and harbors adjacent thereto in case the Republic of Panama should not be, in the judgment of the United States, able to maintain such order.

Concessions

(1) Guaranteed the independence of the Republic of Panama.

(2) Granted the right to have official dispatches of the Government of Panama transmitted over any telegraph and telephone lines established for canal purposes and used for public and private business at rates not higher than those required from officials in the service of the United States.

(3) $10 million in gold coin of the United States and an annual payment of $250,000, beginning 9 years after the date of the exchange of ratifications.

(4) Granted the Republic of Panama the right to transport over the canal its vessels and its troops and munitions of war at all times without paying charges of any kind. The exemption is extended to the auxiliary railway for the transportation of persons in the service of the Republic of Panama, or of the police force charged with the preservation of public order outside of the zone, as well as to their baggage, munitions of war, and supplies.

(5) United States assumes the costs of damages caused to owners of private property of any kind by reason of the grants contained in the treaty or by reason of the operations of the United States, its agents or employees, or by reason of the construction, maintenance, operation, sanitation, and protection of the canal or of the works of sanitation and protection provided for in the treaty.

(6) After 50 years, the system of sewers and waterworks constructed and maintained by the United States shall revert to and become the properties of the cities of Panama and Colon.

Texts of Canal Treaties That Were Initialed by Panama and U.S. in Washington

Following are the texts of the Panama Canal Treaty, the treaty on the neutrality of the Panama Canal and a protocol to the neutrality treaty that were initialed in Washington on September 6, 1977 by the United States and Panama. Also initialed, but not reproduced here, were an ''agreed minute'' to the treaty and an annex on Procedures for the Cessation of Transfer of Activities Carried Out by the Panama Canal Company.

Panama Canal Treaty

The United States of America and the Republic of Panama,

Acting in the spirit of the Joint declaration of April 3, 1964, by the Representatives of the Governments of the United States of America and the Republic of Panama, and of the Joint Statement of Principles of February 7, 1974, initialed by the Secretary of State of the United States of America and the Foreign Minister of the Republic of Panama, and

Acknowledging the Republic of Panama's sovereignty over its territory,

Have decided to terminate the prior treaties pertaining to the Panama Canal and to conclude a new treaty to serve as the basis for a new relationship between them and, accordingly, have agreed upon the following:

Article I
Abrogation of Prior Treaties and Establishment of a
New Relationship

Upon its entry into force; this Treaty terminates and supersedes:

(a) The Isthmian Canal Convention between the United States of America and the Republic of Panama, signed at Washington, November 18, 1903;

(b) the Treaty of Friendship and Cooperation signed at Washington, March 2, 1936, and the Treaty of Mutual Understanding and Cooperation and the related Memorandum of understanding reached, signed at Panama, January 25, 1955, between the United States of America and the Republic of Panama;

(c) all other treaties, conventions, agreements and exchanges of notes between the United States of America and the Republic of Panama, concerning the Panama Canal which were in force prior to the entry into force of this treaty; and

(d) provisions concerning the Panama Canal which appear in other treaties, conventions, agreements and exchanges of notes between the United States of America and the Republic of Panama which were in force prior to the entry into force of the Treaty.

[2]

In accordance with the terms of this Treaty and related agreements, the Republic of Panama, as territorial sovereign, grants to the United States of America, for the duration of this treaty, the rights necessary to regulate the transit of ships through the Panama Canal, and to manage, operate, maintain, improve, protect and defend the canal. The Republic of Panama guarantees to the United States of America the peaceful use of the land and water areas which it has been granted the rights to use for such purposes pursuant to this Treaty and related agreements.

[3]

The Republic of Panama shall participate increasingly in the management and protection and defense of the Canal, as provided in this Treaty.

179

[4]

In view of the special relationship established by this Treaty, the United States of America and the Republic of Panama shall cooperate to assure the uninterrupted and efficient operation of the Panama Canal.

Article II
Ratification, Entry Into Force, and Termination
[1]

This treaty shall be subject to ratification in accordance with the constitutional procedures of the two parties. The instruments of ratification of the Treaty shall be exchanged at Panama at the same time as the instruments of ratification of the Treaty concerning the Permanent Neutrality and Operation of the Panama Canal, signed this date, are exchanged. This treaty shall enter into force, simultaneously with the Treaty Concerning the permanent neutrality and operation of the Panama Canal, six calendar months from the date of the exchange of the instruments of ratification.

[2]

This treaty shall terminate at noon, Panama time, December 31, 1999.

Article III
Canal Operation and Management
[1]

The Republic of Panama, as territorial sovereign, grants to the United States of America the rights to manage, operate, and maintain the Panama Canal, its complementary works, installations and equipment and to provide for the orderly transit of vessels through the Panama Canal. The United States of America accepts the grant of such rights and undertakes to exercise them in accordance with this treaty and related agreements.

[2]

In carrying out the foregoing responsibilities, the United States of America may:

(a) use for the aforementioned purposes, without cost except as provided in this Treaty, the various installations and areas (including the Panama Canal) and waters, described in the agreement in the Implementation of this article, signed this date, as well as such

180

other areas and installations as are made available to the United States of America under this Treaty and related agreements, and take the measures necessary to ensure sanitation of such areas;

(b) Make such improvements and alterations to the aforesaid installations and areas as it deems appropriate, consistent with the terms of this treaty;

(c) Make and enforce all rules pertaining to the passage of vessels through the canal and other rules with respect to navigation and maritime matters, in accordance with this Treaty and related agreements. The Republic of Panama will lend its cooperation, when necessary, in the enforcement of such rules;

(d) Establish, modify, collect and retain tolls for the use of the Panama Canal, and other charges, and establish and modify methods of their assessment;

(e) regulate relations with employees of the United States Government;

(f) provide supporting services to facilitate the performance of its responsibilities under this article;

(g) issue and enforce regulations for the effective exercise of the rights and responsibilities of the United States of America under this Treaty and related agreements. The Republic of Panama will lend its cooperation, when necessary, in the enforcement of such rules; and

(h) Exercise any other right granted under this treaty, or otherwise agreed upon between the two parties.

[3]

Pursuant to the foregoing grant of rights, the United States of America shall, in accordance with the terms of this Treaty and the provisions of United States law, carry out its responsibilities by means of a United States Government agency called the Panama Canal Commission, which shall be constituted by and in conformity with the laws of the United States of America.

(a) The Panama Canal Commission shall be supervised by a Board composed of nine members, five of whom shall be nationals of the United States of America and four of whom shall be Panamanian nationals proposed by the Republic of Panama for appointment to such positions by the United States of America in a timely manner.

(b) should the Republiv of Panama request the United States of

America to remove a Panamanian national from membership on the board, the United States of America shall agree to such a request. In that event, the Republic of Panama shall propose another Panamanian national for appointment by the United States of America to such position in a timely manner. In case of removal of a Panamanian member of the Board at the initiative of the United States of America, both parties will consult in advance in order to reach agreement concerning such removal and the Republic of Panama shall propose another Panamanian national for appointment by the United States of America in his stead.

(c) the United States of America shall employ a national of the United States of America as Administrator of the Panama Canal Commission, and a Panamanian national as Deputy Administrator, through December 31, 1989. Beginning January 1, 1990, a Panamanian national shall be employed as the administrator and a national of the United States of America shall occupy the positions of Deputy Administrator. Such Panamanian nations shall be proposed to the United States of America by the Republic of Panama for appointment to such positions by the United States of America.

(d) Should the United States of America remove the Panamanian national from is position as Deputy Administrator, or Administrator, the Republic of Panama shall propose another Panamanian national for appointment to such position by the United States of America.

[4]

An illustrative description of the activities the Panama Canal Commission will perform in carrying out the responsibilities and rights of the United States of America under this Article is set forth at the Annex. Also set forth in the Annex are procedures for the discontinuance or transfer of those activities performed prior to the entry into force of this Treaty by the Panama Canal Company on the Canal Zone Government which are not to be carried out by the Panama Canal Commission.

[5]

The Panama Canal Commission shall reimburse the Republic of Panama for the costs incurred by the Republic of Panama in providing the following public services in the canal operating areas and in housing areas set forth in the agreement in implementation of Article III of this treaty and occupied by both United States and

Panamanian citizen employees of the Panama Canal Commission: police, fire protection, street maintenance, street lighting, street cleaning, traffic management and garbage collection. The Panama Canal Commission shall pay the Republic of Panama the sume of ten million United States dollars ($10,000,000) per annum for the foregoing services. It is agreed that every three years from the date that this treaty enters into force, the costs involved in furnishing said services shall be re-examined to determine whether adjustment of the annual payment should be made because of inflation and other relevant factors affecting the cost of such services.

[6]

The Republic of Panama shall be responsible for providing, in all areas comprising the former Canal Zone, services of a general jurisdictional nature such as customs and immigration, postal services, courts and licensing, in accordance with this treaty and related agreements.

[7]

The United States of America and the Republic of Panama shall establish a Panama Canal Consultative Committee, composed of an equal number of high-level representatives of the United States of America and the Republic of Panama, and which may appoint such subcommittees as it may deem appropriate. This committee shall advise the United States of America and the Republiv of Panama on matters of policy affecting the Canal's operation. In view of both Parties' special interest in the continuity and efficiency of the Canal operation in the future, the Committee shall advise on matters such as general tolls policy, employment and training policies to increase the participation of Panamanian nations in the operation of the Canal, and international policies on matters concerning the Canal. The Committee's recommendations shall be transmitted to the two governments, which shall give such recommendations full consideration in the formulation of such policy decisions.

[8]

In addition to the participation of Panamanian nationals at high management levels of the Panama Canal Commission, as provided for in paragraph 3 of this Article, there shall be growing participation of Panamanian nations at all other levels and areas of employment in the aforesaid commission, with the objective of preparing, in an orderly and efficient fashion, for the assumption by the Republic of Panama of full responsibility for the management, operation and maintenance of the Canal upon the termination of this Treaty.

[9]

The use of the areas, waters and installations with respect to which the United States of America is granted rights pursuant to this Article, and the rights and legal status of United States Government agencies and employees operating in the Republic of Panama pursuant to this article, shall be governed by the agreement in implementation of this Article, signed this date.

[10]

Upon entry into force of this Treaty, the United States Government agencies known as the Panama Canal Company and the Canal Zone Government shall cease to operate within the territory of the Republic of Panama that formerly constituted the Canal Zone.

Article IV
Protection and Defense

[1]

The United States of America and the Republic of Panama. Each party shall act, in accordance with its constitutional processes, to meet the danger resulting from an armed attack or other actions which threaten the security of the Panama Canal or of ships transiting it.

[2]

For the duration of this treaty, the United States of America shall have the primary responsibility to protect and defend the canal. The rights of the United States of America to station, train and move military forces within the Republic of Panama are described in the agreement in implementation of this article, signed this date. The use of areas and installations and the legal status of the armed forces of the United States of America in the Republic of Panama shall be governed by the aforesaid Agreement.

[3]

In order to facilitate the participation and cooperation and defense of the Canal, the United States of America and the Republic of Panama shall establish a combined Board comprised of an equal number of senior military representatives of each party. These representatives shall be charged by their respective governments with consulting and cooperating on all matters pertaining to the protection and defense of the Canal, and with planning for actions to be taken in concert for that purpose. Such combined protection and defense arrangements shall not inhibit the identity or lines of authority of the armed forces of the United States of America or the Republic of Panama The combined board shall provide for coordination and cooperation concerning such matters as:

(a) The preparation of contingency plans for the protection and defense of the Canal based upon the cooperative efforts of the armed forces of both parties;

(b) the planning and conduct of combined military exercises: and

(c) the conduct of United States and Panamanian military operations with respect to the protection and defense of the canal.

[4]

The combined Board shall, at five-year intervals throughout the duration of the Treaty, review the resources being made available by the two parties for the protection and defense of the Canal. Also, the combined board shall make appropriate recommendations to the two governmentsrespecting projected requirements, the efficient utilization of available resources of the two parties, and other matters of mutual interest with respect to the protection and defense of the Canal.

[5]

To the extent possible consistent with its primary responsibility for the protection and defense of the Panama Canal, the United States of America will endeavor to maintain its armed forces in the Republic of Panama in normal times at a level not in excess of that of the armed forces of the United States of America in the territory of the former Canal Zone immediately prior to the entry into force of this treaty.

Article V
Principle of Nonintervention

Employees of the Panama Canal Commission, their dependents and designated contractors of the Panama Canal Commission, who are nationals of the United States of America, shall respect the laws of the Republic of Panama and shall abstain from any activity incompatible with the spirit of the treaty. Accordingly, they shall abstain from any political activity in the Republic of Panama as well as from any intervention in the internal affairs of the Republic of Panama. The United States of America shall take all measures within its authority to ensure that the provisions of this article are fulfilled.

Article VI
Protection of the Environment
[1]

The United States of America and the Republic of Panama commit themselves to implement this Treaty in a manner consistent with the protection of the natural environment of the Republic of Panama. To this end, they shall consult and cooperate with each other in all appropriate ways to ensure that they shall give due regard to the protection and conservation of the environment.

[2]

A Joint Commission on the Environment shall be established with equal representation from the United States of America and the Republic of Panama, which shall periodically review the implementation of this treaty and shall recommend as appropriate to the two governments ways to avoid or should this not be possible, to mitigate the adverse environmental impacts which might result from their respective actions pursuant to the treaty.

[3]

The United States of America and the Republic of Panama shall furnish the Joint Commission on the Environment complete information on any action taken in accordance with this treaty which, in the judgment of both, might have a significant effect on the environment. Such information shall be made available to the Commission as far in advance of the contemplated action as possible to facilitate the study by the Commission of any potential environmental problems and to allow for consideration of the recommendation of the Commission before the contemplated action is carried out.

Article VII
Flags
[1]

The entire territory of the Republic of Panama, including the areas the use of which the Republic of Panama makes available to the United States of America pursuant to this treaty and related agreements, shall be under the flag of the Republic of Panama and consequently such flag always shall occupy the posiiton of honor.

[2]

The flag of the United States of America may be displayed, together with the flag of the Republic of Panama, at the headquarters of the Panama Canal Commission, at the site of the combined board, and as provided in the agreement in implementation of Article IV of this treaty.

[3]

The flag of the United States of America also may be displayed at other places and on some occasions, as agreed by both parties.

Article VIII
Privileges and Immunities

[1]

The institution owned or used by the agencies or instrumentalities of the United States of America operating in the Republic of Panama pursuant to this treaty and related agreements, and their official archives and documents shall be inviolable. The two parties shall agree on procedures to be followed in the conduct of any criminal investigation at such locations by the Republiv of Panama.

[2]

Agencies and instrumentalities of the Government of the United States of America operating in1 the Republic of Panama pursuant to this Treaty and related agreements shall be immune from the jurisdiction of the Republic of Panama.

[3]

In addition to such other privileges and immunities as are afforded to employees of the United States Government and their dependents pursuant to this treaty, the United States of America may designate up to twenty officials of the Panama Canal Commission who, along with their dependents, shall enjoy the privileges and immunities accorded to diplomatic agents and their dependents under international law and practice. The United States of America shall furnish to the Republic of Panama a list of the names of said officials and their dependents, identifying the pisitions they occupy in the Government of the United States of America, and shall keep such list current at all times.

Article IX
Applicable Laws and Law Enforcement
[1]

In accordance with the provisions of this treaty and related agreements, the law of the Republic of Panama shall apply in the areas made available for the use of the United States of America pursuant to this Treaty. The law of the Republic of Panama shall be applied to matters or events which occurred in the former canal zone prior to the entry into force of this treaty only to the extent specifically provided in prior treaties and agreements.

[2]

Natural or juridical persons who, on the date of entry into force of this treaty, are engaged in business or nonprofit activities at locations in the former canal zone may continue such under the same terms and conditions prevailing prior to the entry into force of this treaty for a thirty-month transition period from its entry into force. The Republic of Panama shall maintain the same operating conditions as those applicable o the aforementioned enterprises prior to the entry into force of this treaty in order that they may receive licenses to do business in the Republic of Panama subject to their compliance with the requirements of its law. Thereafter, such persons shall receive the same treatment under the law of the Republic of Panama as similar enterprises already established in the rest of the territory of the Republic of Panama without discrimination.

[3]

The rights of ownership, as recognized by the United States of America, enjoyed by natural or juridical private persons in buildings and other improvements to real property located in the former Canal Zone shall be recognized by the Republic of Panama in conformity with its laws.

[4]

With respect to buildings and other improvements to real property located in the Canal operating areas housing areas or other areas subject to the licensing procedure established in Article IV of the agreement in implementation of Article III of this treaty, the owners shall be authorized to continue using the land upon which their property is located in accordance with the procedures established in that article.

[5]

With respect to buildings and other improvements to real property located in areas of the former canal zone to which the aforesaid licensing procedure is not applicable, or may cease to be applicable during the lifetime or upon termination of this treaty, the owners may continue to use the land upon which their property is located, subject to the payment of a reasonable charge to the Repubic of Panama. Should the Republic of Panama decide to sell such land, the owners of the buildings or other improvements located thereon shall be offered a first option to purchase such land at a reasonable cost. In the case of nonprofit enterprises, such as churches and fraternal organizations, the cost of purchase shall be nominal in accordance with the prevailing practice in the rest of the territory of the Republic of Panama.

[6]

If any of the aforementioned persons are required by the Republic of Panama to discontinue their activities or vacate their property for public purposes, they shall be compensated at fair market value by the Republic of Panama.

[7]

The provisions of paragraphs 2-6 above shall apply to natural or juridical persons who have been engaged in business or nonprofit activities at locations in the former Canal Zone for at least six months prior to the date of signature of this Treaty.

[8]

The Republic of Panama shall not issue, adopt or enforce any law, decree, regulation, or international agreement or take any other action which purports to regulate or would otherwise interfere with the exercise on the part of the United States of America of any right granted under this Treaty or related agreements.

[9]

Vessles transiting the Canal, and cargo, passengers and crews carried on such vessels shall be exempt from any taxes, fees, or other charges by the Republic of Panama. However, in the event such vessels call at a Panamanian port, they may be assessed charges incident thereto, such as charges for services provided to the vessel. The Republic of Panama may also require the passengers and crew disembarking from such vessels to pay such taxes, fees and charges as are established under Panamanian law for persons entering its territory. Such taxes, fees and charges shall be assessed on a nondiscriminatory basis.

[10]

The United States of America and the Republic of Panama will cooperate in taking such steps as may from time to time be necessary to guarantee the security of the Panama Canal Commission, its property, its employees and their dependents, and their property, the Forces of the United States of America and the members thereof, the civilian component of the United States Forces, the dependents of members of the Forces and the civilian component, and their property, and the contractors of the Panama Canal Commission and of the United States Forces, their dependents, and their property. The Republic of Panama will seek from its Legislative Branch such legislation as may be needed to carry out the foregoing purposes and to punish any offenders.

[11]

The Parties shall conclude an agreement whereby nationals of either State, who are sentenced by the courts of the other State, and who are not domiciled therein, may elect to serve their sentences in their State of nationality.

Article X
Employment With the Panama Canal Commission

[1]

In exercising its rights and fulfilling its responsibilities as the employer, the United States of America shall establish employment and labor regulations which shall contain the terms, conditions and prerequisites for all categories of employees of the Panama Canal Commission. These regulations shall be provided to the Republic of Panama prior to their entry into force.

[2]

(a) The regulations shall establish a system of preference when hiring employees, for Panamanian applicants possessing the skills and qualifications required for employment by the Panama Canal Commission. The United States of America shall endeavor to ensure that the number of Panamanian nationals employed by the Panama Canal Commission in relation to the total number of its employees will conform to the proportion established for foreign

190

enterprises under the law of the Republic of Panama.

(b) The terms and conditions of employment to be established will in general be no less favorable to persons already employed by the Panama Canal Company or Canal Zone Government prior to the entry into force of this Treaty, than those in effect immediately prior to that date.

[3]

(a) The United States of America shall establish an employment policy for the Panama Canal Commission that shall generally limit the recruitment of personnel outside the Republic of Panama to persons possessing requisite skills and qualifications which are not available in the Republic of Panama.

(b) The United States of America will establish training programs for Panamanaian employees and apprentices in order to increase the number of Panamanian nationals qualified to assume positions with the Panama Canal Commission, as positions become available.

(c) Within five years from the entry into force of this Treaty, the number of United States nationals employed by the Panama Canal Commission who were previously employed by the Panama Canal Company shall be at least twenty percent less than the total number of United States nationals working for he Ptanama Canal Company immediately prior to the entry into force of this Treaty.

(d) The United States of America shall periodically inform the Republic of Panama, through the Coordinating Committee, established pursuant to the Agreement in Implementation of Article III of this Treaty, of available positions within the Panama Canal Commission. The Republic of Panama shall similarly provide the United States of America any information it may have as to the availability of Panamanian nationals claiming to have skills and qualifications that might be required by the Panama Canal Commission, in order that the United States of American may take this information into account.

[4]

The United States of America will establish qualification standards for skills, training and experience required by the Panama Canal Commission. In establishing such standards, to the extent they include a requirement for a professional license, the United States of America, without prejudice to its right to require addi-

191

tional professional skills and qualifications, shall recognize the professional licences issues by the Republic of Panama.

[5]

The United States of America shall establish a policy for the periodic rotation, at a maximum of every five years, of United States citizen employees and other non-Panamanian employees, hired after the entry into force of this Treaty. It is recognized that certain exceptions to the said policy of rotation may be made for sound administrative reasons, such as in the case of employees holding positions requiring certain nontransferable or non-recruitable skills.

[6]

With regard to wages and fringe benefits, there shall be no discrimination on the basis of nationality, sex, or race. Payments by the Panama Canal Commission of additional remuneration, or the provision of other benefits, such as home leave benefits, to United States nationals employed prior to entry into force of this Treaty, or to persons of any nationality, including Panamanian nationals who are thereafter recruited outside of the Republic of Panama and who change their place of residence, shall not be considered to be discrimination for the purpose of this paragraph.

[7]

Persons employed by the Panama Canal Company or Canal Zone Government prior to the entry into force of this Treaty, who are displaced from their employment as a result of the discontinuance by the United States of America of certain activities pursuant to this Treaty, will be placed by the United States of America, to the maximum extent feasible, in other appropriate jobs with the Government of the United States in accordance with United States Civil Service regulations. For such persons who are not United States nationals, placement efforts will be confined to United States Government activities located within the Republic of Panama. Likewise, persons previously employed in activities for which the Republic of Panama assumes responsibility as a result of this Treaty will be continued in their employment to the maximum extent feasible by the Republic of Panama. The Republic of Panama shall, to the maximum extent feasible, ensure that the terms and conditions of employment applicable to personnel employed in the activities for which it assumes responsibility are no less favorable than those in effect immediately prior to the entry into force of this Treaty. Non-United States nationals employed by the Panama Canal Company or Canal Zone Government prior to the entry into force of this Treaty who are involuntarily separated from their positions because of the discontinuance of an activity by reason of this Treaty, who are not entitled to an immediate annuity under the United States Civil Service Retirement System, and for whom continued employment in the Republic of Panama by the Government of the United States of America is not practicable, will be provided special job placement assistance by the Republic of Panama for employment in positions for which they may be qualified by experience and training.

[8]

The Parties agree to establish a system whereby the Panama Canal Commission may, if deemed muturally convenient or desirable by the two Parties, assign certain employees of the Panama Canal Commission, for a limited period of time, to assist in the operation of activities transferred to the responsibility of the Republic of Panama as a result of this Treaty or related agreements. The salaries and other costs of employment of any such persons assigned to provide such assistance shall be reimbursed to the United States of American by the Republic of Panama.

[9]

(a) The right of employees to negotiate collective contracts with the Panama Canal Commission is recognized. Labor relations with employees of the Panama Canal Commission shall be conducted in accordance with forms of collective bargaining established by the United States of America after consultation with employee unions.

(b) Employee unions shall have the right to affiliate with international labor organizations.

[10]

The United States of America will provide an appropriate early optional retirement program for all persons employed by the Panama Canal Company or Canal Zone Government immediately prior to the entry into force of this Treaty. In this regard, taking into account the unique circumstances created by the provisions of this Treaty, including its duration, and their effect upon such employees, the United States of America shall, with respect to them:

( )determine that conditions exist which invoke applicable United

States law permitting early requirement annuities and apply such law for a substantial period of the duration of the Treaty;

(b) seek special legislation to provide more liberal entitlement to, and calculation of, retirement annuities than is currently provided for by law.

Article XI
Provisions for the Transition Period
[1]

The Republic of Panama shall reassume plenary jurisdiction over the former Canal Zone upon entry into force of this treaty and in accordance with its terms. In order to provide for an orderly transition to the full application of the jurisdictional arrangements established by this Treaty and related agreements, the provisions of this Article shall become applicable upon the date this Treaty enters into force, and shall remain in effect for thirty calendar months. The authority granted in this Article to the United States of America for this transition period shall supplement, and is not intended to limit, the full application and effect of the rights and authority granted to the United States of America elsewhere in this treaty and in related agreements.

[2]

During this transition period, the criminal and civil laws of the United States of America shall apply concurrently with those of the Republic of Panama in certain of the areas and installations made available for the use of the United States of america pursuant to this treaty, in accordance with the following provisions:

(a) The Republic of Panama permits the authorities of the United States of America to have the primary right to exercise criminal jurisdiction over United States citizen employees of the Panama Canal Commission and their dependents, and members of the United States forces and civilian component and their dependents, in the following cases:

(i) for any offense committed during the transition period within such areas and installations, and

(ii) for any offense committed prior to that period in the former Canal Zone.

The Republic of Panama shall have the primary right to exercise jurisdiction over all other offenses committed by such persons, except as otherwise provided in this treaty and related agreements or as may be otherwise agreed.

(b) either party may waive its primary right to exercise jurisdiction in a specific case or category of cases.

[3]

The United States of America shall retain the right to exercise jurisdiction in criminal cases relating to offenses committed prior to the entry into force of this treaty in violation of the laws applicable in the former Canal Zone.

[4]

For the transition period, the United States of America shall retain police authority and maintain a police force in the aforementioned areas and installations. In such areas, the police authorities of the United States of America may take into custody any person not subject to their primary applicable laws or regulations, and shall promptly transfer custody to the police authorities of the Republic of Panama. The United States of America and the Republic of Panama shall establish joint police patrols in agreed areas. Any arrests conducted by a joint patrol shall the responsibility of the patrol member or members representing the Party having primary jurisdiction over the person or persons arrested.

[5]

The courts of the United States of America and related personnel, functioning in the former Canal Zone immediately prior to the entry into force of this Treaty, may continue to function during the transition period for the judicial enforcement of the jurisdiction to be exercised by the United States of America in accordance with this Article.

[6]

In civil cases the civilian courts of the United States of America in the Republic of Panama shall have no jurisdiction over new cases of a private civil nature, but shall retail full jurisdiction during the transition period to dispose of any civil cases, including admiralty cases, already instituted and pending before the courts prior to the entry into force of this Treaty.

[7]

The laws, regulations, and administrative authority of the United States of America applicable in the former Canal Zone immediately prior to the entry info force of this Treaty shall, to the extent not inconsistent with this treaty, and related agreements, continue in force for the purpose of the exercise by the United States of America of law enforcement and judicial jurisdiction only during the transition period. The United States of America may amend, repeal or otherwise change such laws, regulations and administrative authority. The two parties shall consult concerning procedural and substantive matters relative to the implementation of this Article, including the disposition of cases pending at the end of the transition period and in this respect, may enter into appropriate agreements by an exchange of notes or other instruments.

[8]

During this transition period, the United States of America may continue to incarcerate individuals in the areas and installations made available for the use of the United States of America by the Republic of Panama pursuant to this Treaty and related agreements, or to transfer them to penal facilities in the United States of America to serve their sentences.

Article XII
A Sea-Level Canal or a Third Lane of Locks
[1]

The United States of America and the Republic of Panama recognize that a sea-level canal may be important for international navigation in the future. Consequently, during the duration of this Treaty, both Parties commit themselves to study jointly the feasibility xf a sea-level canal in the Republic of Panama, and in the event they determine that such a waterway is necessary, they shall negotiate terms, agreeable to both Parties, for its construction.

[2]

The United States of America and the Republic of Panama agree on the following:

(a) No new interoceanic canal shall be constructed in the territory of the Republic of Panama during the duration of this Treaty, except in accordance with the provisions of this Treaty, or as the two Parties may otherwise agree; and

(b) During the duration of this Treaty, the United States of America shall not negotiate with third states for the right to construct an interoceanic canal on any other route in the Western Hemisphere, except as the two Parties may otherwise agree.

The Republic of Panama grants to the United States of America the right to add a third lane of locks to the existing Panama Canal. This right may be exercised at any time during the duration of this Treaty, provided that the United States of America has delivered to the Republic of Panama copies of the plans for such construction.

[4]

In the event the United States of America exercises the right granted in paragraph 3 above, it may use for that purpose, in addition to the areas otherwise made available to the United states of America pursuant to this Treaty, such other areas as the two Parties may agree upon. The terms and conditions applicable to Canal operating areas made available by the Republic of Panama for the use of the United States of America pursuant to Article III of this Treaty shall apply in a similar manner to such additional areas.

[5]

In the construction of the aforesaid works, the United States of America shall not use nuclear excavation techniques without the previous consent of the Republic of Panama.

Article XIII
Property Transfer and Economic Participation by the Republic of Panama

[1]

Upon termination of this Treaty, the Republic of Panama shall assume total responsibility for the management, operation, and maintenance of the Panama Canal, which shall be turned over in operating condition and free of liens and debts, except as the two Parties may otherwise agree.

[2]

The United States of America transfers, without charge, to the Republic of Panama all right, title and interest the United States of America may have with respect to all real property, including non-removable improvements thereon, as set forth below:

(a) Upon the entry into force of this Treaty, the Panama Railroad and such property that was located in the former Canal Zone but that is not within the land and water areas the use of which is made available to the United States of America pursuant to this Treaty. However, it is agreed that the transfer on such date shall not include buildings and other facilities, except housing, the use of which is retained by the United States of America pursuant to this Teaty and related agreemetns, outside such areas;

(b) Such pierty located in an area or a portion thereof at such time as the use by the United States of America of such area or portion thereof ceases pursuant to agreement between the two Parties.

(c) Housing units made available for occupancy by members of the Armed Forces of the Republic of Panama in accordance with paragraph 5(b) of Annex B to the Agreement in Implementation of Article IV of this Treaty at such time as such units are made available to the Republic of Panama.

(d) Upon termination of this Treaty, all real property, and non-removable improvements that were used by the United States of America for the purposes of this Treaty and related agreements,

And equipment related to the management, operation and maintenance of the Canal remaining in the Republic of Panama.

[3]

The Republic of Panama agrees to hold the United States of America harmless with respect to any claims which may be made by third parties relating to rights, title and interest in such property.

[4]

The Republic of Panama shall receive, in addition, from the Panama Canal Commission a just and equitable return on the national resources which it has dedicated to the efficient management, operation, maintenance, protection and defense of the Panama Canal, in accordance with the following:

(a) An annual amount to be paid out of Canal operating revenues computed at a rate of thirty-hundredths of a United States dollar ($0.30) per Panama Canl net ton, or its equivalency, for each vessel transiting the Canal, after the entry into force of this Treaty, for which totls are charged. The rate of thirty-hundredths of a United states dollar ($0.30) per Panama Canl net ton, or its equivalency, will be adjusted to reflect changes in the United States wholesale price index for total manufactured goods during biennial periods. The first adjustment shall take place five years after entryinto force of this Treaty, taking into account the changes that occurred in such price index during the preceding two years. Thereafter successive adjustments shall take place at the end of each biennial period.

If the United States of America should decide that another indexing method is preferable, such method shall be proposed to the Republic of Panama and applied if mutually agreed.

(b) A fixed annuity of ten million United States dollars ($10,000,000) to be paid out of Canal operating revenues. This amount shall constitute a fixed expense of the Panama Canal Commission.

(c) An annual amount of up to ten million United States dollars ($10,000,000) per year, to be paid out of Canal operating revenues to the extent that such revenues exceed expenditures of the Panama Canal Commission including amounts paid pursuant to this Treaty. In the event Canal operating revenues in any year do not produce a surplus sufficient to cover this payment, the unpaid balance shall be paid from operating surpluses in future years in a manner to be mutually agreed.

Article XIV
Settlement of Disputes

In the event that any question should arise between the Parties concerning the interpretation of this Treaty or related agreements, they shall make every effort to resolve the matter through consultation in the appropriate committees established pursuant to this Treaty and related agreements, or, if appropriate, through diplomatic channels. In the event the Parties are unable to resolve a particular matter through such means, they may, in appropriate cases, agree to submit the matter to conciliation, mediation, arbitration, or such other procedure for the peaceful settlement of the dispute as they may mutually deem appropriate.

Highlights of Pact

Duration—The treaty will expire Dec. 31, 1999.

Defense—The United States will have primary responsibility for the canal's defense for the duration of the treaty. Panama will participate and will take over defense when the treaty expires. The United States can decide on its own whether to dispose of the 14 American bases in the zone or withdraw the 9,000 United States troops there.

Economic Cooperation—The United States will pay Panama $40 million to $50 million annually from revenue from canal tolls, an additional $10 million annually for the canal's operation and $10 million more if canal revenues permit. Panama will also receive $50 million in military assistance over the next 10 years. Additional aid programs involving almost $300 million in loans and loan guarantees are being developed.

Treaty Concerning the Permanent Neutrality and Operation of the Panama Canal

The United States of America and the Republic of Panama have agreed upon the following:

Article I

The Republic of Panama declares that the Canal, as an international transit waterway, shall be permanently neutral in accordance with the regime established in this Treaty. The same regime of neutrality shall apply to any other international waterway that may be built either partially or wholly in the territory of the Republic of Panama.

Article II

The Republic of Panama declares the neutrality of the canal in order that both in time of peace and in time of war it shall remain secure and open to peaceful transit by the vessels of all nations on terms of entire equality, so that there will be no discrimination against any nation, or its citizens or subjects, concerning the conditions or charges of transit, or for any other reason, and so that the canal, and therefore the Isthmus of Panama, shall not be the target of reprisals in any armed conflict between other nations of the world. The foregoing shall be subject to the following requirements:

(a) Payment of tolls and other charges for transit and other charges for transit and ancillary services, provided they have been fixed in conformity with the provisions of Article III (c);

(b) Compliance with applicable rules and regulations, provided such rules and regulations are applied in conformity with the provisions of Article III (c);

(c) the requirement that transiting vessels commit no acts of hostility while in the canal, and

(d) such other conditions and restrictions as are established by this treaty.

Article III
[1]

For purposes of the security, efficiency and proper maintenance of the Canal the following rules shall apply:

(a) the canal shall be operated efficiently in accordance with conditions of transit through the Canal, and rules and regulations that shall be just, equitable and reasonable, and limited to those necessary for safe navigation and efficient, sanitary operation of the canal;

(b) ancillary services necessary for transit through the canal shall be provided;

(c) tolls and other charges for transit and ancillary services shall be just, reasonable, equitable and consistent with the principles of international law;

(d) as a pre-condition of transit, vessels may be required to establish clearly the financial responsibility and guarantees for payment of reasonable and adequate indemnification, consistent with international practice and standards, for damages resulting from acts or ommissions of such vessels when passing through the canal. In the case of vessels owned or operated by a Sate or for which it has acknowledged responsibility, a certification by that State that it shall observe its obligations under international law to pay for damages resulting from the act or omission of such vessels when passing through the Canal shall be deemed sufficient to establish such financial responsibility;

(e) vessels of war and auxiliary vessels of all nations shall at all times be entitled to transit the canal, irrespective of their internal operation, means of propulsion, origin, destination or armament, without being subjected, as a condition of transit, to inspection, search or surveillance. However, such vessels may be required to certify that they have complied with all applicable health, sanitation and quarantine regulations. In addition, such vessels shall be entitled to refuse to disclose their internal operation, origin, armament, cargo or destination. However, auxiliary vessels may be required to present written assurances, certified by an official at a high level of the Government of the State requesting the exemption, that they are owned or operated by that Government and in this case are being used only on Government noncommercial service.

[2]

For the purposes of this treaty, the terms "Canal," "vessel of war," "auxiliary vessel," "internal operation," "armament" and "inspection" shall have the meanings assigned them in Annex A to this treaty.

Article IV

The United States of America and the Republic of Panama agree to maintain the regime of neutrality established in this Treaty, which shall be maintained in order that the Canal shall remain permanently neutral, notwithstanding the termination of any other treaties entered into by the two contracting Parties.

Article V

After the termination of the Panama Canal Treaty, only the Republic of Panama shall operate the canal and maintain military forces, defense sites and military installations within its national territory.

Article VI

[1]

In recognition of the important contributions of the United States of America and of the Republic of Panama to the construction, operation, mantenance, and protection and defense of the Canal, vessels of war and auxiliary vessels of those nations shall, notwithstanding any other provisions of this treaty, be entitled to transit the Canal irrespective of their internal operation, means of propulsion, origin, destination, armament or cargo carried. Such vessels of war and auxiliary vessels will be entitled to transit the canal expeditiously.

[2]

The United States of America, so long as it has responsibility for the operation of the canal, may continue to provide the Republic of Colombia toll-free transit through the canal for its troops, vessels and materials of war. Thereafter the Republic of Panama may provide the Republic of Columbia and the Republic of Costa Rica with

202

the right of toll-free transit.

Article VII
[1]

The United States of America and the Republic of Panama shall jointly sponsor a resolution in the Organization of American States opening to accession by all States of the world the protocol to this treaty whereby all the signatories will adhere to the objectives of this treaty, agreeing to respect the regime of neutrality set forth herein.

[2]

The Organization of American States shall act as the depositary for this treaty and related instruments.

Article VIII

This treaty shall be subject to ratification in accordance with the constitutional procedures of the two Parties. The instruments of ratification of this Treaty shall be exchanged at Panama at the same time as the instruments of ratification of the Panama Canal Treaty, signed this date, are exchanged. This treaty shall enter into force, simulataneously with the Panama Canal Treaty, six calendar months from the date of the exchange of the instruments of ratification.

Done at Washington this 7th day of September, 1977, in duplicate, in the English and Spanish languages, both texts being equally authentic.

Annex
[1]

"Canal" includes the existing Panama Canal, the entrances thereto, and the territorial seas of the Republic of Panama adjacent thereto, as defined on the map annexed hereto (Annex B), and any other inter-oceanic waterway in which the United States of America is a participant or in which the United States of America has participated in connection with the construction or fininancing, that may be operated wholly or partially within the territory of the Republic if Panama, the entrances thereto and the territorial seas adjacent thereto.

"Vessel of war" means a ship belonging to the naval forces of a State, and bearing the external marks distinguishing warships of its nationality, under the command of an officer duly commissioned by the Government and whose name appears in the Navy List, and manned by a crew which is under regular naval discipline.

[3]

"Auxiliary vessel" means any ship, not a vessel of war, that is owned or operated by a State and used, for the time being, exclusively on Government noncommercial service.

[4]

"Internal operation" encompasses all machinery and propulsion systems, as well as the management and control of the vessel, including its crew. It does not include the measures necessary to transit vessels under the control of pilots while such vessels are in the canal.

[5]

"Armament" means arms, ammunitions, implements of war and other equipment of a vessel which possesses characteristics appropriate for use for warlike purposes.

[6]

"Inspection" includes on-board examination of vessel structure, cargo, armament and internal operation. It does not include those measures strictly necessary for admeasurement, nor those measures strictly necessary to assure safe, sanitary transit and navigation, including examination of deck and visual navigation equipment, nor in the case of live cargoes, such as cattle or other livestock, that may carry communicable diseases, those measures necessary to assure that health and sanitation requirements are satisfied.

Protocol to Treaty Concerning the Permanent Neutrality and Operation of the Panama Canal

Article I

Whereas the maintenance of the neutrality of the Panama Canl is important not only to the commerce and security of the United States of America and the Republic of Panama, but to the peace and security of the Western Hemisphere and to the interests of world commerce as well;

Whereas the regime of neutrality which the United states of America and the Republic of Panama have agreed to maintain will ensure permanent access to the Canal by vessels of all nations on the basis of entire equality;

Whereas the said regime of effective neutrality shall constitute the best protection for the Canal and shall ensure the absence of any hostile act against it;

The Contracting Parties to this Protocol have agreed upon the following:

The Contracting Parties hereby acknowledge the regime of permanent neutrality for the Canal established in the Treaty Concerning the Permanent Neutrality and Operation of the Panama Canal and associate themselves with its objectives.

Article II

The Contracting Parties agree to observe and respect the regime of permanent neutrality of the Canal in time of war as in time of peace, and to ensure that vessels of their registry strictly observe the applicable rules.

Article III

This Protocol shall be open to accession by all States of the world, and shall enter into force for each State at the time of deposit of its instrument of accession with the Secretary General of the Organization of American States.

Statement of Understanding

Following is the text of the statement of understanding agreed to by President Carter and Panamanian leader Brig. Gen. Omar Torrijos Herrera following their meeting at the White House on Oct. 14, 1977:

Under the Treaty Concerning the Permanent Neutrality and Operation of the Panama Canal (the Neutrality Treaty), Panama and the United States have the responsibility to assure that the Panama Canal will remain open and secure to ships of all nations. The correct interpretation of this principle is that each of the two countries shall, in accordance with their respective constitutional processes, defend the Canal against any threat to the regime of neutrality, and consequently shall have the right to act against any aggression or threat directed against the Canal or against the peaceful transit of vessels through the Canal.

This does not mean, nor shall it be interpreted as a right of intervention of the United States in the internal affairs of Panama. Any United States action will be directed at insuring that the Canal will remain open, secure and accessible, and it shall never be directed against the territorial integrity or political independence of Panama.

The Neutrality Treaty provides that the vessels of war and auxiliary vessels of the United States and Panama will be entitled to transit the Canal expeditiously. This is intended, and it shall so be interpreted, to assure the transit of such vessels through the Canal as quickly as possible, without any impediment, with expedited treatment, and in case of need or emergency, to go to the head of the line of vessels in order to transit the Canal rapidly.

Appendix 2:
A Constitutional Scholar Looks at the Treaties
Congressional Record, November 4, 1977

Testimony of Professor Raoul Berger Before Subcommittee on Separation of Powers of Judiciary Committee on Constitutional Issues Concerning Panama Canal Treaties.

Mr. Allen, Mr. President, on November 3, 1977, the Subcommittee on Separation of Powers of the Committee on the Judiciary convened to receive the testimony of Raoul Berger in connection with the subcommittee's investigation of certain constitutional issues associated with the Panama Canal Treaties. Professor Berger is the foremost legal authority on the U.S. Constitution and is the author of the recently published best seller, "Government by Judiciary." He is best remembered for his work, "Executive Privilege," which had tremendous impact on the course of history during the Watergate controversy.

His testimony before the subcommittee yesterday was highly significant in that he stated very forcefully the view that no property belonging to the United States in the Isthmus of Panama can be transferred to Panama by treaty alone, but that authorization by the Congress is specifically required by article IV, section 3(2) of the U.S. Constitution. Professor Berger expressed the further opinion that any treaty purporting to transfer such property, even if ratified by the Senate, would be void.

Inasmuch as the subcommittee has received overwhelming requests for copies of Professor Berger's testimony, I ask unanimous consent that his statement be printed in the *Record,* so that it will be easily available to Members of Congress and interested members of the public.

There being no objection, the testimony was ordered to be printed in the *Record,* as follows:

207

Statement by Professor Raoul Berger Before the Senate Subcommittee on Separation of Powers Hearings on the Panama Canal Treaties

You have invited me to comment on the relation between the Article IV, Section 3(2) power of Congress to dispose of property of the United States and the treaty power, in light of the statements respecting the relation by Herbert J. Hansell, Legal Advisor, Department of State[1] and Ralph E. Erickson, Deputy Assistant Attorney General.[2] Although I am in favor of the Panama Canal Treaty, I share your solicitude for the preservation of constitutional boundaries and your concern lest the function committed to Congress by diminished. I have long held the conviction that all agents of the United States, be they Justices, members of Congress, or the President, must respect these boundaries. No agent of the people may overleap the bounds of delegated power. That is the essence of constitutional government and of our democratic system.

Long experience has led me to be skeptical of arguments by representatives of the Executive branch when they testify with respect to a dispute between Congress and the President, for they are then merely attorneys for a client, the President. It was for this reason that Justice Jackson dismissed his own prior statements in the capacity of Attorney General as mere advocacy, saying, a "judge cannot acept self-serving press statements for one of the interested parties as authority in answering a constitutional question, even if the advocate was himself."[3] The Hansell-Erickson testimony did not serve to diminish my skepticism.

The effect of these hearings ranges beyond the Panama treaty. The Panama cession will constitute a landmark which, should the State Department prevail, will be cited down the years for "concurrent jurisdiction" of the President in the disposition of United States property. Acquiescence in such claims spells progressive attrition of Congressional powers; it emboldens the Executive to make ever more extravagent claims. I would remind you that Congressional acquiescence encourages solo Presidential adventures such as plunged us into the Korean and Vietnam wars. Congressional apathy fostered the expansion of executive secrecy. Then as now the State Department invoked flimsy "precedents," for example, the pursuit of cattle rustlers across the Mexican border, to justify presidential launching of a full-scale war.[4] If Congress slumbers in the face of such claims it may awaken the Samson shorn of his locks.

Earlier judicial statements that this or the other executive practice has been sealed by long-continued Congressional acquiescence[5] need to be reexamined in light of more recent judicial opinions, more conformable to the Constitution, that Congress may not abdicate its powers[6] and a fortiori, it cannot lose them by disuse[7] that usurpation can not be legitimated by repetition.[8] Senatorial insistence on respect for constitutional boundaries will warn the Executive against encroachments on Congress' powers; it will alert foreign nations to the fact that treaties for the cession of United States property must be subject to the consent of the full Congress.

Mr. Erickson, addressing himself to the question whether Article IV, Section 2 (3), "pursuant to which Congress has the power to dispose of property of the United States is an exclusive grant of legislative power to the Congress or whether the Congress and the President and the Senate, through the treaty power, share that authority," handsomely states "the answer to this question is not simple and although free from doubt."[9] That doubt counsels against encroachment on a power explicitly conferred on Congress; a clear case for establishment of "concurrent jurisdiction" is needed in the teeth of that express grant.

In support of the claim that the President and Senate enjoy "concurrent power" to dispose of United States property. Messrs. Hansell and Erickson invoke a melange of dicta, without weighing even stronger statements that Congress' disposal power is "exclusive." Thus the Supreme Court declared that Article IV "implies an exclusion of all other authority over the property which could interfere with this right or obstruct its exercise."[10] Echoing such judicial statements, an opinion of the Attorney General stated in 1899 that "The power to dispose permanently of the public lands and public property in Puerto Rico rests in Congress, and in the absence of a statute conferring such power, can not be exercised by the Executive Department of the Government."[11]

Such statements respond to two cardinal rules of construction. First here is the rule that express mention signifies implied exclusion, which the Supreme Court has employed again and again: "When a statute limits a thing to be done in a particular mode, it

209

includes the negative of any other mode."[12] The rule was invoked by the Founders; for example, Egbert Benson said in the First Congress, in which sat many Framers and Ratifiers, that "it cannot be rationally intended that all offices should be held during good behaviour, because the Constitution has declared [only] one office to be held by this tenure."[13] The fact, emphasized by Hansell, that "The property clause contains no language excluding concurrent jurisdiction of the treaty power" is therefore of no moment. Having given Congress the power to dispose of public property, it follows that the President and Senate were "impliedly excluded" therefrom. Second there is the settled rule that the specific governs the general:

Where there is in an act a specific provision relating to a particular subject, that provision must govern in respect to that subject as against general provisions in other parts of the act, although the latter, standing alone, would be broad enough to include the subject to which the more particular provision relates.[14]

In terms of the present issue, the specific power of disposition governs the general treaty provision.

Under these rules it is of no avail that according to Hansell, "there is no restraint expressed in respect to dispositions" in the treaty power itself. For this Mr. Hansell relies on *Geofroy v. Riggs*: The treaty power, as expressed in the Constitution, is in terms unlimited except by those restraints which are found in that instrument against the action of the . . . departments. . .[15]

Only the treaty power is "expressed"; Geofroy does not call for express restraints—it suffices that they can be found in the Constitution. The "implied exclusion" is "found" in the Constitution by virtue of the express grant of disposal power to Congress under the rule of express mention, and of the fact that the general treaty power is limited by the special Congressional power of disposition. These principles are reflected in the Supreme Court's statement in *Sioux Tribe of Indians v. United States:* Since the Constitution places the authority to dispose of public lands exclusively in Congress, the Executive's power to convey any interest in the lands must be traced to Congressional delegation of its authority.[16] To this the State Department responds that Sioux Tribe "did not deal with the relation between the treaty power and the Congressional power under Article IV, Section 3, cl. 2;" Hansell labelled it "dicta."[17] By this test the Hansell-Erickson collection of dicta falls to the ground, for almost all were not uttered in the context of that relation.

The Executive branch employs a double standard—what is dictum when the language is unfavorable to it becomes Holy Writ when the dictum reads in its favor. Erickson, for example, tells us that—

"Jones against Meehan is cited as an example by reason of the quote and the language there, which it seems to me is of significance, irrespective of the particular facts involved."[18]

Messrs. Erickson and Hansell can not have it both ways. In truth, dicta carry little weight when a particular issue has not been decided. Chief Justice Marshall dismissed his own dicta in *Marbury v. Madison* when they were pressed upon him in *Cohens v. Virginia,* 19 U.S. 264, 399 (1821), on the ground that dicta do not receive the careful consideration accorded to the question "actually before the court." The statements here quoted respecting "exclusivity" carry weight because they reflect traditional canons of construction. The foregoing considerations should suffice to dispose of a number of other Hansell-Erickson arguments for "concurrent jurisdiction," but I shall consider them for the sake of completeness.

To escape from the exclusivity of Congress disposal power Mr. Erickson argues:

"To begin with, Article IV, Section 3, clause 2, uses the same terminology, 'Congress shall have power,' as Article I, Section 8, which in our opinion, permits treaty provisions relating to such matters to be self-executing [i.e., without Congressional action], at least to the extent that the inherent character of the power or other constitutional provisions do not make the power exclusive to Congress."[19]

Erickson's qualification is a concession that some Article I powers can not be concurrently exercised by the President. The Department of State concedes that "treaties may [not] impose taxes."[20] Why is that power more "inherently" exclusive than such other Article I, Section 8 powers as the power to establish post offices, to provide and maintain a navy, to declare war, to coin money, etc., all of which manifestly can not be exercised by treaty. Erickson proves too much.

211

Second, he urges:

"Article IV, Section 3, clause 2, is included in a portion of the Constitution which deals with the distribution of authority between the Federal and State governments. It does not purport to allocate powers exercisable by Congress or pursuant to treaty."[21]

But Section 3 (2) unmistakably does "allocate powers exercisable by Congress": "The Congress shall have power to dispose of . . . property belonging to the United States." Hansell argues that the placement of the property article in clause 4 . . . provides strong evidence that the property clause does not restrict the treaty power."[22] That the "placement of a power in one or another Article is without significance for its scope is readily demonstrable: (a) "Congress shall have power to declare the punishment of treason" is located in the Judiciary Article III; (b) Congress' powers to make "exceptions and regulations" respecting the Supreme Court's appellate jurisdiction is lodged in Article III, Section 2; (c) The provision that "Congress may determine the time of choosing the electors" is placed in the Executive Article II, Section 1 (4). Does this authorize the President by treaty to declare the punishment of treason, to regulate the Court's appellate jurisdiction, or to interpose in the choice of electors? Whether located in Article I or Article IV, "Congress shall have power" means on and the same thing—the power resides in Congress, not in the President. It needs constantly to be borne in mind that the President has circumvented Senate participation in treaty-making by affixing the label "Executive Agreements" to treaties, without constitutional warrant,[23] so that claims made on behalf of the Senate and the President can be turned to his own advantage.

Mr. Hansell also attaches significance to the close linkage between the Article IV "power to dispose" and "the power to make all needful rules and regulations" respecting the Territory or other property belonging to the United States, and cites *Geofroy v. Riggs* for the proposition that "the treaty power can be used to make rules and regulations governing the territory belonging to the United States, even in the District of Columbia."[24] Geofroy presented the question whether a citizen of France could take land in the District of Columbia by descent from a citizen of the United States. Local law withheld the right, but in keeping with national solicitude for protection of citizens abroad, a treaty provided for reciprocal rights of inheritance in such circumstances for citizens of both signatories. In consequence the treaty overrode the local provision; but this hardly stretches to the "making of rules and regulations" by treaty for the District of Columbia. Were this true, the President could by treaty take over the governance of the District of Columbia, in spite of the Article I, Section 8 (17) provision that "The Congress shall have power to exercise exclusive jurisdiction in all cases whatever over such district." Assume notwithstanding that the treaty power does indeed comprehend the "making of rules and regulations governing the . . . District of Columbia," does the "close" linkage with the "power to dispose" comprehend a disposition of the White House by treaty? Such arguments verge on absurdity.

Messrs. Hansell and Erickson have cited a string of cases in support of "The power to dispose of public land . . . by treaty."[25] Some, such as *Holden v. Joy,* 84 U.S. 211 (1872), and *Jones v. Meehan,* 175 U.S. 1 (1899), have frequently been cited in your hearings. Let me begin with Hansell's citation of *Missouri v. Holland,* 252 U.S. 416 (1920), for it quickly illustrates how farfetched are the State Department's interpretations. *Missouri v. Holland* arose out of a State challenge to the treaty with Great Britain for the protection of migratory birds which annually traversed parts of the United States and Canada. Justice Holmes, addressing the argument that the treaty infringed powers reserved to the States by the Tenth Amendment, stated:

"Wild birds are not in the possession of any one, and possession is the beginning of ownership. The whole foundation of the State's rights is the presence within their jurisdiction of birds that yesterday had not arrived, tomorrow may be in another State, and in a week a thousand miles away."[26]

Consequently the State could assert no "title" in migratory birds. By the same token, the United States could lay no claims to "ownership" of the birds, and *Missouri v. Holland* is therefore wholly irrelevant to the power by treaty to dispose of property belonging to the United States.

Holden v. Joy and *Jones v. Meehan* will repay close analysis because they involve Indian treaties which constitute one of the pillars of the argument, to quote Erickson, that "the United States can convey its title by way of self-executing treaty and that no imple-

213

menting legislation is necessary.''[27] To begin with Jones, both Hansell and Erickson quote: ''It is well settled that a good title to parts of the lands of an Indian tribe may be granted to individuals by a treaty between the United States and the tribe, without any act of Congress, or any patent from the Executive authority of the United States.''[28] The treaty had ''set apart from the tract six hundred and forty acres . . .'' for an individual Indian; and the issue was what kind of title did he take. The Court quoted from an opinion of Attorney General Roger Taney, destined before long to succeed Chief Justice Marshall:

''These reservations are excepted out of the grant made by the treaty, and did not therefore pass with it; consequently the title remains as it was before the treaty; that is to say, the lands reserved are still held under the original Indian title.''[29]

The Court held that ''the reservation, unless accompanied by words limiting its effect, is equivalent to a present grant of a complete title in fee simple.''[30] That explanation presumably responded to the fact that tribal lands were generally held in common; individual titles were all but unknown, so that such title had to be secured through the machinery of the treaty. But that is far from a disposition of government land because, as Taney explained, the ''reserved'' title remained in the Indians. Many, if not most, of the cases of Indian treaties involve just such ''reserve'' provisions.[31]

The quotation from *Holden v. Joy*, Erickson acknowledges, is dictum; notwithstanding Hansell relies on it as ''a clear statement of the law'':[32]

''It is insisted that the President and the Senate, in concluding such a treaty, could not lawfully covenant that a patent should be issued to convey lands which belonged to the United States without the consent of Congress, which cannot be admitted. On the contrary, there are many authorities where it is held that a treaty may convey to a grantee a good title to such lands without an act of Congress, and that Congress has no constitutional power to settle or interfere with rights under treaties, except in cases purely political.''[33]

What bearing the last clause has on Congress' ''power to dispose'' of public lands escapes me; this Delphic utterance surely does not overcome the clear terms of Article IV. As to the ''many authorities,'' the Court's citation could hardly be farther afield. To avoid cluttering this statement with a minute analysis of each case cited by the Court for the assertion that "a treaty may convey to a grantee a good title . . . without an act of Congress," I have abstracted them in an appendix attached hereto, so that you may see for yourself that half of the cases thus cited are altogether irrelevant, and that the rest concern "reserves" under which, as Taney observed, no title had passed to the United States but remained in the given Indiana. In considering such dicta, it is well to bear in mind Chief Justice Taney's statement that the Court's opinion upon the construction of the Constitution is always open to discussion when it is supposed to have been founded in error, and that its judicial authority should hereafter depend altogether on the force of the reasoning by which it is supported.[34]

By that standard the Holden dictum is no authority at all. The inappositeness of Holden is underscored by the facts. In May, 1828, and February, 1833, "the United States agreed to possess the Cherokees of seven million acres of land west of the Mississippi." It "was the policy of the United States to induce Indians . . . to surrender their lands and possessions to the United States and emigrate and settle in the territory provided for them in the treaties," so an exchange of land was provided. But a third treaty, that of December, 1835, proved necessary, hwereby the Indians ceded their lands to the United States in consideration of $5,000,000 to be invested in the manner stipulated. The Indians considered that the prior treaties, confirmed by the new, did not contain a sufficient quantity of land, so the United States agreed to convey an additional tract in consideration of $500,000 to be deducted from the $5,000,000.[35] This may be viewed either as a purchase and sale or an exchange: "the Cherokees were competent to make the sale to the United States and to purchase the lands agreed to be conveyed to them . . ." And the transaction was authorized by the Act of 1830, which empowered the President to set aside land west of the Mississippi for the reception of such tribes as chose to emigrate, and to "exchange" such lands with any tribe.[36] The 1830 act served to ratify the Act of 1828, and "ratification is equivalent to original authority:"[37] It is well settled that Congress may . . . 'ratify . . . acts which it might have authorized' . . . and give the force of law to official action unauthorized when taken."[38] Although the subsequent 1833 and 1835 treaties differed in some

215

particulars from the authorization, the purpose was the same—"to induce the Indians . . . to emigrate and settle in the country long before set apart for that purpose."[39] When, therefore, the Court, speaking to the contention that the President and the Senate "could not lawfully covenant that a patent should issue to convey lands which belonged to the United States without the consent of Congress," stated that "a treaty may convey to a grantee a good title to such lands without an act of Congress conferring it," it was making a statement that was unnecessary to the decision, because Congress had authorized the conveyance.

As to other treaties, Hansell tells us, "the precedents look two ways." Some have been "contingent upon congressional authorization." The "precedents supporting the power to dispose of property by treaty alone," he states, "can be found in the boundary treaties with neighboring powers, especially in the treaties between the United States and Great Britain of 1842 and 1846 for the location of our northeast and northwest boundaries . . ."[40] Settlement of boundary disputes are not really cessions of United States property. The Oregon boundary dispute proceeded from an inflated claim: "Fifty-Four Forty or Fight"; the British, on the other hand, claimed land down to the forty-second parallel. Only when the dispute was settled by treaty—at 49 degrees—could either party confidently assert that it had title.[41] Consequently, as Samuel Crandall, a respected commentator, stated, "A treaty for the determination of a disputed line operates not as a treaty of cession, but of recognition."[42]

Among other examples of alleged treaty transfers of property, Hansell instances the return to Japan of the Ryukyu Islands.[43] By Article III of the 1951 Treaty of Peace with Japan, the United States received the right to exercise "all and any powers of administration, legislation and jurisdiction over the territory and inhabitants of those islands. . . ." While Japan renounced in Article II, "all right, title and claim" to various territories, it made no similar renunciation with respect to the Ryukyus.[44] Quoting the Legal Advisor of the State Department, that "sovereignty over the Ryukyu Islands . . . remains in Japan . . .", a District Court stated that "Sovereignty over a territory may be transferred by an agreement of cession," but it concluded that there had been no cession.[45] The Fourth Circuit Court of Appeals quoted a statement by

216

Ambassador John Foster Dulles, a delegate to the Japanese Peace Conference, that the aim was "to permit Japan to retain residual sovereignty," and held that the treaty did not make "the island a part of the United States, and it remains a foreign country for purposes of" the Federal Tort Claims Act.[46]

"In the history of transfers of property to Panama," Hansell tells us, "we have had a mixed practice,"[47] By the 1903 Panama Convention, Panama granted to the United States "all the rights, power and authority within the Zone . . . which the United States would possess if it were the sovereign of the territory . . . to the entire exclusion of the exercise by the Republic of Panama of any such sovereign rights, power, or authority . . ."[48] The words "if it were sovereign" signal an intent to stop short of a cession of sovereignty. That is confirmed by an Opinion of the Attorney General. Considering the Tariff Act levy of duties on articles imported "into the United States of into any of its possessions," he stated that "the Canal Zone is not one of the possessions of the United States within the meaning of that term as used by Congress in the tariff act, but rather is a place subject to the use, occupation, and control of the United States for a particular purpose."[49] In *Luckenback S.S. Co. v. United States,* Chief Justice Taft stated, "Whether the grant in the treaty amounts to a complete cession of territory and dominion to the United States or is so limited as to leave titular sovereignty in the Republic of Panama, is a question which has been the subject of diverging opinions," which he found it unnecessary to decide,[50] and is therefore still open. Instead he relied on a "long continued course of legislation and administrative action [that] has operated to require that the ports in the Canal Zone are to be regarded as foreign ports within the meaning" of the Act governing the transport of "mail between the United States and any foreign port,"[51] itself a hint that the Panama Treaty is no more a cession than the Japanese Treaty respecting the Ryukyus.

It does not follow, however, that the interests of the United States do not constitute "property of the United States." The grant of "use and occupation . . . in perpetuity" constitutes "property" no less than the familiar lease of realty for 99 years. Then there are the installations that cost billions of dollars. Disposition of these no less requires the consent of Congress than does that of territory. In 1942, the President by Executive Agreement promised to transfer

217

certain installations to Panama subject, however, to Congressional approval.[52] A similar provision is to be found in the Treaty of 1955.[53] These are executive constructions that speak against Messrs. Hansell and Erickson.

In sum, Messrs. Hansell and Erickson have failed to make out a case for "concurrent jurisdiction" with Congress in the disposition of United States property. If the President is to fly in the face of the express "power of Congress to dispose" it must be on a sounder basis than the arguments they have advanced. In my judgment, the Panama Treaty should contain a provision making it subject to approval of the Congress.

Footnotes

[1]Hearings on the Panama Canal Treaty before the Senate Subcommittee on Separation of Powers (95th Cong. 1st Sess.) Part II, p. 3 (July 29, 1977), hereafter cited as Hansell.

[2]Hearings before the House Subcommittee on the Panama Canal on "Treaties Affecting the Operations of the Panama Canal," (92 Cong. 2d Sess.) p. 95 (December 2, 1971), hereafter cited as Erickson.

[3]*Youngstown Sheet & Tube Co. v. Sawyer,* 343 U.S. 579, 647 (1952), concurring opinion.

[4]R. Berger, *Executive Privilege: A Constitutional Myth* 75–88 (1974).

[5]Congress "uniformly and repeatedly acquiesced in the practice." "It may be argued that while the facts and rulings prove a usage they do not establish its validity. But government is a practical affair intended for practical men. Both officers, lawmakers and citizens naturally adjust themselves to any long continued action of the Executive Department—on the presumption that unauthorized acts would not have been allowed to be so often repeated as to crystallize into a regular practice." *United States v. Midwest Oil Co.,* 236 U.S. 459, 471 (1915). But as Justice Frankfurter later declared, "Deeply embedded traditional ways of conducting a government cannot supplant the Constitution or legislation . . ." Youngstown Sheet, supra, n. 3 at 610, concurring opinion.

[6]*Panama Refining Co. v. Ryan,* 293 U.S. 388, 421 (1935).

[7]*United States v. Morton Salt Co.,* 338 U.S. 632, 647 (1950).

[8]"That an unconstitutional action has been taken before surely does not render that same action less unconstitutional at a later date." *Powell v. McCormack,* 395 U.S. 486, 546–547 (1969). *Zweibon v. Mitchell,* 516 F.2d 594, 616 (D.C. Cir. 1975); "there can be no doubt that an unconstitutional practice, no matter how inveterate, cannot be condoned by the judiciary." *United States v. Morton Salt Co.,* 338, U.S. 632, 647 (1950): "non-existent powers can [not] be prescripted by an unchallenged exercise . . ."

[9]Erickson 97.

[10]*Wisconsin Cent. R.R. Co. v. Price County,* 133 U.S. 496, 504 (1890); see also

Swiss Nat. Ins. Co. v. *Miles,* 289 Fed. 571, 574 (App. D.C. 1923).

[11]22 Op. Atty. Gen., 544, 545 (1899). 2 J. Story, *Commentaries on the Constitution of the United States, Section* 1328, p. 200 (4th ed. 1873): "The power of Congress over the public territory is clearly exclusive and universal . . ." Cf. *Osborne* v. *United States,* 145, F. 2d 892, 896 (9th Cir. 1944).

[12]*Botany Worsted Mills* v. *United States,* 278 U.S. 282, 289 (1929); *T.I.M.E.* v. *United States,* 359 U.S. 464, 471 (1959): "we find it impossible to impute to Congress an intention to give such a right to shippers under the Motor Carrier Act when the very sections which established that right in Part I [for railroads] were wholly omitted in the Motor Carrier Act."

[13]*1 Annals of Cong.* 505 (2d ed. 1936) (print bearing running head "History of Congress"); and see Alexander White, id. 517.

[14]*Swiss Nat. Ins. Co.* v. *Miller,* 289 Fed. 570, 574, (App. D.C. 1923). *Ginsberg & Son* v. *Popkin,* 285 U.S. 204, 208 (1932): "General language of a statutory provision, although broad enough to include it, will not be held to apply to a matter specifically dealt with in another part of the same enactment." *Buffum* v. *Chase Nat. Bank,* 192 F.2d 58, 61 (7th Cir. 1951). In this light, the fact, stressed by Hansell, that the Framers contemplated that a treaty could affect "territorial" rights, Hansel 5, is not decisive, for the treaty would yet be subject to the special Congress "power to dispose." There is no evidence in the records of the Convention that the Framers intended in any way to curtail that power, or to give the President a share in it. Were the matter less clear, we should yet "prefer a construction which leaves to each element of the statute a function in some way different from the others" to one which causes one section to overlap another. *United States* v. *Dinerstein,* 362 F.2d 852, 855–856 (2d Cir. 1966).

[15]Hansell 4; 133 U.S. 258, 267 (1890), emphasis added. One might with equal force argue that no limitation on Congress' "power to dispose" is "expressed" in Article IV.

[16]316 U.S. 317, 326 (1942). *Turner* v. *American Baptist Missionary Union,* 24 Fed. Cas. (No. 14, 251) 344, 346 (C. Ct. Mich. 1852): "Without a law the president is not authorized to sell the public lands. . . . The [Indian] treaty, in fact appropriated the above tract of 160 acres for a particular purpose, but, to effectuate that purpose, an act of Congress was passed."

[17]Hansell 27, 22.

[18]Erickson 105.

[19]Id. 97.

[20]Hansell 25.

[21]Erickson 97.

[22]Hansell 4–5, emphasis added.

[23]Berger, supra n. 4 at 140–162.

[24]Hansell 5.

[25]Id.; Erickson 97.

[26]252 U.S. at 434.

[27]Erickson 97.

[28]Hansell 6; Erickson 97.

[29]175 U.S. at 12, emphasis added.

[30]Id. 21.

31See infra Appendix.

[32] Erickson 97; Hansell 22.

[33] Quoted by Hansell 5–6; 84 U.S. at 247.

[34] The Passenger Cases, 48 U.S. (7 How.) 283, 470 (1849), dissenting opinion.

[35] 84 U.S. at 237, 238, 241.

[36] Id. 245, 238–239.

[37] *Wilson* v. *Shaw*, 204 U.S. 24, 32 (1907).

[38] *Swayne & Hoyt, Ltd.* v. *United States,* 300 U.S. 297, 301–302 (1937).

[39] 84 U.S. at 240.

[40] Hansell 6.

[41] S. E. Morison, *Oxford History of the American People,* 538, 546–547 (1965).

[42] S. Crandall, *Treaties, Their Making and Enforcement,* 226 (2d ed. 1916).

[43] Hansell 6.

[44] 3 U.S.T. 3169, 3172, 3173.

[45] *United States* v. *Ushi Shiroma,* 123 F. Supp. 145, 149, 148 (D. Hawaii, 1954).

[46] Hansell 7.

[48] Quoted Hearings, supra n. 1, Part I, p. 5, emphasis added.

[49] 27 Op. Atty. Gen. 594, 595 (1909).

[50] 280 U.S. 173, 177–178 (1930).

[51] Id. 178.

[52] "When the authority of the Congress . . . shall have been obtained therefore . . ." Agreement of May 18, 1942, 59 Stat. (Pt. 2) 1289.

[53] Agreement of January 25, 1955, 6 U.S.T. 2273, 2278.

Appendix

i

Holden v. *Joy*: its citations for treaty power to dispose of property.

A. "Reserve" cases (title remains in Indians)

(1) *United States* v. *Brooks,* 51 U.S. (10 How.) 442 (1850).

Indian cession to United States; supplement to treaty provided that Grappe's representatives "shall have their right to the said four leagues of land reserved to them. . ." (450, 451). Held: treaty "gave to the Grappes a fee simple title to all the rights the [Indians] had in these lands . . ." (460).

(2) *Doe* v. *Wilson,* 64 U.S. (23 How.) 457 (1859). Indian treaty ceded land to United States, making reservations to individual Indians. "As to these, the Indian title remained as it stood before the treaty was made; and to complete the title to the reserved lands, the United States agreed that they would issue patents to the respective owners." (461–462).

(3) *Crews* v. *Burcham,* 66 U.S. (1 Black) 352 (1861). Cession by Indians with reserves (355). "The main and controlling

220

questions involved in this case were before this court in the case of *Doe* v. *Wilson*, 23 How. 457 . . ." (356).

(4) *Mitchel* v. *United States*, 34 U.S. (9 Pet.) 711 (1835). Prior to the Spanish cession of Florida to the United States, the Indians had made a cession to Spain, "reserving to themselves full right and property" in certain lands. (749). Held: "by the treaty with Spain the United States acquired no lands in Florida to which any person had lawfully obtained" title. (734, 756). Issue: title of purchaser from Indians to reserved lands.

(5) *The Kansas Indians*, 72 U.S. (5 Wall.) 737 (1866). Treaty exchange of lands; Indians reserved lands for each individual (739, 741). Issue: was such land taxable by Kansas.

B. Irrelevant Cases:

(1) *Meigs* v. *McClung*, 13 U.S. (9 Cranch) 11 (1815). Held: land claimed from defendants did not lie within territory ceded to the United States by the Indians. (17).

(2) *Wilson* v. *Wall*, 73 U.S. (6 Wall.) 83 (1967). Treaty provided that certain Indians would be entitled to 640 acres for self, and additional acres, roughly speaking, for each child. (84). Issue: whether an Indian held land governed by the latter clause in trust for his children. (86). Court said "Congress has no constitutional power to settle the rights under treaties except in cases purely political," (89) the clause quoted in *Holden* v. *Joy*. The reason, it explained, was that "The Construction of them is the peculiar province of the judiciary . . ." id. In other words, interpretations of treaties is for the courts.

(3) *American Insurance Co.* v. *Canter*, 26 U.S. (1 Pet.) 511 (1828). Insurer brought a libel in the District Court, South Carolina, to obtain restitution of 356 bales of cotton carried by ship that was wrecked on the Florida coast. A Florida territorial court had earlier awarded 76% salvage to salvers, who sold the Canter. (540). Issue: did the territorial court have jurisdiction. No mention of grant by United States.

(4) *Worcester* v. *Georgia*, 31 U.S. (6 Pet.) 515 (1832). Worcester, a white missionary was convicted of residing within Indian territory without a State license. The treaty with the Indians placed them under the protection of the United States, gave it the sole right of "managing all their affairs." Held: the Georgia act can have no force in the Indian territory. (561).

221

(5) *Foster* v. *Neilson*, 27 U.S. (2 Pet.) 253 (1829). Re grants made in the ceded territory by Spain prior to January 24, 1815, the article provides "that those grants shall be ratified and confirmed like Indian "reserves . . . the ratification and confirmation which are promised must be by the Act of the Legislature," i.e. Congress. (314–315).

ii

Some additional Hansell citations for power to dispose by treaty.

(1) *Reid* v. *Covert*, 354, U.S. 1 (1957). Military Code provided for trial by court martial of "all persons . . . accompanying the armed forces" of the United States in foreign countries. Wife of Army Sergeant convicted by court martial in England of his murder. Held: Bill of Rights requires jury trial after indictment.

(2) *Asakura* v. *Seattle*, 265 U.S. 322 (1924). Seattle ordinance restricted pawnship license to United States citizen. (339–340). Japanese attacks as violation of treaty provision: citizens or subjects of each signatory "shall have liberty . . . to carry on trade, wholesale and retail . . . upon the same terms as native citizens or subjects . . ." (340). Held: can't deny the Japanese equal opportunity. (342).

(3) *Santovicenza* v. *Egan*, 284 U.S. (1931). Italian subject dies in New York, leaving no heirs or next of kin. (351). Italian consul claims under "most favored nation" treaty clause. Held: The treaty-making power is broad enough" to cover "the disposition of the property of aliens dying within the territory of the respective parties . . ." Any "conflicting law of the State must yield." (40).

iii

Some additional Erickson citations for self-executing treaty conveyances.

(1) *Francis* v. *Francis*, 203 U.S. 233 (1906). Indian treaty ceded land to United States, but reserved certain tracts for use of named persons. (237). Quotes *Jones* v. *Meehan*; when treaty makes "a reservation of a specified number of sections of land . . . the treaty itself converts the reserved sections into individual property . . ." (238). It was in these circumstances that the Court said, "a title in fee may pass by treaty without the aid of an act of Congress, and without a patent," (241–242) the reason being that title to the reserved land remained in the Indians.

(2) *Best* v. *Polk*, 85 U.S. (18 Wall.) 112 (1873). By Indian

treaty "reservation of a limited quantity [of land] were conceded to them. (113). One section "had been located to an Indian." (113, 116). Thereafter, the United States issued a patent to James Brown. Held (117), "the Indian reservee was held to have a preference over the subsequent patentee."

Addendum to Statement by Raoul Berger Before the Subcommittee on Separation of Powers of the Committee on the Judiciary

The statement by Attorney General Griffin B. Bell (hereafter cited as A.G.) before the Senate Foreign Relations Committee, September 29, 1977, reached me on Saturday afternoon, October 29, 1977, too late for inclusion of my comments in the body of my statement. Only three points made by the Attorney General seem to me to call for additional comment, and of these I shall speak in turn.

I

The Percheman Case

The Attorney General cites *United States* v. *Percheman*, 32 U.S. (7 Pet.) 511, 88–89 (1833) to prove that "the Court held self-executing certain clauses of the Florida Treaty with Spain which related to the regulation of property rights in newly acquired territory." A. G. at p. 10. At the cited pages it appears that Article 8 of the treaty provided:

"All the grants of land made before the 24th of January, 1818, by his Catholic Majesty . . . in the said territory ceded by his Majesty to the United States, shall be ratified and confirmed to the persons in possession of the lands . . .

This Article, Chief Justice Marshall remarked, "must be intended to stipulate expressly for that security of private property which the laws and usages of nations would, without express stipulation, have conferred . . . Without it (Article 8), the title of individuals would remain as valid under the new government as they were under the old . . . the security of (pre-existing) private property was intended by the parties . . .

In short, the treaty provided that prior Spanish grants to *private* persons should be ratified and confirmed, a provision far removed from presidential "regulation" of public territory. Moreover, *Foster* v. *Neilson*, 27 U.S. (2 Pet.) 253, 314–315 (1829), a case cited

223

by the Attorney General (A.G. at p. 3), held with respect to the self-same provision that "the ratification and confirmation which are promised must be by the Act of the Legislature," i.e. Congress. The citation to Percheman illustrates why I approach an Attorney General's statement with something less than awe.

II
Remarks in the Legislative History of the Constitution

(1)The Attorney General asserts that "the members of the Convention were fully aware of the possibility that a treaty might dispose of the territory or property of the United States," (A.G. at p. 5). He begins with the remark of George Mason in the Constitutional Convention: "The Senate by means of a treaty might alienate territory etc. without legislative sanction." A.G. at p. 6; 2 Farrand 297. This was during a debate on a resolution that "Each House shall possess the right of originating bills," when Mason seconded Strong's motion to "except bills for raising money for the purposes of revenue, or for appropriating the same." The Senate, said Mason, "could already sell the whole Country by means of Treaties," plainly an extravagant overstatement, made at a time when the treaty was not under discussion. His "alienate territory" remark may merely represent a strategic retreat from his untenable "sell the whole country" remark.

There follow a group of utterances that have reference to boundary disputes, i.e. conflicting claims to ownership to be settled by treaties of peace.

(2) When the treaty power was under discussion. Williamson and Spaight moved "that no Treaty of Peace affecting territorial rights should be made without concurrence of two thirds of the [members of the Senate present]." A.G. at p. 6; 2 Farrand 543: Similarly, Gerry, speaking for a greater proportion of votes on "treaties of peace", said that here:

"The dearest interests will be at stake, as the fisheries, territories, etc. In treaties of peace also there is more danger to the extremities of the Continent" has reference to boundary disputes which do not really involve territory owned by the United States.

(3) "Sherman and Morris proposed but did not formally move," the Attorney General states, "the following proviso:

"But no treaty (of peace) shall be made without the concurrence of the House of Representatives, by which the territorial boundaries

224

of the United States may be contracted . . ."

A.G. at p. 6; 4 Farrand 58. Farrand adds that "The subject was then debated, but the motion does not appear to have been made." id. Why was the motion not made after debate? Presumably, the matter was postponed for consideration with Article IV. Section 3(2) would come up for discussion. During this subsequent discussion of "The Legislature shall have power to dispose of . . . the territory . . .", it is singular that no mention was made of an exception for disposition under the treaty power. 2 Farrand 466. Nonmention is the more remarkable because such an exception would carve out an area of undefined magnitude from the power conferred, a matter which would affront the democratically minded who placed their faith in the House. It seems more reasonable to infer from the history that Article IV, Section 3(2) was designed to set at rest the fears that territory might be ceded without the concurrence of the House.

(4) The Attorney General cites an amendment proposed by the Virginia Ratification Convention as exhibiting the "awareness of the Founding Fathers that the Constitution authorizes self-executing treaties disposing of the territory and property of the United States":

"No commercial treaty shall be ratified without the concurrence of the members of the Senate [not merely of those present]; and no treaty ceding, contracting . . . the territorial rights or claims of the United States . . . shall be made, but in cases of extreme necessity; nor shall any such treaty be ratified without the concurrence of tree-fourths of the whole number of the members of both Houses respectively."

A.G. at p. 7; 3 Elliot. Debates on the Federal Constitution 660. The Attorney General's reading paradoxically transforms Virginia's anxiety to have greater safeguards, i.e., three-fourths of both Houses rather than the bare majority that satisfies Article IV, into an argument for excluding the House altogether. Like the earlier remarks, the Virginia proposal testifies to the importance that the Founders attached to the disposition of territory—no cession except "in cases of extreme necessity"—and it counsels against reading the equivocal "treaty-making" to encroach upon the "power to dispose" that requires the vote of both Houses, not merely the Senate. In any event, it may be asked, should the post-Convention view of one State be permitted to override the plain terms of Article IV.

(5) Hugh Williamson, a delegate to the Convention, wrote to Madison some nine months after its close, to recall to him "a Proviso in the new Sistern which was inserted for the express purpose of preventing a majority of the Senate . . . from giving up the Mississippi. It is provided that two-thirds of the members present in the Senate shall be required in making treaties. . . ."

A.G. at p. 7–8; 3 Farrand 306–307. The Mississippi presented a gnawing boundary question which threatened the expansion of the West and was only settled by the Louisiana Purchase. Boundary treaties do not really involve the disposition of territory or property of the United States but the adjustment of conflicting claims, even when some believe their claims to be more valid than those of the opposing party.

To my mind, the history is at best inconclusive; the remarks quoted by the Attorney General are confined to adjustment of boundary disputes, with one exception, by treaties of peace. Treaties of peace present special problems, and such citations do not add up to general concurrent jurisdiction over the disposition of government territory or property. To go beyond such territorial adjustments collides with the rationale of *Pierson* v. *Ray*, 386 U.S. 547, 554–555 (1967). With respect to the common law immunity of judges from suit for acts performed in their official capacity, the Court declared:

"We do not believe that this settled principle was abolished by Section 1983, which makes liable 'every person' who under color of law deprives another of his civil rights . . . we presume that Congress would have specifically so provided had it wished to abolish the doctrine."

Thus, the all-inclusive "every person" was held not to curtail an existing common law immunity in the absence of a specific provision. The more equivocal treaty-making power demands an even more exacting standard. Before it be concluded that it in any way diminishes the explicit grant to Congress of "power to dispose" of territory, a clearly expressed intention to do so is required. That requirement is not satisfied by the random remarks collected by the Attorney General.

The Attorney General concedes that:

"The specific power granted to the House of Representatives and Congress in fiscal matters (Article I, Section 7, clause 1 and Article I, Section 9, clause 7, money bills and appropriations power) preclude making treaties self-executing to the extent that they involve the raising of revenue or the expenditure of funds. Were it otherwise, President and Senate could bypass the power of Congress and in particular of the House of Representatives over the pursestrings."

A. G. at p. 4–5. Now, sections nine and seven are couched in quite dissimilar terms. One, Section 9(7), is framed in terms of flat prohibition: "No money shall be withdrawn from the Treasury but in consequence of appropriations made by law. . . ." Section 7 (1), on the other hand, merely provides that "All bills for raising revenue shall originate in the House." Yet, the Attorney General reads Section 7(1) to preclude the President and Senate from "bypass[ing] the power of Congress and in particular of the House of Representatives over the pursestrings." What is there that distinguishes "All bills . . . shall originate in the House" from "The Congress shall have power to dispose. . . ."? The impalpability of the distinction is underlined by the State Department's concession that "treaties may [not] impose taxes." Nothing in this Article I, Section 8(1) "The Congress shall have power to lay and collect taxes" distinguishes it from the Article IV "The Congress shall have power to dispose. . . ."

If the President may not by treaty "bypass" the power of the House to originate revenue-raising bills, or the power of Congress to tax, no more may he "bypass" its "power to dispose" of the territory and property of the United States.

227

Appendix 3:
Address of Dr. Romulo Escobar Bethancourt, Head of the Panamanian Negotiating Team, Before the National Assembly of Panama, August 19, 1977

[This highly emotional speech, delivered by Dr. Bethancourt to prove to Panamanian radicals and ultranationalists that he and the Torrijos regime hadn't "sold out," reveals what the Panamanian government really interprets the neutrality treaty to mean. After reading Dr. Bethancourt's incendiary speech, no one can say that America has not been warned just how dangerous it would be to surrender the canal to Panama. All emphases are mine.]

The original [American] position was that to reach an agreement with Panama there would have to be a neutrality treaty and a military treaty. The military treaty would be made before the end of this century to be operative after the year 2000. This kept the negotiations stalled for a long time, because Panama opposed the enactment of a military treaty. Such a treaty would have implied two things: First, the continued U.S. military presence in Panama after the end of the present treaty [2000]; and second, the United States, as a great power, is a country frequently involved in wars in other parts of the world, and we did not want that, because of the existence of a military treaty, the future youth of our country to have to go fight in the American battlefields with the pretext that this related to the defense of the Panama Canal. This was a position that Panama maintained until the United States withdrew the idea of a military treaty. We were then able to negotiate a neutrality treaty alone.

With regard to the neutrality pact, the following situation arose: The United States asked if Panama would disagree with the idea of the canal being neutral. We told them we didn't, that on the contrary, a long-standing aspiration of Panama had been that the Panama Canal would be neutral. They said that they wanted the Panama Canal to be neutral and we said we entirely agreed with them. Differences then arose only in what they understood by neutrality and what we understood by neutrality. They proposed that Panama and the United States declare that the canal was neutral and that the United States would guarantee that neutrality. Panama was opposed to this concept, explaining that we did not want the United States to maintain a guarantee over the State of Panama, using the neutrality issue as an excuse. This was another source of debate that kept the negotiations stalled *until the United States gave up the idea of its guaranteeing the canal's neutrality.*

Another of the positions they presented was that Panama must agree to maintain the canal permanently neutral and permanently open. We told them that Panama could commit herself to maintain the canal permanently neutral because that was her wish. Panama has no interest in having anything other than a neutral canal, the Panama Canal, because otherwise the Isthmus of Panama could become a battlefield. But we said *Panama could not promise to maintain the canal permanently open* because of three circumstances that might arise. One, because of natural causes; we explained that an earthquake could take place, for instance, which would close the canal, and, in such a situation, Panama could not be under an obligation to keep it open. Another possibility was temporary disruptions—landslides could take place and the canal would have to be closed to carry out clean-up operations. *The third possibility was that the canal could become unprofitable for Panama; in such a situation, Panama could not be tied down to keeping open a canal which was not earning revenue.* They [United States negotiators] accepted the first two reasons—natural causes and temporary disruptions—but they did not accept the third reason, lack of profits. This too kept the negotiations stalled for a long time.

They argued that if the canal was not profitable, Panama couls obtain money from the United States or the other countries that use the canal to keep it open. We told them that when the new treaty with the United States ended, we did not want Panama to be under either direct or indirect obligation to turn to the United States or any other country to request money to keep the canal open. Our respective positions remained unchanged until we reached the agreement I am about to describe. They said, we can't present to our Congress an article that states you will close the canal because of insufficient revenues. *And we said we could not present an arti-*

cle committing us to operating the canal permanently when we have no way of knowing if the canal someday will yield no profit. We finally agreed to eliminate that article, and so Panama was freed of the obligation to maintain the canal open permanently. The negotiations then went exclusively to the issue of neutrality.

The United States then proposed that there be a neutrality treaty between Panama and the United States and no one else. Because *they did not want for either the Russians, the Cubans or the Chinese—they said so exactly—to intervene in the neutrality of the Panama Canal.* Our position was that neutrality didn't make any sense if limited to two countries as a result of a treaty between the United States and Panama and that we opposed the other countries not having the right to join in that treaty. They changed their position and agreed to allow the countries of the American continent (except for Cuba), but no others, to join. We said no, that this was meaningless, because in case of a war between the United States and Russia or China, those countries not being a part of the neutrality agreement would be under no commitment to respect the canal or the Isthmus of Panama. That was another reason for long delays, until *they finally accepted the idea that all the countries of the world could join the neutrality treaty.*

Later, there arose the problem of choosing a forum for all the nations of the world the join the pact. We said it had to be done in the United Nations. They answered that they did not much like the idea of the United Nations because of their problems with the nonaligned countries, the Third World, the Arabs, etc. They proposed the O.A.S. We agreed, provided that this body only serve as a depository, as the physical location where all the nations of the world would sign the treaty, and that O.A.S. would have no say in determining which countries would sign. This was another cause for discussion. It was solved through a protocol of neutrality—that famous protocol which has been attacked as giving the United States the right to intervene in Panama by some who apparently read such a description in a Miami newspaper. This protocol is only a note* indicating the existence of the neutrality pact. It summarizes the agreement and sets down that country such-and-such

---

*The meaning of *note* is not clear. It could mean a note of explanation or a small piece of paper.

agrees to abide by it. That is the famous protocol. It is the same thing as the neutrality treaty but in the form of a protocol (that is what it is called), and the O.A.S. is the depository.

Another issue was preferential right of way through the canal for American warships. The Americans said that they had two problems. First, they had to please the Pentagon—they had to present it with something it liked so it would support the treaty; and second, that as they would be leaving Panama as soon as the treaty ended, they should be allowed at least that much, if nothing else, because they built the canal. We pointed out that we recognized they had indeed built the canal, but that writing in the neutrality pact that the United States warships would have preferential right of way over the rest of the vessels violated the neutrality treaty and that was contrary to the objective of the treaty we were negotiating. This was another cause for lengthy discussion and much analysis. They searching through their books and we searching through ours; they invoking their treaty writers and we involing ours. This is how these discussions are carried out. Changing their position, *they asked for preferential right of way during times when the United States was at war—originally they wanted it in times of peace and war—and that this right be granted only when requested by the ship's captain. We said no—that wartime was the least appropriate moment to grant preferential passage rights since it would be a violation of neutrality.* After long discussions *they accepted that U.S. warships could not be granted preferential rights.* Then both countries set about looking for a formula which would not involve preferential rights, and we came to the agreement that the warships of the United States, in times of peace or in times of war, and the warships of Panama—we still don't have any now, but maybe by the year 2000 we will have some—will have the right to speedy passage through the canal. This means that they will have the right to as rapid a passage as possible. We were able to agree on this because it's not in any country's interest to have another nation's warships delaying for long in its territorial waters; so the faster they go through, the better.

Another of the issues in the neutrality pact that we were—I should explain that I am giving you the true picture of what the neutrality agreement will consist of. *We did not give in either to the American's insistence that the United States and Panama jointly declare the neutrality of the canal. We said that the declaration of the canal's neutrality was an act relating to Panama's sovereignty, and that it would have to be a unilateral declaration. After long discussion, they accepted that the declaration would be made by Panama alone, in other words, that Panama be the one to declare the canal permanently neutral.* They proposed that in our declaration we say that the state of neutrality was intended to prevent the canal from becoming a theater of war. We answered that we were declaring the canal neutral so that neither the Panama Canal nor the Isthmus of Panama would become a theater of war. They wanted to separate the canal and the isthmus. We told them that we could not do that, that the canal was part of our isthmus, and that our neutrality only made sense if it covered both the canal and the rest of the country. We wouldn't be any better off if, rather than dropping a bomb in the canal, they dropped it, for example, on Ocu or Santiago. *They accepted that the declaration of neutrality be worded in such a way that neither the canal nor any part of the Isthmus of Panama could be the object of reprisals in the course of another nation's conflict.*

The other point we made in relation to our concept of neutrality is that it is not a neutrality which will allow the United States ships to transit peacefully, but rather one which will allow ships flying all the flags in the world to transit peacefully, notwithstanding what country may be involved, its being a communist country, a fascist country, or a monarchy—that we were not insistent on its being a democratic country to allow it peaceful passage. And finally, that the pact was to be made between the two countries, and it is stated there that Panama declared the neutrality of the canal, in the manner that I already explained to you, following the establishment of a neutrality pact with the United States and a commitment being made on the part of both nations to maintain that neutrality. This concept of maintaining the neutrality was that which replaced their original position of guaranteeing the neutrality. The upholding of the neutrality is indicated within the treaty and in the protocol all other countries are committing themselves to this protocol.

Later came a discussion on their proposal that the two countries commit themselves to upholding this neutrality under all circumstances. We said that if the phrase "under all circumstances" was included, two important exceptions would have to be made.

The first was that this would apply only so long as internal order was not involved, since these are problems for one country or our national guard to address; and second, in the case of an attack on the isthmus or the Panama Canal by a third country. This was cause for much discussion, and in the end, they preferred to leave out the phrase so that we would not include the exception. We also pointed out that the neutrality pact must indicate clearly that after 31 December 1999 at 12 o'clock noon—or at 12 noon as [Edwin] Fabroga says or at 12 midnight as [Adolfo] Ahumada says—that from that date on, the American troops could not be in Panama. After much discussion, they said, "We don't like that phrase—that there can be Russian troops or Cuban troops." Then a proposal was made to change the phrase to read that from 31 December 1999 on only Panamanian troops could be stationed in Panama. We were in perfect agreement with this. They were happy, because they had been half-thinking that we are going to call in the Russians, and we were happy because one of our aspirations was precisely that our troops be the only ones here.

So this is the "problem" with the neutrality pact. The criticisms made of it—some that you have heard or have read—indicate that we give the United States the right to intervene in our country after the year 2000. These critics think that rights of intervention are granted in the treaty. To the great powers, no one gives the right of intervention; they intervene whenever they feel like it with or without a treaty. When they [the Americans] landed in Santo Domingo, they had no military treaty with Santo Domingo, nor had any right of intervention in Santo Domingo, and they landed anyway. But there are people here who think that it is in the articles of a [law] code that tell a country if it has the right to intervene or not, and they don't know that it is the bayonets, the guns, and the atomic bomb that gives a country the strength to intervene. And so a country like the United States can land in Panama whenever it feels like it after the year 2000 with or without a neutrality pact. But it cannot land, for example, in Russia, even if Russia tells it to land. *Those are the facts of the matter so that with the neutrality pact, we are not giving the United States the right of intervention.* What we are giving is an assurance that the canal will be permanently neutral, that we are not going to close the canal so that their ships or this ship or that ship cannot go through. Why this neutrality pact? Because they are thinking, "By the year 2000 this country [Panama] may have gone socialist and become our enemy and we now want to make sure that even if they become socialist, they cannot close our passage."

And, frankly speaking, they do not need this neutrality pact to intervene or not intervene. They need it to present it to their Congress, to tell their Congress, "Look, we are giving the canal to those Panamanians, but we retain the right to watch over it so that they behave themselves." That's the truth. It's an internal political problem; they are trying to solve an internal problem with a Congress intensely opposed to these negotiations and one which, in addition, includes members who have not been elected by the American people but rather who have become members of Congress of their own accord—these are certain Panamanians living here and others in Miami.*

So about the neutrality pact, there are its *real* contents, distinguished Representatives. It was very carefully thought out, as you can see from my description of how its final form was arrived at. I might add that we feel very proud of the way the matter has been resolved. You should have seen the original draft they presented along with the military treaty. Agreeing totally to that would have been shameful; *I would not have dared to sit at this table now to give you any kind of explanation if I'd brought with me their original draft for the military treaty and the neutrality treaty.*

The other problem concerned the option for the construction of the sea-level canal. Two months ago, almost on the day of the opening of the Alaskan pipeline, President Carter delivered a speech in which he said that his government was deeply interested in the construction of a sea-level canal either through Panama or through another point in Central America, and right after President Carter's speech the American negotiators brought the question of the option to the negotiating table. During the earlier negotiations of 1966 and 1968 this issue had been intensely debated by the negotiators of that time, Doctor Diogenes de La Rosa and others since it was at that time that they [the Americans] were making the studies which they later completed and they wanted to speed up the timetable for possible construction. But in the present round of

*Bethancourt refers here to exiles opposed to the Torrijos regime.

negotiations it appears they had put the problem aside until now, with President Carter's speech and the Alaskan oil.

And so the discussion of the option began. We talked about this option approximately two times and we arrived at no conclusion. Then came the Bogota conference.

There, the problem of the option truly made for a crisis, because there a very complete proposal was laid out for agreement by all the presidents, with Carter working through negotiators Linowitz and Bunker, and our side being represented by our chancellor, Gonzales Revilla, and our negotiating team. They [the Americans] proposed that Panama have an option to build a sea-level canal at an unspecified time, and second, that Panama commit herself to the idea that no other country could construct a sea-level canal. They presented that proposal in Bogota, and we read it to the presidents. It was the proposal that the negotiators had brought and we read it to them, and as a result the negotiations between the two countries were practically broken off.

The general [Torrijos] said in his statement that we had come to this Bogota conference to celebrate a new treaty only to find that we had come to a wake. There, the struggle between the two countries began, with Bogota taking part also, since the other presidents were meddling as if they were Panamanians too.

There was no way to reach an agreement on what they proposed. Panama's delegation wrote a proposal which met with general approval. Read word for word, it is more or less like this:

Article 3—The possibility of constructing a third set of locks or a sea-level canal.

1. The Republic of Panama and the United States agree that a sea-level canal could be important in the future or in the context of international relations.

Consequently, after its approval, the question of construction will be dealt with. There isn't even an option. The option relates only to studying the matter. We will sit down and analyze with the United States if it is feasible. If it is, the two countries will build it, maybe during the next ten or fifteen years. The generations of the future will be much more prepared. We do not give you a copy of the treaty because its release is pending on the announcement of President Carter and of General Torrijos, and its becoming an official document. We will publish it wholly when it does become [official], and we will debate it publicly.

The ones who cannot prove that this treaty is better than the one of 1903, that perpetuity is better, will have the problem. That the two million dollars a year is better than what is proposed now. We don't care if they say that General Torrijos is a dictator; those who are opposed and say that we are not revolutionaries—let them grab their knapsack and their grenade and go prove it with deeds.

Appendix 4:
Violation of Human Rights and Civil Liberties in Panama

Study by Dr. Gustave Anguizola
(Prepared for the Council for Inter American Security
919 18th Street, N.W., Washington, D.C. 20036)

About the Author

A native of Panama, Dr. Gustave Anguizola is currently Professor of History and Political Science at the University of Texas. Educated at Indiana University, the Classical School at Athens, Greece, and Stanford University, Dr. Anguizola has had a distinguished career teaching at Purdue University, New York State University, Morris College and North Carolina State University, where he served as Chairman of the Department of Social Science.

Author of many articles in professional journals, Dr. Anguizola has been the recipient of numerous academic awards, including the Fulbright-Hays award. Panamanian-United States relations have been of special interest to Dr. Anguizola, for his grandfather was Panama's Secretary of the Treasury and an intimate acquaintance of Phillipe Bunau-Varilla, primary negotiator of the 1903 canal treaty. Among his works on the subject are *Isthmian Political Suitability: 1921–1976*, and *The Power of Persistence: Life of Phillipe Bunau-Varilla.*

Introduction

General Omar Torrijos seized power in Panama on October 11, 1968, through action of the Panamanian National Guard. The successful military *coup* ousted the populist Dr. Arnulfo Arias who had been in office only eleven days.[1]

Since that time, charges of corruption and repression have been leveled against the Torrijos government. Torrijos has presented himself as a nationalist revolutionary leader. It has been suggested that his personal style, similar to that of Fidel Castro, has been developed by Torrijos to help him legitimize and stabilize his own position.

The record of repression, human rights violations, and corruption since October, 1968 is not consistent. These activities seem to vary according to the government's perception of its own stability and short-term objectives.

Though the Torijos government has received military equipment[2] and training from the United States, it would be a mistake to seriously contemplate conclusion of major political agreements with this regime. In particular, to conclude a settlement changing the status of the Panama Canal would sanction the Torrijos government in its present form. It would also endanger the safety of the citizens of the Canal Zone.

President Carter has stirred world opinion through his focus on the issue of human rights.[3] If the United States is to hold to its own historic principles of human dignity and freedom, this moral position must remain at the base of his diplomacy. To conclude in haste a major agreement with the present government of Panama would call into question the credibility of the Administration's advocacy of human rights. A Canal treaty with Torrijos could undermine U.S. foreign policy as well as do a grave injustice to the people of Panama.

The following charges raise serious questions as to the advisability of concluding major agreements with the Torrijos government. They also raise important questions about the character of the Torrijos regime.

Misuse of Political Power

Omar Torrijos has exercised power in a highly personal way. In fact his government has been called a "personality cult." His powers are so broad and ill-defined as to permit regular misuse of executive authority. Only in Haiti, in fact, does a national constitution grant such absolute powers to one man by name.[4]

Article 277 of the Panamanian constitution, promulgated in 1972, refers to General Omar Torrijos, Commander-on-Chief of the

National Guard, as the "recognized Maximum Leader of the Panamanian Revolution." In order to insure the fulfillment of this revolution, he is formally granted the power to:

1. Appoint commanders and officers of the armed forces and military hierarchy.
2. Appoint, with Cabinet approval, all Supreme Court magistrates, Attorney General, Attorney of the Administration, and their alternates.
3. Approve all government contracts, negotiate all government debts, and direct foreign relations.
4. Appoint the Comptroller General and Sub-Comptroller General, Director of the Autonomous and Semi-Autonomous institutions and Magistrates of the Electoral Tribunal which are to be named by the executive branch according to the Constitution and laws.
5. Coordinate all the work of public administration.
6. Participate with voting rights in all Cabinet meetings, meetings of the Legislative Commission, National Assembly of Representatives, Provincial Councils of Coordination, and the Communal Committees.[5]

Torrijo's enumerated powers extend beyond the executive sector, and vest both judicial and legislative functions in the hands of one man. Legislation in Panama, since 1968, has been both vague and abundant. Almost 4,000 new laws have been issued during the years 1968–1976. It has not been uncommon for new laws to be voided soon after passage. Contrary to Constitutional guarantees prohibiting such practice, retroactive law has also been enforced. Also, as will be detailed later, Torrijos only permits one political party to operate.

**Violation of Fundamental
Human Rights and
Civil Liberties**

Violation of the Right to Life

Since the coming to power of Torrijo's regime, not only arbitrary arrest, but also torture and murder at the hands of the powerful G-2 State Security Police have become increasingly more frequent. The accusation is frequently made that arrested parties have evidenced opposition to the regime, or have associated with those considered opponents.

One of the most notable recorded cases constituting abuse involves a combination of human rights violations: the case of Roman Catholic Priest Hector Gallego.

In the summer of 1968, Father gallego was appointed "Parroco"[6] of the Santa Fe parish, located in Veraguas Privince of Panama. His subsequent work, organizing agricultural cooperatives in his parish, was found damaging to the commercial interests of some powerful local relatives of Omar Torrijos. On June 9, 1971, G-2 agents entered Father Gallego's home while he slept and arrested him. There has been no word of him since that date, and the government has forbidden the Catholic Church to employ private investigators[7]. The regime has also failed to carry out the full public investigation which had been promised. It was widely conjectured, however, that Father Gallego was tortured and murdered[8]. Father Pedro Hernandez Robal stated on August 21, 1972 that "The Colombian priest, Father Hector Gallego, 30 years of age, was thrown into the sea from an airplane on June 9, 1971 by order of General Omar Torrijos, head of the Panamanian National Guard[9].

During September of 1976, a number of women related or married to known critics of the government were victimized by the National Guard:

Mrs. Blanca de Marchosky, wife of lawyer Eusebio Marchosky.

Mrs. Alma Robles de Samos, sister of Ivan and Winston Robles, lawyers in exile in Miami.

Mrs. Fulvia Morales.

These women were arrested and held incommunicado. Deprived of food and water, they were subjected to long periods of interrogation. G-2 agents and some Cuban interrogaters who assist in G-2 training were involved in the questioning. The subsequent jailings included depriving the accused of beds, change of clothing, and contact with relatives.

During this period, a list of women who were married to reputed dissidents was publisked in the government-controlled newspapers. These same women, accused of "collaborating" with the women previously jailed, were also threatened with arrest. Arrest of persons by the government's special G-2 National Guard section is reportedly often carried out without either formal charges or warrant. The authorities may refuse to acknowledge the arrest, and may prohibit arrested persons from contacting friends or family members.

The list of persons murdered by the G-2 police is a lengthy one, and attempts by relatives or associates to investigate are reportedly usually squelched[10].

In addition to the reported murder of Father Gallego, a more recent case of note is that of Miss Marlene Mendizabal and her fiancé, Jorge E. Falconet. Both young people were members of student groups which opposed communist-oriented organizations at the University of Panama. These revolutionary leftist organizations openly supported General Torrijos.

Mr. Falconet, a student at the National University of Panama, simply disappeared, but Miss Mendizabal's body was found. The National Guard prevented an autopsy from being performed. Several student organizations at the Instituto Nacional, Miss Mendizabal's high school, sent letters to the Attorney General which accused the authorities of covering up the incident and of intimidating the victims' family members. Miss Mendizabal's mother, for example, was allegedly so badly beaten by government agents during her attempt to investigate her daughter's May, 1976, murder, that a considerable period of hospitalization was required. It is also said that the tombstone, purchased by some of Miss Mendizabal's relatives, was destroyed two days after it was placed over her grave.

It has been found that torture is widely employed by G-2 guards. Bodies which have been discovered and examined show evidence of *various* types of corporal abuse such as the body of Ruben Miro, a lawyer, who was tortured and murdered after his arrest.

Eduardo White died of injuries to stomach and chest inflicted by a rubber hose during his arrest.

Miss Dorita Moreno, a University of Panama medical student and member of a group opposing deposition of Arnulfo Arias, was sexually assaulted by members of the National Guard.

Three persons, Nat Mendes, Jr., Fernando Ayala, and Francisco Mata, were tortured for condemning the unexplained disappearance of Father Gallego.

241

Sammy Sitton was tortured by National Guard members for speaking out against the Torrijos government.

Enrique Moreno, after torture, was able to leave Panama to reside in Miami.

Father Luis Medrano was forced to wear a black hood while being driven to his execution. However, because one of the directors of "Radio Hogar" recognized the G-2 chief as one of the priest's abductors, Father Medrano was not murdered.

Antonio Poole, a British national born in Argentina, experienced during imprisonment beatings, clubbings, and prodding in "sensitive" body areas with a stick. He also underwent electric shocks administered by a 12-volt car battery attached to two cables. Mr. Poole has also related a mock execution during which he was driven with his eyes taped shut to a location away from his place of incarceration. Here he was put through a thorough pre-execution preparation, only to discover that the ritual was only a hoax[11].

Methods of torture have reportedly included the following:

1. Sexual abuse by sexual deviants placed in prisoner's cells.
2. Insertion of prisoners' hands in bone crushing machines.
3. Beating with a rubber hose which leaves no scars.
4. Blows with the fist.
5. Long periods of interrogation without recesses for sleep, under strong lights, and without clothing.
6. Bathing of prisoners in *ice water*.
7. Electric shocks applied to sensitive body parts.
8. Simulated execution, a psychological torture, usually accompanied by physical abuse.
9. Forcing prisoners to stand for long periods away from a wall with legs spread, hands on the neck, and forehead touching the wall. Any movement results in beating with a rubber hose[12].

Denial of Freedom of Assembly and Association

When the military seized power in Panama in 1968, ten political parties were disolved[13]. Though parties are allowed to exist, according to the 1972 Constitution, only the *People's Party* (The Communist Party) is sanctioned by the Torrijos regime. This party alone, headed by Sexretary General Rugen Dario Sousa, operates freely and openly. In addition to Omar Torrijos, other prominent People's Party members include: Romulo Escobar Bethencourt,

242

Chairman of the National Information Commission; Juan Materno Vasquez, President of the Supreme Court; and Marcelino Jaen, President of the National Legislative Assembly.

Various other political organizations have reportedly been forced underground. The Social Democratic Movement, begun in February, 1976; the Movement of Independent Lawyers; the Odontologist Association; the Engineers and Architexts Society; and other professional and political groups are said to be constantly faced with G-2 repression. For example:

Several of the organizations' directors have been removed from their positions by Torrijos.

According to sources, two former Chamber of Commerce Presidents, the President-elect, and one of its directors were exiled[14].

The headquarters and records of the Panama Business Executive Association were confiscated in January, 1976.

For criticizing at a public meeting the government's economic policies, corruption, and repression, the presidents of the Cattlemen's Association and the Rice-growers of Panama were also exiled.

In addition to coercing enlistment of government employees into a state-controlled political organization, G-2 squads have been known to take more violent actions against labor unions. It has been disclosed that during September, 1976, the offices of the Christian Democrat-associated labor unions were broken into and ravaged. All the leaders were arrested.

Labor unions of all types are expected to join the Federacion Sindical, a communist-dominated labor federation through which organized labor could be controlled by the government. The leaders of the Federacion Sindical include long-time Communist Party members Domingo Barrio and Marta Matamoros.

The unions which have managed to maintain an independent status have faced extreme difficulties in seeking benefits from the Labor Ministry. It has been revealed that in government institutions where labor has traditionally been well represented, these groups are not allowed a voice. The pressures to which the Christian Democrat-associated groups have been subjected are said to be increasingly felt by other non-Sindical members.

When students gathered in September, 1976, for a march protesting the government's increase of milk and rice prices, and the continued lack of basic freedoms, the Torrijos government reacted swiftly. First, the state-controlled Student Federation (FZP), made up largely of non-student government agents, was sent to foment an "inter-student clash". However, what followed was a seven-day protest, resulting in disruption of Panama City's main traffic artery and damage to a large portion of the commercial sector[15].

When the regime's initial attempt to place blame for the disruptions on U.S. agencies collapsed, protest became widespread. Finally, sections of the Army were deployed with tear gas, rubber hoses, anti-riot pellets, and dogs[16].

At least two students died, one of whom reportedly "disappeared" from a government hospital. Three hundred to five hundred students, including some non-involved bystanders, were said to have been arrested and given the option of attending indoctrination classes at the City Jail, or of being sent to the panal colony at Coiba. It is reported that some of the imprisoned youths were tortured by electric shock. A number of those arrested were forced to stand outdoors from 13-15 hours, deprived of food, in a stationary position. After finally being given breakfast, the youths were made to attend a political awareness seminar.

This major disruptive incident compromises the regime's credibility. Especially noteworthy was the apparent absence of border crossings, anti-American demonstrations, posters, etc. which typically accompany student upheavals. Instead, the primary grievances this time were over Panama's internal problems.

Violations of Freedoms of Press and Speech

Both the press and radio are controlled in Panama by the Torrijos government. Media expressing opinions considered hostile to the regime are faced with the prospects of censorship or confiscation. Prominent media personnel may receive harsh sanctions.

Five radio stations, "La Vox de Colon," "Ondas Instmenas," "Radio Aeropuerto," "Radio Soberna," and "Radio Impacto" have been confiscated by the government since the 1968 *coup*.

Great pressure has reportedly been exerted on privately owned newspapers to bring them in line with the official press bureau, Editora Renovacion. This agency is owned by the government and managed by Rodrigo Gonzales, a close Torrijos assistant. It has been disclosed that two new private papers, *Quibo* and *La Opinion Publica* were squelched even before full-scale publication could begin, Editora La Verdad, which was to publish *La Opinion Publica*, was closed down for having previously printed subversive materials. Resolution "099" of March 6, 1975, which decreed suspension of publication was, it is reported, signed by the Minister of Justice, and was authorized by Torrijos. When the Movement of Independent Lawyers published a bulletin exposing in detail the *Quibo* and *La Opinion Publica* confiscations, its directors were threatened with release of a press decree which would label their actions a crime[17].

Such violations have reportedly become so flagrant that the Inter-American Press Society (SIP at its March, 1975 meeting in San Salvador, El Salvador, published a resolution (#6) which exposed and condemned the Torrijos regime for acts of censorship and other violations of free speech and press:

> Considering that the regime of Panama, which has the Press under direct or indirect control, has again censored the publication of a weekly newspaper which would have been called *La Opinion Publica (Public Opinion)* even before it appeared; considering that all the measures pursued by the SIP to the government of Panama to revoke the measure as to allow the publication of *La Opinion Publica* have failed; considering that this measure is the culmination of a series of arbitrary acts against the Free Press that have been carried out by the regime of dictator Omar Torrijos, the Board of Directors has determined to condemn the arbitrary resolution that prevented the publication of *La Opinion Publica* and to renew its efforts to promote a Forum of World Opinion where the repressive methods of the regime of dictator Omar Torrijos are exposed[18].

Exile and Persecution of Nationalists

It is widely known that the right to live in one's own country without fear of arbitrary deportation or expatriation has been consistently violated by the Torrijos government.

Exiled persons have told of being accused of anti-government subversion. For example, three lawyers involved in the Movement of Independent Lawyers were exiled in January, 1969, and a fourth entered Miami after a period of physical and mental torture. Altogether, in the right years from 1968–1976, at least 1,300 Panamanian professionals, businessmen, students, and labor union members have been exiled[19].

The public record shows that Dr. Ruben D. Calres, Jr. was exiled in January, 1976, after attending a public meeting in Chiriqui Province, Panama. Open public meetings were called by community leaders in David, Chiriqui Province, to discuss grievances against the Torrijos regime. Public officials and representatives of both public and private organizations were invited to attend. Soon after attending this meeting, Dr. Carles and fourteen other businessmen and professionals were arrested and exiled.

After his arrest, Carles was transported to a National Guard headquarters where he encountered several other men who had attended the Chiriqui meeting. The prisoners were searched; and personal documents, identification cards, and family photographs were confiscated. They were then ordered to remove all clothing and watch while their billfolds were searched. Most of the group were allowed to retain only their identification cards.

Following questioning, Carles and his associates were ordered into a DC-3, and flown to Guayaquil, Ecuador. The Panamanian government explained the deportations, it is reported, as its response to an alleged conspiracy which had sought to promote class struggle. According to Dr. Carles, the Panamanian government tried to prevent the exiles from obtaining visas from other countries by pressuring officials in Ecuador to prohibit their departure. Ecuadorian authorities also informed them that two Panamanian agents had been assigned to spy on them in Guayaquil[20].

The *first American citizen* and a legal resident of Panama who was deported by the Torrijos government is David Dale Mendelson. On the afternoon of April 3, 1977, Mr. Mendelson was taken against his will by the Panamanian secret police. He was not only denied his rights as an American citizen and Panamanian resident, but was also brutally beaten. His beating resulted in a contusion of the kidney, causing blood in the urine, and requiring hospitalization. He was held incommunicado and prohibited from making telephone calls to an attorney or to the American Consulate. On April 4, 1977, he was deported, via Braniff Flight 948, to the United States. In his subsequent letter of April 29, 1977, to two Panamanian lawyers, Mr. Mendelson sought assistance in suing the

Panamanian government for violation of human rights, beating, defamation of character, loss of business and personal property, and denial of contact with an attorney or the American Consulate[21].

It has also been discovered that the Torrijos regime has sent G-2 agents to other South, Central, and North American countries to arrest and intimidate Panamanian exiles. Often posing as officials of consulates and embassies, G-2 agents are able to seek out and persecute former Panamanian citizens. Mr. Ruben Carles has also discussed the awareness and fear of Panamanian agents which he and his associates felt while in Ecuador.

Leopoldo Aragon, then in exile in Costa Rica (presently in Sweden), was actually arrested by Panamanian agents. It is also suspected that in Costa Rica, Panamanian National Guards have murdered several opponents of the Torrijos regime who sought refuge there. Agents have reportedly been extremely active in Venezuela, Colombia, Miami, New York, and Washington, D.C. A portion of a 1975 G-2 payroll sheet lists Edgardo Lopez, now the Panamanian Consul in Miami. Although Lopez is called a *guardia* (common soldier) by occupation, he receives a salary comparable to that of the highly-paid G-2 chief, Manual Noriega.

Denial of the Right to Counsel

Officials of the Torrijos government have written laws which deny the accused the right to defense, if such person has allegedly engaged in subversive activities directed against the Panamanian state. In fact, some feel that the situation has become so serious that in November 1969, the Panamanian National Bar Association published a statement concerning the new relationship between the individual and the law:

> With the implementation of this system, the power the Judiciary enjoys is such as to exercise both the legislative and the judicial functions. For this reason, the National Bar Association, when protesting the fact that power was given to the executive branch to sanction a crime, following the procedure of a police indictment, it does so, convinced that the defendant has no access to the guarantees of the due process of law. For this reason, the National Bar Association considers the re-establishment of the constitutional guarantees a mere formality since the decrees that

247

have been issued consider that the practice of the citizen's inherent rights is a crime.[22]

Violation of the Right to Privacy and Freedom from Unwarranted Searches and Seizures

As previously noted, unwarranted entry into private homes has reportedly occurred repeatedly under the Torrijos regime. The unwarranted search of domiciles is known to be a frequent violation of privacy of individuals and their personal effects.

Both wiretapping and interference with private correspondence by the military police are reportedly routinely carried out by the military police. The Movement of Independent Lawyers was initially formed after fourteen Panamanian nationals had all their property confiscated before they were exiled to Ecuador.

Corruption

Nepotism

Over forty members of Omar Torrijos' extended family hold high government positions. Family members so favored include three brothers and their wives, six sisters and their husbands, three nephews, and at least twelve cousins. Among Torrijos' cousins is Panama's Vice-President, Gerardo Bonzales. Other powerful positions into which Torrijos' relations have been placed are those of Director of the National Lottery and Director of the government-owned gambling casinos. Torrijos' older brother, Hugo Torrijos, Director of the gambling casinos, is also involved in "Juliano Internacional" This establishment sells and rents gambling machines. Hugo Torrijos also controls the prostitution business for Panama and Latin America and the white slave market through his company "Espectaculos Nacionalas, S.A."[23]

Roberto Diaz Hererra, Torrijos' first cousin, was recently promoted to lieutenant colonel in the Panamanian National Guard. Diaz Hererra's brothers are Efebo Diaz Hererra, Panamanian Ambassador to Cuba, Nitido Diaz Hererra, Chief of Customs in the Republic of Panama, and Edison Diaz Hererra, Municipal Treasurer

248

Marcelino Jaen is married to Omar Torrijos' sister, Toya Torrijos Hererra, and serves as president of the National Legislative Committee.

Involvements of Omar Torrijos Outside Panama

Omar Torrijos is reportedly compiling vast holdings both in Panama, Spain and Belize. His brother Moises Monchi is Panamanian Ambassador to Spain, and is said to be engaged in procuring large real estate holdings. The Torrijos government has also changed Panamanian banking laws to permit special Euro-dollar accounts.

Since Fidel Castro came to power in Cuba on January 1, 1959, only three heads of State have visited him. Omar Torrijos is one of these three leaders. He arrived in Cuba on January 10, 1976.[24]

Involvement in Narcotics Traffic

In spite of public concern about international narcotics traffic, it has been found that members of Torrijos' family and other national officials are deeply involved in Mafia-connected narcotics trade. Though not a diplomatic official, Rafael Richard, Jr. WAs awarded a diplomatic passport under orders of the Panamanian Minister of Foreign Affairs. Richard entered New York, under diplomatic immunity, with 70 kilos of heroin given to him by the then Panamanian Ambassador to Argentina, Moises Torrijos. When arrested, Richard was in the company of Guillermo Gonzales and Nicolas Polanco, who are closely related to Torrijos' brother, Moises.[25]

Joaquin Him Gonzales, chief of the control tower of Panama City's Tocumen International Airport, was reportedly arrested in the Canal Zone for involvement in the smuggling of drugs into Dallas, Texas. As tower chief, this Torrijos confidant was in a position to prevent searches of air cargo by the Immigration Department. Altogether, from 1971 to 1972, 641 pounds of heroin were intercepted enroute from Panama to the United States, according to the Draft Report of the Panama Canal Subcommittee of the Merchant Marine and Fisheries Committee, March 8, 1972.[26]

249

Popular Organized Protest: Professional, Labor, and Student Groups

Several civic groups of various types have been formed in Panama to articulate grievances and to work for reform. One of the largest is the *Movimiento Civico Nacional*, formed on December 11, 1973. The original Declaration of Principles was signed by 35 organizations, including the Kiwanis Club, Lions Club, Housewive's Association, and National Medical Association. The organization claimed that its members were "concerned for the restless and unsure climate in which all the classes are living in this country, and because of the absence of public and individual liberties."

The objective of the organization is the pursuit of basic greedoms which are considered lacking in Panama. Among these are: freedom of information, freedom of expression, complete independence of the judiciary, freedom to form political parties and to see political liberties recognized. Also, the group calls for permanent and complete information on Canal negotiations in order to guarantee effective sovereignty.

In a speech given before the organization by (Rotarian) Dr. Osvaldo Velasquez, the speaker suggested that the call for total Canal Zone sovereignty is used as proof of popular support for the Torrijos government. Dr. Velasquez stated that because Panamanians lack civil liberties, any new draft document on the Canal submitted to the plebiscite, as constitutionally required, undoubtedly would have been approved in advance by the Foreign Office. Because any opposition to a draft treaty would likely be met with reprisals, the plebiscite "would be nothing more than a pseudo-democratic subterfuge." Furthermore, he questioned whether the U.S. Senate would consider approval of a treaty imposed in such a fashion.[27]

Among others in Panama who were concerned about a Torrijos-imposed agreement was Jerry Dodson, who said in his letter of resignation from his consular post (to Secretary of State William Rogers, June 5, 1969): "American citizens have been arrested on a large scale for no apparent reason. In a large number of cases, the National Guard has denied consular access to the citizens. There have been numerous cases of mistreatment as well."[28]

Conclusion

General Omar Torrijos, since assuming power in 1968, has, as evidence illustrates, repeatedly violated the rights of Panamanian citizens. He has rewritten the Panamanian constitution to give himself extraordinary powers and he has supplemented these powers with arbitrary arrests, torture, and murders. While the principal targets of his oppression are political opponents, even non-political individuals like Father Gallego fall victim.

These reported violations of human rights have stirred protests in Panama. Along with evidence of profiteering by Torrijos and his family, they have led groups like the Movimiento Civico Nacional to reject Torrijo's legitimacy and his right to negotiate a new Panama Canal settlement.

In light of this, it seems that the best course for the United States is not to conclude a treaty which could augment and perpetuate Torrijos' power over Panamanians and extend it to Canal Zone residents.

Notes

1. Panama, *La Estrella de Panama*, Oct. 11, 1968, p. 1 cc 1-6.
2. On October 2, 1976, the first of a group of 16 tanks, armed with 50 caliber machine guns, arrived in Panama via Miami. (See "Canal Protection Division Activity Report No. 2205", Oct. 2, 1976.)
3. See *New York Times*, June 20, 1977, p. 3, cc 4-6; and June 25, 1977, p. 1, c5, p. 6, c5.
4. Haitian Constitution, 1964, revised 1970.
5. See Constitution of the Republic of Panama, (Panama City, 1977), article 277.
6. Parish priest.
7. Agence France Presse, Aug. 21, 1972. *El Sol de Mexico*.
8. Ibid. Statement by Reverend Pedro Hernandez Robadal.
9. Ibid.
10. Report of Panamanian Committee on Human Rights, Sept. 15, 1976.
11. Notorized statement from Antonio Poole to Ruben D. Carles, Jr., Sept. 15, 1976, Miami. *Panamanian Committee on Human Rights*.
12. Ibid.
13. Political parties include:
    Christian Democratic Party (PDC)
    Panamenista Party (PP)
    Republican Party (PR)
    National Patriotic Coalition (CPN)
    Democratic Action (AD)

Third National Party (TPN)
Liberal Party (PLN)
Agrarian Labor Party (PAL)
National Liberation Movement (MLNP)
Progressive Party (PPN)
14. Two former Presidents of the Chambers of Commerce, Guillermo Ford and Roberto Eisenmann, Sr.
15. *The Dallas Morning News*, Jan. 24, 1976, p. 30E, c4, and *New York Times*, Sept. 23, 1976, p. 48A, c8.
16. Ibid.
17. Editorial *Miami Herald*, Jan. 19, 1974.
18. See Panamanian Committee for Human Rights, Document, Sept. 1976, Vol. 1.
19. Ibid.
20. Ruben D. Carles, Jr., "The Constitution of Panama, Article 29", (Washington, D.C., Library of Congress Research Service, 1976), pp. 48-50.
21. David D. Mendelson reported these happenings in conversations with Phillip Harman.
22. Panama, *La Estrella de Panama*, No. 13, 1969, p. 1, cc 1-4.
23. Ibid. Also Martin C. Needler, "Omar Torrijos: The Panamanian Enigma," in *Intellect*, Feb. 1977, pp. 242-243.
24. The other two are Salvador Allende and Luis Esheverria.
25. Panamanian Committee For Human Rights, Document, Sept. 1976.
26. See U. S. House of Representatives, Panama Canal sub-Committee on Merchant Marine and Fishing, "Draft Report", (Washington, D.C. March 8, 1972.)
27. Address by Osraldo Velasquez before the Movimiento Civico Nacional, Nov. 4, 1976.
28. Dodson to Secretary William Rogers, June 5, 1969.

Partial List of Persons Reported Murdered by the Torrijos Government

Arrieta, Abdiel
Britton, Floyd
Cadeno, Anibal
Cubas Perez, Hipolito
Cubas Perez, Narciso
Cruz, Mojica
Cruz, Ramon
Falconnet, Jorge
Fistonich, Andres
Frederic, Jaime Alberto
Gallego, Hector (Rev.)
Generoso, Elisondro

Gonzales, Encarnacion
Gonzales, Felix
Gonzales, Elias
Gonzales, Ariosto
Gantez, Belisario
Medrano, Jorge Tulio
Moreno, Dorita
Mendizabal, Marlene
Monterosa, Luis Carlos
Miro, Ruben
Manson, Hildebrando
Osorio, Waldemedo
Palacios, Teodoro
Portugal, Heliodoro
Quintanar, Herbert
Rivera, Basilio
Sanchez, Ubaldo
Sarmiento, Cesar
Sarmiento, Genaro
Tejada, Cesareo
Tunon, Jose del C.
White, Eduardo
Document, *Panamanian Committee for Human Rights*, Vol. II, November, 1976.

Partial List of Persons Reported Exiled by the Torrijos Government

Abood, Tito
Achurra, Serafin (Major of the National Guard)
Aizpurua, Jaime (Agronomist Engineer)*
Alvarado, Osvaldo (Lt. of the National Guard)
Alvarez, Antonio*
Aragon, Leopoldo
Arauz, Angel
Arias, Gilberto
Arias, Madrid, Dr. Arnulfo (former President of Panama, M.D.)
Arias, Tomas
Avila, Victor

Beecher, Clarence (Professor)

Bernal, Dr. Migel Antonio (Lawyer, University Professor)*

Berriman, Felipe (Priest)

Boyd, Federico (Lt. Col. of the National Guard)

Boyd, Dr. Julio (D.D.S.)

Britton, Federico (Brother of Floyd who was murdered by the National Guard)

Calamari, Humberto (Lawyer)

Carles, Querube S. de (Civic Leader)

Carles, Ruben Dario (Economist, University Professor)*

Chen, Demetrio

Crespo, Bolivar

Crocamo, Abraham (Captain of the National Guard)

De Arco, Gilberto

De Arco, Juan Manuel

De Arco, Tare

De La Guardia, Rodolfo

Diaz, Duque Luis Carlos (Lt. Col. of the National Guard)

Dominiguez, Antonio (Business and Civic Leader)*

Dominiguqz, Domingo

Dominiguez, Julio

Dubois, Cesar

Eisenmann, Jr., I. Roberto (Businessman, Former President of the Chamber of Commerce, Banker)*

Ford, Guillermo (Businessman, Banker, Former President of the Chamber of Commerce)*

Francheschi, Adolfo

Gonzales, Gabriel

Gonzales de la Lastra, Carlos Ernesto (Former President of the APEDE and Executive Secretary of the Social Democratic Movement)

Guevara, Guillermo (University Student)

Harris, Humberto

Huertematte, Max

Jimenez, Humberto (Major of the National Guard)

Jurado, Dr. Alonso (M.D.)

King, Thelma

Lecuona, Julian (Priest)

Lekas, Juan

Lopez, Eudoro
Lopez, Humberto (Law Student, Member of the Executive Committee of the Social Democratic Movement)
Mandura, Eduardo
Marchosky, Eusebio (Lawyer)
Martinez, Boris (Colonel of the National Guard)
Martinez, Luis
Martinez, Jr., Luis
Mayo, Jesus
Menendez Franco, Gonzalo (Lawyer)
Miro Jr., Ruben
Mong, Enrique
Morales, Marcos
Moran, Diana (Lawyer)
Moreno, Quico
Nicosia, Hildebrando
Nieda, Harmodio
Perez del Rosario, Juan
Pitti, Jorge
Quiros Guardia, Alberto (Newsman, University Professor)*
Richard, Jose Alexis
Robinson, Carlos (Newsman)
Robles, Ivan (Lawyer)*
Robles, Dr. Winston (Lawyer, University Professor)*
Rodriguez, Bolivar
Rodriguez, Felix Rolla, Pimentel, Dr. Guillermo (M.D.)
Romero, Buenaventura
Romero, Maximo
Saavedra, Canilo (Lt. Col. of the National Guard)
Sagel, Diogenes (Newsman)
Salas, Jacobo
Samudio, David
Sanchez, Pascual
Sanjur, Amando (Col. of the National Guard)
Sanjur, Fidencio
Sanjur, Ruben
Silvera, Ramior (Col. of the National Guard)
Solis Palma, Manuel
Turner, David

Turner, Domingo
Turner, Jorge
Velasquez, Gilberto
Weeden, Alvin (Lawyer)*
Weeden, George (Businessman, Director of the Chamber of Commerce)*
Wilson, Carlos
Yanez, Victor
Young Adames, Dr. Carlos (M.D.)
Zappi, Humberto

*Exiled in January and February, 1976, to Ecuador.

Bibliography

Note: Throughout *Surrender In Panama*, sources for all quotes have been identified in the text. The purpose of this bibliography is neither to relist all those sources nor to supply an encyclopedic general reading list on Panama, but to give the reader a good selection of basic historical, military, diplomatic, and political background material to aid in a deeper understanding of the canal, the treaties, and the debate about them.

Key Books

Dubois, Jules, *Danger over Panama* (Indianapolis, 1964).

DuVal, Miles P., Jr., *Cadiz to Cathay* (Stanford, 1944).

——— *And Mountains Will Move* (Stanford, 1947).

Ealy, Lawrence O., *Yanqui Politics and the Isthmian Canal* (University Park, Pennsylvania, 1971).

Ryan, Paul B., *The Panama Canal Controversy: U.S. Diplomacy and Defense Interests* (Stanford, 1977).

Torrijos, Omar, *Nuestra Revolución* [*Our Revolution*] (Panama, 1974).

Key Congressional Testimony

Panama Canal Treaties (Hearings before the Committee on Foreign Relations, United States Senate, Ninety-fifth Congress, First Session, September 26, 27, 29, 30, and October 19, 1977).

Panama Canal Treaty—Disposition of United States Territory (Hearings before the Subcommittee on Separation of Powers of the Committee on the Judiciary, United States Senate, Ninety-fifth Congress, First Session, July 22, and 29, 1977).

Key Periodical Articles

Flood, Daniel J., "The Challenge to Congress over the Panama Canal" (*Manion Forum*, no. 1151, October 31, 1976).

Hudson, Richard, "Storm over the Canal" (*New York Times Magazine*, May 16, 1976).

Krulak, W.H., "Panama: Strategic Pitfall" (*Strategic Review*, vol. 4, Winter 1976).

Maechling, Charles, Jr., "The Panama Canal: A Fresh Start" (*Orbis,* vol. 20, Winter 1977).

Prewett, Virginia, "The Panama Canal: Past and Present in Perspective" (*Sea Power*, vol. 19, August 1976).

Rosenfeld, Stephen S., "The Panama Negotiations—A Close-run Thing" (*Foreign Affairs*, vol. 54, October 1975).

Simpson, Michael D., "Panama: The Proposed Transfer of the Canal and the Canal Zone By Treaty" (*Georgia Journal of International and Comparative Law*, vol. 5, Winter 1975).

Strother, Robert S., "The Panama Question: An Alternative to U.S. Defeatism" (*National Review*, vol. 27, September 12, 1975).

Bibliographical Source Book

Bray, Wayne D.: *The Controversy over a New Canal Treaty between the United States and Panama: A Selective Annotated Bibliography of United States, Panamanian, Colombian, French, and International Organization Sources* (Washington, D.C. 1976).